An Introduction to
Modern Jewish Thinkers

An Introduction to Modern Jewish Thinkers

From Spinoza to Soloveitchik

Second Edition

Alan T. Levenson

ROWMAN & LITTLEFIELD PUBLISHERS, INC.
Lanham • Boulder • New York • Toronto • Oxford

I would like to thank the following for granting permission to use material reprinted in this book: Moses Mendelssohn, trans. Allan Arkush. *Jerusalem: Or On Religious Power and Judaism*. pp. 103–110 © 1983 Brandeis University Press/University Press of New England. Hanover and London. Reprinted with permission. Feldheim Publishers for permission to reprint from *The Nineteen Letters* by Samson Raphael Hirsch and Bernard Drachman, 1988 (reprint); The Jewish Publication Society for permission to reprint from Theodor Herzl's *The Zionist Idea*, Arthur Hertzberg, 1979; A. J. Heschel, *Man Is Not Alone: A Philosophy of Religion*, 1951; *Abraham Geiger and Liberal Judaism: The Challenge of the Nineteenth Century*, Max Wiener, 1962; and *Judaism as a Civilization*, Mordechai Kaplan, 1981; Indiana University Press for permission to reprint from *Scripture and Translation* by Martin Buber; Bloch Publishing Company, Inc. for permission to reprint from *Israel Salanter* by Menachem Glenn, 1979; From *The Lonely Man of Faith* by Joseph B. Soloveitchik. Copyright © 1965 by Joseph B. Soloveitchik. Used by permission of Doubleday, a division of Random House, Inc.; Dover Publications, Inc. for permission to reprint from *Political-Theological Treatise* by H. M. Elwes and Baruch Spinoza, 1951; Henry Holt and Company, LLC for permission to reprint from *The Star of Redemption* by Franz Rosenzweig, English-language translation © 1964, 1970, 1971.

ROWMAN & LITTLEFIELD PUBLISHERS, INC.

Published in the United States of America
by Rowman & Littlefield Publishers, Inc.
A wholly owned subsidiary of The Rowman & Littlefield Publishing Group, Inc.
4501 Forbes Boulevard, Suite 200, Lanham, Maryland 20706
www.rowmanlittlefield.com

PO Box 317
Oxford
OX2 9RU, UK

British Library Cataloguing in Publication Information Available

Library of Congress Cataloging-in-Publication Data
Levenson, Alan T.
  [Modern Jewish thinkers]
  An introduction to modern Jewish thinkers : from Spinoza to Soloveitchik / Alan T. Levenson.— 2nd ed.
     p. cm.
  Includes bibliographical references and index.
  ISBN 13: 978-0-7425-4606-6 (cloth : alk. paper)
  ISBN 10: 0-7425-4606-3 (cloth : alk. paper)
  ISBN 13: 978-0-7425-4607-3 (pbk. : alk. paper)
  ISBN 10: 0-7425-4607-1 (pbk. : alk. paper)
  1. Judaism—History—Modern period, 1750– I. Klein, Roger C. II. Title.
  BM190.L48 2006
  296.309'03—dc22   2005026333

Printed in the United States of America

♾™ The paper used in this publication meets the minimum requirements of American National Standard for Information Sciences—Permanence of Paper for Printed Library Materials, ANSI/NISO Z39.48-1992.

Contents

Acknowledgments

This page allows me to give some small measure of thanks to the wonderful support that I have enjoyed for so many years from so many quarters. Teachers at Brown University, including Jacob Neusner, Wendell Deitrich, Kurt Raaflaub, and Bryce Lyon, first taught me to think about religion and history in a sophisticated manner. At Ohio State University, I received support from the History Department and the Melton Center of Jewish Studies. Dagmar Lorenz, with whom I took several courses, gave me my grounding in German-Jewish literature. Jeremy Cohen's tutelage and example has been a continually helpful model of academic rigor. Most of all, Ohio State University introduced me to my mentor, Marc Lee Raphael. The professional happiness I have found as a teacher of Judaica is in large measure Marc's doing. Marc excels as a teacher, scholar, intellectual, and *mentsch.* It gives me the greatest pleasure to be able to thank him here.

Siegal College of Judaic Studies has been my professional home, and everyone associated with the college has my thanks. The support staff and library staff have handled my outrageous photocopying demands and frantic interlibrary loan requests with tolerance and grace. This book has benefited from the comments of my faculty colleagues including David Ariel, Lifsa Schachter, Moshe Berger, Ron Brauner, Jeff Schein, and Roger Klein (who authored the chapter on A. J. Heschel). Susannah Heschel, who taught in Cleveland for several years before moving to Dartmouth, encouraged this project from the outset. Most of all, as a rabbinic dictum has it, I have learned from my students, many of whom are also colleagues and friends. Videoconferencing classes in Milwaukee and Kansas City also deserve notice for pushing me to better clarify my thinking on the thinkers presented here. Fred and Pearl's book club reassured me that the format developed here was effective without a teacher in the room. Anyone who has never had the pleasure of teaching or learning with mature adults is missing the living embodiment of "Torah L'Shma"—learning for learning's sake. A generous grant from the Littauer Foundation gave me a little time off from my heavy teaching schedule to transform very informal lectures into the still informal chapters presented below. It will be obvious that the remaining errors, lapses, and misjudgments in this book are my own.

When I met Hilary Seltzer, at a party in Jerusalem, her friends skeptically suspected that I was interested in her washing machine. As we approach our tenth anniversary, I hope her friends are now convinced of my honorable motives—I know Hilary is. Hilary's love and support has brightened our good times and seen me through our rough times, including the seemingly endless quest for our son Benjamin, who finally arrived from Russia in February of 1998. Finally, I would like to dedicate this book to my parents, Doris and Harlan Hettmansberger, and to Larry and Davida Levenson, for everything else.

I am delighted that Rowman & Littlefield decided to issue this revised edition, and I thank Brian Romer for his guidance, patience, and interest in the revision process. I would also like to thank, once again, Rabbi Dr. Roger Klein for allowing me to reproduce his introduction to the Heschel reading. Rabbi Barbara Penzner's insightful questions, developed for the "Yad Mordecai" project of the Reconstructionist movement's adult education initiative, have been liberally incorporated in this edition. Finally, my very deep gratitude goes to Mr. David Genshaft for his generosity in assuming the permissions and scanning costs that have made this edition affordable.

Alan T. Levenson
August 2005 / Av 5765

Introduction

Preparing a class on modern Jewish thinkers, I was surprised to discover that no single work offered what I wanted: an accessible, nontechnical survey directed at adult learners and also appropriate for undergraduate-level college classes. Many distinguished scholars have contributed to modern Jewish philosophy and constructive Jewish theology, but for whatever reasons, none had written an unthreatening welcome to the world of modern Jewish thought. Purely academic works on Jewish thought either assumed or treated as irrelevant the historical circumstances and biographical details that beginning and intermediate students find so helpful and interesting. Perhaps because my training was in history and not philosophy, I am never satisfied with an idea until I know something about the person and the times that generated it.

I also wanted my students to read the original works of the great Jewish thinkers and not only summaries or critiques of their thoughts. But this is easier said than done. One of my bicycling buddies told me that he had picked up Buber's *I and Thou* three times, only to find it too daunting an undertaking. It is equally daunting to ask a college or public librarian to recommend a work of Mordechai Kaplan's or Abraham Joshua Heschel's, only to be told that there are dozens of items authored by each. Certain classics of Jewish thought, Emil Fackenheim's *To Mend the World* or Franz Rosenzweig's *The Star of Redemption*, for instance, begin with a couple of hundred pages of philosophical critique sure to put off all but the most intrepid readers. Where to begin?

My role in this book is chiefly to give the reader access to these classics. I have designed these introductions and questions to help students grapple with primary sources selected for their accessibility and/or centrality and then come to their own conclusions. The student who works his or her way through this "user's manual" will, at the very least, have made the acquaintance of most of the important Jewish thinkers in the modern era, understand a great deal more about the problems that have perplexed modern Jews, and possess a good springboard from which to dive into the sea of modern Jewish thought, whether for academic or personal growth. As diverse as these figures are, all have insights to contribute to the eclectic Judaism practiced by most American Jews—including me.

Before starting this book, the reader has a legitimate right to ask: Why bother with modern Jewish thought at all? I offer the following (partial) responses as a teacher and as a committed Jew; as such, my responses are both intellectual and personal. Since the time of Spinoza, there has existed a distinctively modern, distinctively Jewish discourse that constitutes a distinguished piece of our intellectual inheritance. For those committed to this tradition, ignorance of Mendelssohn or Hirsch or Rosenzweig is no more desirable than ignorance of the midrash or of medieval Jewish philosophy. Biblical and rabbinic texts remain the basic touchstone of Judaism. But our modern perplexities concerning God, revelation, selective observance of the Commandments, and the nature of Jewish identity have been addressed more directly in the last three hundred years than in any previous period. By ignoring modern Jewish thought, we fail to take our own contemporary dilemmas seriously, and, ironically, we disarm, "the power most able to deliver us," as Martin Buber put it in *People Today and the Jewish Bible* (1925).

While rabbinic materials require considerable tutelage to master and enjoy, modern Jewish thought provides a surprisingly accessible means for the untutored Jew (or interested non-Jew) who wishes to grapple with the eternal questions in a recognizable language. One additional factor demands mention. The lives of the modern Jewish thinkers are relatively easy to reconstruct as compared with the sages who composed the Talmud. This invites integration of the biographical and the intellectual. The figures portrayed here were products of their times and needed to wrestle with various contemporary dilemmas on their way to mature and enduring understandings of Jewishness. It is inspiring and empowering to know that the figures presented here (and a more interesting group of characters would be difficult to assemble), were embarked on a personal as well as an intellectual voyage.

The structure of this book is designed to forward the goals just described. Each major section is preceded by a brief overview of the historical circumstances and an explanation of the key issues or tendencies that seem (to me) to tie the thinkers in that section together. Each individual chapter offers the following:

- a historically and biographically oriented introduction to the thinker presented in that chapter

- a short description of each author's overall intellectual contributions
- some of the more important scholarly interpretations of the thinker under discussion
- critical passages or chapters from these modern Jewish classics
- a series of questions that invite the reader, through the eyes of the figure under consideration, to confront the issues raised
- some suggestions for further reading, chosen on the criteria of interest and comprehensibility

For instance, in my first chapter, I place Spinoza in the context of the Marrano experience and the developing Amsterdam Jewish community, then describe the role that the *Theological-Political Treatise* plays in Spinoza's overall theological project. Next, I reproduce Spinoza's discussions in the *Theological-Political Treatise* on the utility of Scripture, accompanied by questions designed to elicit his view of Scripture, the possibilities of relating to Scripture without belief in its divine origins, and the methods of determining what ethical and social values Scripture actually propounds. Finally, I conclude this discussion and selection from Spinoza with works by and about this brilliant heretic.

With every thinker or *movement*, I try to link my exposition to questions of personal relevance, bringing the reader into dialogue with the material presented. Most of the thinkers presented here have generated a substantial body of interpretation. My suggestions for further readings differentiate historical background from philosophical critiques, indicate which works I consider the most exciting, and warn readers when the level of difficulty may prove too demanding for most lay readers. These suggestions for further reading generally concentrate on books, which are so much easier to locate than journal articles; they are not meant as exhaustive bibliographies, but rather as guides for the individual reader who wishes to pursue the lives and thought of these figures beyond the borders of this introduction.

As to my choice of thinkers, it should be clear that other worthy figures could be presented. By and large, my criterion of selection has been my sense of what would speak most powerfully to the lay reader. I will confess to feeling guilty about not including Hermann Cohen, one of my favorites, but I am already giving German-Jewish thinkers pride of place. Emanuel Levinas, a French contemporary of Rosenzweig and Buber, seems to me too convoluted to interest most readers. Nachman Krochmal, despite the title of his major opus (*Guide of the Perplexed of Our Time*), strikes me as appealing mainly to the very learned and profoundly committed. I have deliberately represented several thinkers associated with Orthodox Judaism, who have generally received inadequate treatment in earlier works, but have excluded Orthodox figures whose creativity lay principally in their roles as legal (halachic) adjudicators. Also omitted are a host of technically gifted philosophers (Steinheim and Formstecher come to mind) whom I cannot imagine doing anything for contemporary readers except bore them to tears. The absence of women in this book, a glaring omission, is addressed on pp. 225–27.

One last note: This book introduces modern Jewish thinkers, *not* modern Jewish philosophy. A colleague of mine related that Eliezer Berkowitz, a rabbi and a scholar, once quipped that modern Jewish thinkers were more impressive than modern Jewish philosophies. What Berkowitz meant, I presume, was that these figures were often more accomplished as teachers, communal activists, rabbis, and role models than as thinkers. I would consider nearly all of the figures introduced here impressive in both respects. Ultimately, what makes this exploration interesting is precisely that the issues raised here are more than academic.

For many years, in a wide variety of classes, I have tried to bring students into productive dialogue with modern Jewish thinkers and modern Jewish thought. This work extends that effort, I hope, to a wide variety of readers including adult learners looking for a systematic overview of modern Jewish thought, the Jewish "seeker" looking for an entry point from which to engage Judaism thoughtfully, interested non-Jews who want learn what issues have preoccupied Jewish thinkers for the last two or three centuries, and university professors looking for a text that will provide both a coherent overview and a basis for further discussion.

Part One

MODERN JUDAISM
Attack and Defense

INTRODUCTION

The story of Jewish historiography—the writing of Jewish history—is a fascinating one. With a dozen or so exceptions, mainly during the Renaissance, no Jew after Flavius Josephus, who died around the year 100 CE, bothered to write a history of Jews, although several Christians did. In the nineteenth century, this situation changed radically. The first modern Jews to write histories tended to focus on the preceding century (the eighteenth century) as the onset of modernity. They reasoned that that century marked the beginnings of a new political status for the Jews and the stirrings of Jewish Enlightenment (*Haskalah*). Today, most scholars date the beginnings of Jewish modernity earlier, noting that in Western Europe at least, the rise of the nation-state, more secular influences on politics, and more capitalistic economies were well underway by the end of the Thirty Years' War (1648). European Jewry, which was expelled from West to East in the Late Middle Ages, began to travel westward in the search for better living conditions as the political situation in Poland and Russia deteriorated. Salo Baron of Columbia University, the first person to hold a chair in post-biblical Jewish history anywhere, emphasized time and again how much external forces mattered in the passage from medieval to modern times.

Yet a good case can also be made for the predominance of internal changes within the Jewish world. Gershom Scholem, a German Jew who emigrated to British-controlled Palestine in the 1920s, and the pioneer scholar of Jewish mysticism, explained the breakdown of the medieval system largely with reference to Jewish developments. The phenomenon of baptized Jews trying to reclaim Jewish identity (e.g., Marranism), the appearance of more secular Jewish communities, and the disastrous repercussions of the Sabbatian movement (the followers of the false Messiah, Shabbetai Sevi) all pointed to a period distinctly different from the medieval world that preceded it. Basically, Scholem held that the Spanish Expulsion of 1492 ended the medieval Jewish experience and the Sabbatian Explosion of 1665–1666 began the modern. Both Baron and Scholem had merit to their claims: external and internal changes dramatically reshaped Jewish life from the seventeenth to the nineteenth centuries.

One thing is certain: whenever and wherever Jews entered modernity, they entered it on an uneven playing field. In the medieval world, the Christian assault on Judaism was straightforward and theologically driven. Jewish–Christian relations in the eighteenth century became more complex. The *philosophes* of the European Enlightenment criticized Christianity, but they had an even lower opinion of Judaism. They generally regarded Judaism as an atavistic faith, which, in exchange for the right to cultivate pure humanity, would soon be dropped. The rulers of Europe would entertain an improvement in Jewish political status, but at the cost of Jewish self-rule. Asked what the French nation owed the Jews, Clermont de Tonnere replied, "as individuals everything; as a nation, nothing." This formula, perhaps oversimplified, was basically accurate. The masses continued to harbor deep anti-Semitic prejudices that carried over from medieval to modern times. By the end of the nineteenth century, anti-Jewish sentiment would be organized into modern political movements and would borrow the "science" of race to find new ways of justifying old prejudices.

But the Jewish entry into modernity was hardly negative overall. Jews eagerly sought the advantages (social, economic, legal, and political) that citizenship offered. Many of the Jewish leaders most eager to see an end to the Jews' pariah status agreed that their nation was woefully behind the times and that fundamental reforms would be necessary to allow Jewry to thrive in very different circumstances. Medieval figures such as Maimonides and Nachmanides had their qualms about certain aspects of Jewish life; they had no doubts, however, that Judaism was superior to Christianity (or Islam) as a religious and intellectual system. In the nineteenth century, many Jews no longer confided in this as a certainty. Nobody from either side, it should be recalled, could clearly visualize what role Jews would play individually or corporately in European life once they left the ghetto.

It should follow from the preceding paragraph that the early responses to this radical change partook of a defensive, reactive, and apologetic nature. This is not to say that Mendelssohn, Geiger, and Hirsch failed to produce works of enduring relevance and value. They did. But we will not understand what motivated their thinking, nor understand why later generations of Jewish thinkers found them so inadequate, if we do not grasp that they were all involved in a process of "catching up."

Ironically, one of the first and most profound challenges to traditional Judaism was articulated by a Jewish heretic named Benedict (Baruch) Spinoza. As will be explained in greater detail in the first chapter, Spinoza attacked all revealed religions and the divine origins of the Hebrew Scripture. While Spinoza—once excommunicated—could be safely ignored by the Jewish community in his own lifetime, Spinoza's ideas made their way into general European culture and needed to be faced by Moses Mendelssohn a century later. While I will suggest the ways in which Spinoza may be regarded as the first modern Jewish thinker, to Mendelssohn belongs the dubious honor of being the first to formulate a Jewish answer to the question: What role will the Jews play in a new era? Deeply committed to traditional *halachic* life and to greater participation in European culture, Mendelssohn attempted to focus on *religion* as the principal factor separating Jew from Christian. This seemed the best prescription for justifying both greater participation of Jews as nationals and the retaining of Jewish religious practices in a context where all nations had religious minorities but were increasingly hostile to any other obstacles to centralization. (This focus on religion as the critical distinguishing factor between Jews and Christians is not as obvious as it sounds. I grew up in suburban New York in the 1960s where being a Jew meant never eating a blueberry bagel, voting liberal, reading the *New York Times*, eating a great deal but drinking very little, and doing everything to send your children to the best schools possible. The difference between the Levensons and the Cristofaros was considerable, but only tangentially related to the fact that Joe, my best friend, went to church and that I occasionally went to synagogue. In the course of the nineteenth century, Jews became loyal citizens, abandoned many of their religious traditions, and yet remained a distinct ethnicity—or subculture.)

Mendelssohn's overemphasis on religion as the defining factor of "Jewishness" guaranteed dissension over Jewish beliefs and practices. An even more important factor generating infra-Jewish debate was the integration of Western European Jews into their respective nations. As Jews began to share many of the same aspirations and values as Frenchmen, Englishmen, Germans, and so forth, a host of questions emerged. Would one work on the Sabbath in order to afford the same clothing and housing and transportation as one's neighbor? Would one eat only kosher food and absent oneself from the voluntary societies that played such a large role in European culture? Would one send one's child to *heder*, or to the best high school in the area? Would one encourage one's son to go to Tuebingen University to get a law degree, even if it meant the temptations of baptism for career advancement or intermarriage? I could multiply these examples, but I am certain the point is obvious: religion is a part of life, and if every dimension of one's life changes, so too will one's religious behavior. All accommodation, including the orthodoxy of Samson Raphael Hirsch, is "reform" with a lower-case *r*.

The opening chapter of this book discusses Baruch Spinoza, but I had better emphasize that he is highly unrepresentative in one important way. Every other figure treated here believed deeply in the continuation of Jewish life and in the eternal worth of Jewish teachings. It will serve the reader well to keep that in mind when she or he is struck by Mendelssohn's forced arguments, or Hirsch's dogmatism, or Geiger's cavalier attitude to time-honored traditions. For all of these figures—with the exception of Spinoza—saw their task in life as the preservation of Judaism under circumstances that seemed to be unprecedented.

Chapter One

Baruch Spinoza's Critique of Traditional Religion

SPINOZA'S LIFE AND TIMES (1632–1677)

He was of middle size, he had good features in his face, the skin somewhat black, black curled hair, and long eyebrows of the same color, so that one might easily know by his looks that he was descended from Portuguese Jews. He was plain and simple in his clothes and paid little attention to how he was dressed. One of the most eminent councillors of state went to see him and found him in a shabby morning gown, whereupon the councillor blamed him for it and offered him another. Spinoza answered him, that a man was never the better for having a finer gown.[1]

Modest, philosophical, and nonconformist, Spinoza was recognized in his own day as a unique figure, and subsequent generations have confirmed this verdict. Discussions of modern Jewish thought often begin with the figure of Benedict Spinoza, but it is worthwhile asking, Why? Spinoza's most important work, the *Ethics*, purports to be a universally valid work of philosophy, transcending any religious tradition.[2] The subject matter of the *Ethics* has nothing Judaic about it, and the format owes much more to the French Catholic philosopher René Descartes than to any Judaic traditions.[3] Spinoza's audience, limited in those days to a few fellow freethinkers, was certainly not Jewish. And none of Spinoza's preserved writings are in a Jewish language, though Spinoza knew Hebrew well. Spinoza's main philosophic works were in Latin, with some occasional letters in Dutch. Most dramatically, after his excommunication from the community in 1657, Spinoza had no contacts with Jewish life whatsoever, even bringing his sister to court to sue for his share of their parents' estate. (Spinoza won the case on its merits and then took only a bed for his settlement.) Steven Nadler, Spinoza's best biographer, emphasizes

5

Spinoza's complete lack of Jewish self-identification. Clearly, the usual criteria of what makes a thinker's thought Jewish—language, audience, subject matter, and ultimate loyalties—disqualify Spinoza.

According to Jewish law, or *halachah*, Spinoza was indeed Jewish. His parents probably called him Bento or Baruch. Hannah, Spinoza's mother, died when the boy was only a child. His father, Michael, a successful merchant, died when Spinoza was in his early twenties. In 1492, Spain had expelled the largest, most accomplished, and one of the oldest European Jewish communities, and the story of the resettlement of these deportees is long and complex. Many of the exiled Jews found refuge in the (Islamic) Ottoman Empire. Many others accepted the invitation of the nearby King of Portugal. The latter, however, in order to marry the daughter of Ferdinand and Isabella, agreed to eliminate Jewish culture in Portugal too, and forcibly converted the newly arrived emigrants along with the native Portuguese Jews in 1496. The Spinozas, then, descended from the many Jews who had fled from Portugal in the century after the forced conversion in order to resume a Jewish life elsewhere. (Seventeenth-century Amsterdam, where Spinoza was born, had more Ashkenazim than Sephardim, but both groups were well represented.)[4]

These returning Jews, called variously *Marranos*, *conversos*, or *anusim*, had a difficult time reintegrating into normative Jewish communities of Eastern European origins.[5] The sources of this difficulty can be easily imagined. There was no public practice of Judaism anywhere in the Iberian peninsula. Private observance of Judaism could very well land you before the Inquisition. There were no Jewish ritual items or books available for use or purchase. There was no Jewish education. Open displays of Christianity were a necessary safety measure and any "New Christian" who went on for higher education became an active participant in the culture of Catholic Spain or Portugal. How many ex-Jews remained determined to reclaim their Jewish identity? How many tried and succeeded in becoming good Catholics? The historians debate this issue. But for those in the former category, the difficulty in bridging the world of Iberian crypto-Judaism and that of normative, rabbinic Judaism was considerable.

The Israeli philosopher Yirmiyahu Yovel has made an interesting case that much of Spinoza's intellectual endeavors must be seen in the context of the converso experience.[6] Not only Spinoza, but many other converso descendants, found their own private faiths incompatible with the detailed prescriptions of rabbinic Judaism as practiced by the Ashkenazic community. As a boy growing up in Amsterdam, which had a fairly cosmopolitan Jewish community, Spinoza may have heard about the public humiliation and suicide of Uriel D'Accosta, a converso who escaped Spain to resume Jewish life but found the rabbinic Judaism of Amsterdam much different from the religion he sought. In his pathetic memoir, D'Accosta professed shock that seventeenth-century Judaism was not the religion of the Bible—whether this really could have surprised D'Accosta is debatable, but it is certain that he tried and failed to make the leap from Catholicism to Judaism. Spinoza also came under the influence of Juan De Prado, another converso who oscillated between orthodoxy and heterodoxy.

To return to our central question: Is Jewish birth alone an adequate criterion to count one as a Jewish thinker? Surely not, for one can list a slew of distinguished intellectuals of Jewish birth in the arts and sciences whose contributions have had nothing to do with matters Jewish. They may be Jews who are thinkers, but they are not Jewish thinkers in the sense that interests us here. Similarly, the fact that Spinoza's correspondents regarded him as Jewish is irrelevant to the question of the content of his thought. Henry Oldenburg of the British Royal Society, clearly presuming Spinoza had some "inside information," asked his opinion of the messianic claims of Shabbetai Sevi in late 1665—Spinoza never replied.

While the *Ethics* has nothing especially Jewish about it,[7] Spinoza's other major work, the *Tractatus Theologico-Politicus* (1670), or *Theological-Political Treatise* (TPT), qualifies him, at the very least, as a formidable critic of the Judaic tradition. In the TPT, Spinoza subjects the Hebrew Scriptures to historical-critical analysis. Spinoza took many of his hints from medieval Jewish exegetes who were well aware that Moses did not write every word of the Torah. Rabbi Abraham Ibn Ezra (eleventh-century Spain), for instance, clearly did not believe that the last few verses of Deuteronomy, which describe Moses's death and unknown place of burial, were actually written by Moses. (A charming rabbinic legend imagines Moses writing these verses "with tears in his eyes." This piece of lore, however, was not stated as a dogma.)

Spinoza's concept of Bible scholarship and the bluntness with which he stated his conclusions were quite revolutionary. In terms of method, Spinoza advocated techniques of Bible scholarship that have become accepted practice in the secular academy. Spinoza analyzed editorial measures, earlier and later traditions, the social conditions in which texts were originally produced, and manuscript variations and corruptions. These considerations were to become the predominant concerns of subsequent Bible scholarship, but they were revolutionary in Spinoza's day. Spinoza's willingness to draw radical conclusions from these investigations was equally striking: "It is thus clearer than the sun at noonday that the Pentateuch [the Five Books of Moses] was not written by Moses, but by someone who lived long after Moses." Statements like these did not lead to a movement to reinstate the excommunicate.

Since earlier Jewish scholars were also aware of these textual problems, we ought to emphasize the premises of the TPT that drew Spinoza in so radical a direction. To begin with, while Abraham Ibn Ezra and others may have regarded several verses as having been composed by a different hand than Moses's, none of these sages considered the sanctity of the Torah impugned by this recognition. If Moses did not scribe a particular verse, then Joshua did; and if not Joshua, then Ezra or one of the prophets. That God's word ultimately stood behind the text was clear. Moreover, that the Torah represented the way of life for Jewish society, all medievals accepted without reservation. This last point requires elaboration. All Jewish holidays begin the evening of the day before the holiday because the first rabbis decided, on the basis of a mistaken exegesis of chapter 1 of Genesis, that the Bible means to say that each day begins on the evening preceding that day. Rashbam, one of the greatest medieval exegetes, recognized this misunderstanding. Did he then propose to begin the Sabbath on Saturday morning at dawn instead of Friday evening at sundown? Of course not, because any custom ratified by centuries of practice, and with the intention of carrying out God's Torah, could not be wrong. Rashbam said his Sabbath prayers Friday evening. When the Torah Scrolls were read in synagogue, Ibn Ezra stood up and affirmed along with the rest of the congregation that "This is the Torah that Moshe placed before Israel by the word of God."

To the rabbis, as to all Jews, the Torah's meaning went beyond the text and into the living life of the Jewish community. To Spinoza, the Scriptures were a humanly produced document, subject to the same rules of observation and analysis that apply to an astronomical or a meteorological event. As Spinoza baldly stated in chapter 7 of the TPT, "the method [e.g., his method] of interpreting Scripture does not differ widely from the method of interpreting nature—in fact, it is almost the same." In early TPT chapters dealing with prophecy, miracles, and Israel's election (i.e., "Chosenness"), Spinoza uses his rationalism to cut the Hebrew Scriptures down to human size, while being sufficiently veiled in his formulations to avoid persecution.[8] A careful reader will nevertheless recognize that prophecy, miracles, and the doctrine of Israel's election (or Chosenness) are divested of their usual meaning and radically reinterpreted along natural as opposed to supernatural lines.

Armed with this attitude, a superb Jewish education, and one of the most original and penetrating minds Western civilization has ever produced, Spinoza set out to demonstrate that the Bible is a human document written for one people (Jews), in one place (Israel), and at one time (before the Exile of 70 CE). The Bible, therefore, unlike philosophy, has no claim to eternal or universal truth. And here is perhaps the most extraordinary thing about the *Theological-Political Treatise*. Spinoza's revolution in Bible scholarship is not even the main point of the work, but was meant to be principally a groundclearing to establish the basis for a political state in which people are left unmolested in their religious ideas. As the title to the last chapter of the TPT puts it: "That in a free state every man may think what he likes, and say what he thinks." Proclaiming that "the true aim of government is liberty," and living his adult life as a true independent, possibly the first European who belonged to no religious community, it is no wonder that Spinoza ultimately came to be regarded as a hero to dozens of young Jews in the nineteenth century who sought to break the bonds of traditional Jewish community without lapsing into another orthodoxy such as the majority Christian culture offered. The Hebrew Commonwealth, in which heresy was tantamount to treason, since God was the recognized head of state, was for Spinoza a onetime occurrence that could not and should not be reproduced in seventeenth-century Europe. In other words, Spinoza's ideas clearly tend toward a separation of church and state.

But can a Jewish thinker be purely negative in his or her approach to the Judaic tradition? If we raise this question with respect to Karl Marx, I would argue that Marx cannot be considered a Jewish thinker. For one, he was baptized as a child, was raised without exposure to Jewish life, and was hardly Spinoza's equal as a student of the Bible, or religion. Marx not only dismissed religion in general as "the opiate of the masses" but also had particularly nasty things to say about Judaism in his only extended treatment of the subject. Marx saw the task of the day as the emancipation of all people from the spirit of Judaism, which he equated with the spirit of money. Dissolving Judaism entirely could be the only possible outcome, as a mere byproduct, of abolishing capitalism in general.

For Spinoza, however, a variety of Jewish possibilities needed to be broached. While he himself was not interested in making a positive contribution in this regard, Spinoza held out the possibility of complete assimilation, were the nations to cease their Jew-hatred. But he also imagined a national restoration, were the Jews to shake off the emasculating effects of their religious superstitions and have a better run of luck. Since Spinoza drew up his own set of essential principles based on the Hebrew Scriptures, it is even possible to see him as a forerunner of later religious reformers who distinguished between the ethical and the ceremonial commandments. So Spinoza can—and has been—portrayed as the first Assimilationist, the first Zionist, the first Religious Reformer. This mental exercise, of course, only highlights that none of these options were open to a seventeenth-century European Jew. Exiled from the Jewish community and unwilling to join the Christian, Spinoza lived on a modest pension, ground glass lenses (less for the money than to keep abreast of developments in optics), and described himself as a good and loyal citizen of the Dutch Republic.

The contrasting attitudes exhibited in Spinoza and Marx toward the future of the Jews marks another difference between their lives and times. Spinoza felt a special need to explain the Jews' national survival, which most Europeans took as a proof of God's active involvement in human history. (In

Christian tradition, Jewish survival represented a testimony to the truth of Christianity and the dire consequences of denying that truth.) Spinoza attempted to explain the nature of Jew-hatred, which he attributed mainly to the Jewish determination to remain distinct. This was symbolized, above all, by the practice of circumcision, on which this descendant of conversos naturally placed great emphasis. He also reflected at length on the nature of Jewish history and survival, including the martyrdom suffered by conversos during the Inquisition, all of which his own philosophy forced him to explain as somehow neither unique nor miraculous. Even at a distance of several centuries, one can hear how irked Spinoza must have been by the common attitude toward Jewish survival: "As to their continuance so long after their dispersion and the loss of empire, there is nothing marvelous in it, for they so separated themselves from every other nation as to draw down upon themselves universal hate, not only by their outward rites, but also the sign of circumcision which they observe most scrupulously" (TPT 3:55).[9]

To sum up the difference between these two rebellious spirits, while Marx was able to dismiss all religion and Judaism along with it as inconsequential, Spinoza's life and times forced him to confront the Western religious tradition, and that entailed a confrontation with Judaism too. Does that entitle us to consider Spinoza a Jewish thinker? If one considers his Jewish birth, his converso background, his grappling with Judaism as a religion, his gnawing awareness of the peculiarities of Jewish existence, and the belated influence he exerted on later Jewish thinkers on Jewish themes, I think the answer is clear. Despite his excommunication, despite his professed indifference to the Jewish future, despite his self-conception as a universalistic philosopher, we may consider Baruch Spinoza as the first modern Jewish thinker—perhaps, above all, because his presentation needed to be engaged again and again by his Jewish successors.

Obviously, Spinoza wanted the Bible to play a greatly reduced role in European culture. I have opted to reproduce those chapters of the TPT that include Spinoza's cagey answer to the question of what role the Scriptures should and could play in European life. (Please note, since Spinoza wrote for Jews and Christians alike, *Scripture* includes both Old and New Testaments.)

QUESTIONS FOR SPINOZA, *THEOLOGICAL-POLITICAL TREATISE*, CHAPTERS 12–13

The philosopher Leo Strauss contends that Spinoza often concealed his true intentions for fear of persecution. Do you see any evidence of this in the chapters that you are reading?

Spinoza clearly dissented from the traditional view that saw the Torah as the divinely revealed, eternally valid guideline of a living Jewish culture. Yet he claimed it taught "justice and charity." Did Spinoza see the Bible as being with or without positive value?

What is the value of the Bible in Spinoza's eyes? What is the value, purpose, and authority of the Bible in the eyes of Judaism? Of Christianity? In your eyes?

Does the Bible's value rely on its *source* or on its *content?* Is the Torah "holy" because of its author (God) or because of its teachings? Or, because of both?

What does Spinoza mean by the words *sacred* and *Divine?*

Why is Spinoza's list of basic teachings preferable to the Ten Commandments? Or preferable to the injunction to "Love the Lord with all your heart and with your soul and with all your might" (Deut. 6:5)?

Can one try to make Spinoza compatible with traditional revealed religion by focusing on the "ends" or "goals" of the Bible's teachings as opposed to its origins? Why or why not?

Are the questions that Spinoza raises about the Bible still significant and relevant today? Are they still radical?

STUDIES BY AND ABOUT SPINOZA

Steven Nadler, *Spinoza: A Life* (Cambridge: Cambridge University Press, 1999), offers the best biography in any language. Nadler's *Spinoza's Heresy: Immortality and the Jewish Mind* (New York: Oxford University Press, 2001) focuses on the most tantalizing question of all: Why was Spinoza excommunicated? Spinoza's letters, though not serious philosophy, are a good starting place to savor his intellectual milieu. His correspondents included such scientific heavyweights as Christian Huygens and Robert Boyle. Jacob Rader Marcus, in *The Jew in the Medieval World* (Cincinnati, Ohio: Hebrew Union College Press, 1990), excerpts an early biographical sketch of Spinoza and the curriculum (if somewhat idealized) of the Amsterdam Jewish community. Spinoza's general philosophy has generated scholarship that is usually difficult and technical. The *Cambridge Companion to Spinoza*, ed. Don Garrett (Cambridge: Cambridge University Press, 1996), is the best place to start. Harry Wolfson's *From Philo to Spinoza* (New York: Behrman, 1977) is accessible and clear. The same cannot be said for Leo Strauss's *Spinoza's Critique of Religion* (New York: Schocken, 1961), but his prefatory memoir offers a wonderful portrait of a twentieth-century German-Jewish intellectual. The first volume of Yirmiyahu Yovel's *Spinoza and Other Heretics* (Princeton, N.J.: Princeton University Press, 1989) seems to me well worth the effort; volume 2 is only fit for those well versed in European philosophy. Steven Smith, *Spinoza, Liberalism and the Question of Jewish Identity* (New Haven, Conn.: Yale University Press, 1997) addresses Spinoza's political legacy. James Samuel Preus, *Spinoza and the Irrelevance of Biblical Authority* (Cambridge: Cambridge University Press, 2001) is suitable for advanced students. With the background provided here, I hope that the TPT itself will be accessible without further supplementary material.

From *Theological-Political Treatise*

Baruch Spinoza

Chapter XII

Of the true original of the Divine Law, and wherefore scripture is called sacred, and the Word of God. How that, in so far as it contains the Word of God, it has come down to us uncorrupted.

Those who look upon the Bible as a message sent down by God from Heaven to men, will doubtless cry out that I have committed the sin against the Holy Ghost because I have asserted that the Word of God is faulty, mutilated, tampered with, and inconsistent; that we possess it only in fragments, and that the original of the covenant which God made with the Jews has been lost. However, I have no doubt that a little reflection will cause them to desist from their uproar: for not only reason but the expressed opinions of prophets and apostles openly proclaim that God's eternal Word and covenant, no less than true religion, is Divinely inscribed in human hearts, that is, in the human mind, and that this is the true original of God's covenant, stamped with His own seal, namely, the idea of Himself, as it were, with the image of His Godhood.

Religion was imparted to the early Hebrews as a law written down, because they were at that time in the condition of children, but afterwards Moses (Deut. xxx. 6) and Jeremiah (xxxi. 33) predicted a time coming when the Lord should write His law in their hearts. Thus only the Jews, and amongst them chiefly the Sadducees, struggled for the law written on tablets; least of all need those who bear it inscribed on their hearts join in the contest. Those, therefore, who reflect, will find nothing in what I have written repugnant either to the Word of God or to true religion and faith, or calculated to weaken either one or the other: contrariwise, they will see that I have strengthened religion, as I showed at the end of Chapter X.; indeed, had it not been so, I should certainly have decided to hold my peace, nay, I would even have asserted as a way out of all difficulties that the Bible contains the most profound hidden mysteries; however, as this doctrine has given rise to gross superstition and other pernicious results spoken of at the beginning of Chapter V., I have thought such a course unnecessary, especially as religion stands in no need of superstitious adornments, but is, on the contrary, deprived by such trappings of some of her splendour.

Still, it will be said, though the law of God is written in the heart, the Bible is none the less the Word of God, and it is no more lawful to say of Scripture than of God's word that it is mutilated and corrupted. I fear that such objectors are too anxious to be pious, and that they are in danger of turning religion into superstition, and worshipping paper and ink in place of God's Word.

I am certified of thus much: I have said nothing unworthy of Scripture or God's Word, and I have made no assertions which I could not prove by most plain argument to be true. I can, therefore, rest assured that I have advanced nothing which is impious or even savours of impiety.

I confess that some profane men, to whom religion is a burden, may, from what I have said, assume a license to sin, and without any reason, at the simple dictates of their lusts conclude that Scripture is everywhere faulty and falsified, and that therefore its authority is null; but such men are beyond the reach of help, for nothing, as the proverb has it, can be said so rightly that it cannot be twisted into wrong. Those who wish to give rein to their lusts are at no loss for an excuse, nor were those men of old who possessed the original Scriptures, the ark of the covenant, nay, the prophets and apostles in person among them, any better than the people of to-day. Human nature, Jew as well as Gentile, has always been the same, and in every age virtue has been exceedingly rare.

Nevertheless, to remove every scruple, I will here show in what sense the Bible or any inanimate thing should be called sacred and Divine; also wherein the law of God consists, and how it cannot be contained in a certain number of books; and, lastly, I will show that Scripture, in so far as it teaches what is necessary for obedience and salvation, cannot have been corrupted. From these considerations everyone will be able to judge that I have neither said anything against the Word of God nor given any foothold to impiety.

A thing is called sacred and Divine when it is designed for promoting piety, and continues sacred so long as it is religiously used: if the users cease to be pious, the thing ceases to be sacred: if it be turned to base uses, that which was formerly sacred becomes unclean and profane. For instance, a certain spot was named by the patriarch Jacob the house of God, because he worshipped

God there revealed to him: by the prophets the same spot was called the house of iniquity (see Amos v. 5, and Hosea x. 5), because the Israelites were wont, at the instigation of Jeroboam, to sacrifice there to idols. Another example puts the matter in the plainest light. Words gain their meaning solely from their usage, and if they are arranged according to their accepted signification so as to move those who read them to devotion, they will become sacred, and the book so written will be sacred also. But if their usage afterwards dies out so that the words have no meaning, or the book becomes utterly neglected, whether from unworthy motives, or because it is no longer needed, then the words and the book will lose both their use and their sanctity: lastly, if these same words be otherwise arranged, or if their customary meaning becomes perverted into its opposite, then both the words and the book containing them become, instead of sacred, impure and profane.

From this it follows that nothing is in itself absolutely sacred, or profane, and unclean, apart from the mind, but only relatively thereto. Thus much is clear from many passages in the Bible. Jeremiah (to select one case out of many) says (chap. vii. 4), that the Jews of his time were wrong in calling Solomon's Temple, the Temple of God, for, as he goes on to say in the same chapter, God's name would only be given to the Temple so long as it was frequented by men who worshipped Him, and defended justice, but that, if it became the resort of murderers, thieves, idolaters, and other wicked persons, it would be turned into a den of malefactors.

Scripture, curiously enough, nowhere tells us what became of the Ark of the Covenant, though there is no doubt that it was destroyed, or burnt together with the Temple; yet there was nothing which the Hebrews considered more sacred, or held in greater reverence. Thus Scripture is sacred, and its words Divine so long as it stirs mankind to devotion towards God: but if it be utterly neglected, as it formerly was by the Jews, it becomes nothing but paper and ink, and is left to be desecrated or corrupted: still, though Scripture be thus corrupted or destroyed, we must not say that the Word of God has suffered in like manner, else we shall be like the Jews, who said that the Temple which would then be the Temple of God had perished in the flames. Jeremiah tells us this in respect to the law, for he thus chides the ungodly of his time, "Wherefore say you we are masters, and the law of the Lord is with us? Surely it has been given in vain, it is in vain that the pen of the scribes" (has been made)—that is, you say falsely that the Scripture is in your power, and that you possess the law of God; for ye have made it of none effect.

So also, when Moses broke the first tables of the law, he did not by any means cast the Word of God from his hands in anger and shatter it—such an action would be inconceivable, either of Moses or of God's Word—he only broke the tables of stone, which, though they had before been holy from containing the covenant wherewith the Jews had bound themselves in obedience to God, had entirely lost their sanctity when the covenant had been violated by the worship of the calf, and were, therefore, as liable to perish as the ark of the covenant. It is thus scarcely to be wondered at, that the original documents of Moses are no longer extant, nor that the books we possess met with the fate we have described, when we consider that the true original of the Divine covenant, the most sacred object of all, has totally perished.

Let them cease, therefore, who accuse us of impiety, inasmuch as we have said nothing against the Word of God, neither have we corrupted it, but let them keep their anger, if they would wreak it justly, for the ancients whose malice desecrated the Ark, the Temple, and the Law of God, and all that was held sacred, subjecting them to corruption. Furthermore, if, according to the saying of the Apostle in 2 Cor. iii. 3, they possessed "the Epistle of Christ, written not with ink, but with the Spirit of the living God, not in tables of stone, but in the fleshy tables of the heart," let them cease to worship the letter, and be so anxious concerning it.

I think I have now sufficiently shown in what respect Scripture should be accounted sacred and Divine; we may now see what should rightly be understood by the expression, the Word of the Lord; *debar* (the Hebrew original) signifies word, speech, command, and thing. The causes for which a thing is in Hebrew said to be of God, or is referred to Him, have been already detailed in Chap. I., and we can therefrom easily gather what meaning Scripture attaches to the phrases, the word, the speech, the command, or the thing of God. I need not, therefore, repeat what I there said, nor what was shown under the third head in the chapter on miracles. It is enough to mention the repetition for the better understanding of what I am about to say—viz., that the Word of the Lord when it has reference to anyone but God Himself, signifies that Divine law treated of in Chap. IV.; in other words, religion, universal and catholic to the whole human race, as Isaiah describes it (chap. i. 10), teaching that the true way of life consists, not in ceremonies, but in charity, and a true heart, and calling it indifferently God's Law and God's Word.

The expression is also used metaphorically for the order of nature and destiny (which, indeed, actually depend and follow from the eternal mandate of the Divine nature), and especially for such parts of such order as were foreseen by the prophets, for the prophets did not perceive future events as the result of natural causes, but as the fiats and decrees of God. Lastly, it is employed for the command of any prophet, in so far as he had perceived it by his peculiar faculty or prophetic gift, and not by the natural light of reason; this use springs chiefly from the usual prophetic conception of God as a legislator, which we remarked in Chap. IV. There are, then, three causes for the Bible's being called the Word of God: because it teaches true religion, of which God is the eternal Founder; because it narrates predictions of future events as though they were decrees of God; because its actual authors generally perceived things not by their ordinary natural faculties, but by a power peculiar to themselves, and introduced these things perceived, as told them by God.

Although Scripture contains much that is merely historical and can be perceived by natural reason, yet its name is acquired from its chief subject matter.

We can thus easily see how God can be said to be the Author of the Bible: it is because of the true religion therein contained, and not because He wished to communicate to men a certain number of books. We can also learn from hence the reason for the division into Old and New Testament. It was made because the prophets who preached religion before Christ, preached it as a national law in virtue of the covenant entered into under Moses; while the Apostles who came after Christ, preached it to all men as a universal religion solely in virtue of Christ's Passion: the cause for the division is not that the two parts are different in doctrine, nor that they were written as originals of the covenant, nor, lastly, that the catholic religion (which is in entire harmony with our nature) was new except in relation to those who had not known it: "it was in the world," as John the Evangelist says, "and the world knew it not."

Thus, even if we had fewer books of the Old and New Testament than we have, we should still not be deprived of the Word of God (which, as we have said, is identical with true religion), even as we do not now hold ourselves to be deprived of it, though we lack many cardinal writings such as the Book of the Law, which was religiously guarded in the Temple as the original of the Covenant, also the Book of Wars, the Book of Chronicles, and many others, from whence the extant Old Testament was taken and compiled. The above conclusion may be supported by many reasons.

I. Because the books of both Testaments were not written by express command at one place for all ages, but are a fortuitous collection of the works of men, writing each as his period and disposition dictated. So much is clearly shown by the call of the prophets who were bade to admonish the ungodly of their time, and also by the Apostolic Epistles.

II. Because it is one thing to understand the meaning of Scripture and the prophets, and quite another thing to understand the meaning of God, or the actual truth. This follows from what we said in Chap. II. We showed, in Chap. VI., that it applied to historic narratives, and to miracles: but it by no means applies to questions concerning true religion and virtue.

III. Because the books of the Old Testament were selected from many, and were collected and sanctioned by a council of the Pharisees, as we showed in Chap. X. The books of the New Testament were also chosen from many by councils which rejected as spurious other books held sacred by many. But these councils, both Pharisee and Christian, were not composed of prophets, but only of learned men and teachers. Still, we must grant that they were guided in their choice by a regard for the Word of God; and they must, therefore, have known what the law of God was.

IV. Because the Apostles wrote not as prophets, but as teachers (see last Chapter), and chose whatever method they thought best adapted for those whom they addressed: and consequently, there are many things in the Epistles (as we showed at the end of the last Chapter) which are not necessary to salvation.

V. Lastly, because there are four Evangelists in the New Testament, and it is scarcely credible that God can have designed to narrate the life of Christ four times over, and to communicate it thus to mankind. For though there are some details related in one Gospel which are not in another, and one often helps us to understand another, we cannot thence conclude that all that is set down is of vital importance to us, and that God chose the four Evangelists in order that the life of Christ might be better understood; for each one preached his Gospel in a separate locality, each wrote it down as he preached it, in simple language, in order that the history of Christ might be clearly told, not with any view of explaining his fellow-Evangelists.

If there are some passages which can be better, and more easily understood by comparing the various versions, they are the result of chance, and are not numerous: their continuance in obscurity would have impaired neither the clearness of the narrative nor the blessedness of mankind.

We have now shown that Scripture can only be called the Word of God in so far as it affects religion, or the Divine law; we must now point out that, in respect to these questions, it is neither faulty, tampered with, nor corrupt. By faulty, tampered with, and corrupt, I here mean written so incorrectly that the meaning cannot be arrived at by a study of the language, nor from the authority of Scripture. I will not go to such lengths as to say that the Bible, in so far as it contains the Divine law, has always preserved the same vowel-points, the same letters, or the same words (I leave this to be proved by the Massoretes and other worshippers of the letter), I only maintain that the meaning by which alone an utterance is entitled to be called Divine, has come down to us uncorrupted, even though the original wording may have been more often changed than we suppose. Such alterations, as I have said above, detract nothing from the Divinity of the Bible, for the Bible would have been no less Divine had it been written in different words or a different language. That the Divine law has in this sense come down to us uncorrupted, is an assertion which admits of no dispute. For from the Bible itself we learn, without the smallest difficulty or ambiguity, that its cardinal precept is: To love God above all things, and one's neighbour as one's self. This cannot be a spurious passage, nor due to a hasty and mistaken scribe, for if the Bible had ever put forth a different doctrine it would have had to change the whole of its teaching, for this is the corner-stone of religion, without which the whole fabric would fall headlong to the ground. The Bible would not be the work we have been examining, but something quite different.

We remain, then, unshaken in our belief that this has always been the doctrine of Scripture, and, consequently, that no error sufficient to vitiate it can have crept in without being instantly observed by all; nor can anyone have succeeded in tampering with it and escaped the discovery of his malice.

As this corner-stone is intact, we must perforce admit the same of whatever other passages are indisputably dependent on it, and are also fundamental, as, for instance, that a God exists, that He foresees all things, that He is Almighty, that by His decree the good prosper and the wicked come to naught, and, finally, that our salvation depends solely on His grace.

These are doctrines which Scripture plainly teaches throughout, and which it is bound to teach, else all the rest would be empty and baseless; nor can we be less positive about other moral doctrines, which plainly are built upon this universal foundation—for instance, to uphold justice, to aid the weak, to do no murder, to covet no man's goods, &c. Precepts, I repeat, such as these, human malice and the lapse of ages are alike powerless to destroy, for if any part of them perished, its loss would immediately be supplied from the fundamental principle, especially the doctrine of charity, which is everywhere in both Testaments extolled above all others. Moreover, though it be true that there is no conceivable crime so heinous that it has never been committed, still there is no one who would attempt in excuse for his crimes to destroy the law, or introduce an impious doctrine in the place of what is eternal and salutary; men's nature is so constituted that everyone (be he king or subject) who has committed a base action, tries to deck out his conduct with spurious excuses, till he seems to have done nothing but what is just and right.

We may conclude, therefore, that the whole Divine law, as taught by Scripture, has come down to us uncorrupted. Besides this there are certain facts which we may be sure have been transmitted in good faith. For instance, the main facts of Hebrew history, which were perfectly well known to everyone. The Jewish people were accustomed in former times to chant the ancient history of their nation in psalms. The main facts, also, of Christ's life and passion were immediately spread abroad through the whole Roman empire. It is therefore scarcely credible, unless nearly everybody consented thereto, which we cannot suppose, that successive generations have handed down the broad outline of the Gospel narrative otherwise than as they received it.

Whatsoever, therefore, is spurious or faulty can only have reference to details—some circumstances in one or the other history or prophecy designed to stir the people to greater devotion; or in some miracle, with a view of confounding philosophers; or, lastly, in speculative matters after they had become mixed up with religion, so that some individual might prop up his own inventions with a pretext of Divine authority. But such matters have little to do with salvation, whether they be corrupted little or much, as I will show in detail in the next chapter, though I think the question sufficiently plain from what I have said already, especially in Chapter II.

Chapter XIII

It is shown that Scripture teaches only very simple doctrines, such as suffice for right conduct.

In the second chapter of this treatise we pointed out that the prophets were gifted with extraordinary powers of imagination, but not of understanding; also that God only revealed to them such things as are very simple—not philosophic mysteries,—and that He adapted His communications to their previous opinions. We further showed in Chap. V. that Scripture only transmits and teaches truths which can readily be comprehended by all; not deducing and concatenating its conclusions from definitions and axioms, but narrating quite simply, and confirming its statements, with a view to inspiring belief, by an appeal to experience as exemplified in miracles and history, and setting forth its truths in the style and phraseology which would most appeal to the popular mind (cf. Chap. VI., third division).

Lastly, we demonstrated in Chap. VII. that the difficulty of understanding Scripture lies in the language only, and not in the abstruseness of the argument.

To these considerations we may add that the Prophets did not preach only to the learned, but to all Jews, without exception, while the Apostles were wont to teach the gospel doctrine in churches where there were public meetings; whence it follows that Scriptural doctrine contains no lofty speculations nor philosophic reasoning, but only very simple matters, such as could be understood by the slowest intelligence.

I am consequently lost in wonder at the ingenuity of those whom I have already mentioned, who detect in the Bible mysteries so profound that they cannot be explained in human language, and who have introduced so many philosophic speculations into religion that the Church seems like an academy, and religion like a science, or rather a dispute.

It is not to be wondered at that men, who boast of possessing supernatural intelligence, should be unwilling to yield the palm of knowledge to philosophers who have only their ordinary faculties; still I should be surprised if I found them teaching any new speculative doctrine, which was not a commonplace to those Gentile philosophers whom, in spite of all, they stigmatize as blind; for, if one inquires what these mysteries lurking in Scripture may be, one is confronted with nothing but the reflections of Plato or Aristotle, or the like, which it would often be easier for an ignorant man to dream than for the most accomplished scholar to wrest out of the Bible.

However, I do not wish to affirm absolutely that Scripture contains no doctrines in the sphere of philosophy, for in the last chapter I pointed out some of the kind, as fundamental principles; but I go so far as to say that such doctrines are very few and very simple. Their precise nature and definition I will now set forth. The task will be easy, for we know that Scripture does not aim at imparting scientific knowledge, and, therefore, it demands from men nothing but obedience, and censures obstinacy, but not ignorance.

Furthermore, as obedience to God consists solely in love to our neighbour—for whosoever loveth his neighbour, as a means of obeying God, hath, as St. Paul says (Rom. iii. 8), fulfilled the law,—it follows that no knowledge is commended in the Bible save that which is necessary for enabling all men to obey God in the manner stated, and without which they would become rebellious, or without the discipline of obedience.

Other speculative questions, which have no direct bearing on this object, or are concerned with the knowledge of natural events, do not affect Scripture, and should be entirely separated from religion.

Now, though everyone, as we have said, is now quite able to see this truth for himself, I should nevertheless wish, considering that the whole of Religion depends thereon, to explain the entire question more accurately and clearly. To this end I must first prove that the intellectual or accurate knowledge of God is not a gift, bestowed upon all good men like obedience; and, further, that the knowledge of God, required by Him through His prophets from everyone without exception, as needful to be known, is simply a knowledge of His Divine justice and charity. Both these points are easily proved from Scripture. The first plainly follows from Exodus vi. 2, where God, in order to show the singular grace bestowed upon Moses, says to him: "And I appeared unto Abraham, unto Isaac, and unto Jacob by the name of El Sadai (A. V. God Almighty); but by my name Jehovah was I not known to them"—for the better understanding of which passage I may remark that *El Sadai*, in Hebrew, signifies the God who suffices, in that He gives to every man that which suffices for him; and, although *Sadai* is often used by itself, to signify God, we cannot doubt that the word *El* (God) is everywhere understood. Furthermore, we must note that Jehovah is the only word found in Scripture with the meaning of the absolute essence of God, without reference to created things. The Jews maintain, for this reason, that this is, strictly speaking, the only name of God; that the rest of the words used are merely titles; and, in truth, the other names of God, whether they be substantives or adjectives, are merely attributive, and belong to Him, in so far as He is conceived of in relation to created things, or manifested through them. Thus *El*, or *Eloah*, signifies powerful, as is well known, and only applies to God in respect to His supremacy, as when we call Paul an apostle; the faculties of his power are set forth in an accompanying adjective, as *El*, great, awful, just, merciful, &c., or else all are understood at once by the use of *El* in the plural number, with a singular signification, an expression frequently adopted in Scripture.

Now, as God tells Moses that He was not known to the patriarchs by the name of Jehovah, it follows that they were not cognizant of any attribute of God which expresses His absolute essence, but only of His deeds and promises — that is, of His power, as manifested in visible things. God does not thus speak to Moses in order to accuse the patriarchs of infidelity, but, on the contrary, as a means of extolling their belief and faith, inasmuch as, though they possessed no extraordinary knowledge of God (such as Moses had), they yet accepted His promises as fixed and certain; whereas Moses, though his thoughts about God were more exalted, nevertheless doubted about the Divine promises, and complained to God that, instead of the promised deliverance, the prospects of the Israelites had darkened.

As the patriarchs did not know the distinctive name of God, and as God mentions the fact to Moses, in praise of their faith and single-heartedness, and in contrast to the extraordinary grace granted to Moses, it follows, as we stated at first, that men are not bound by decree to have knowledge of the attributes of God, such knowledge being only granted to a few of the faithful: it is hardly worth while to quote further examples from Scripture, for everyone must recognize that knowledge of God is not equal among all good men. Moreover, a man cannot be ordered to be wise any more than he can be ordered to live and exist. Men, women, and children are all alike able to obey by commandment, but not to be wise. If any tell us that it is not necessary to understand the Divine attributes, but that we must believe them simply without proof, he is plainly trifling. For what is invisible and can only be perceived by the mind, cannot be apprehended by any other means than proofs; if these are absent the object remains ungrasped; the repetition of what has been heard on such subjects no more indicates or attains to their meaning than the words of a parrot or a puppet speaking without sense or signification.

Before I proceed I ought to explain how it comes that we are often told in Genesis that the patriarchs preached in the name of Jehovah, this being in plain contradiction to the text above quoted. A reference to what was said in Chap. VIII. will readily explain the difficulty. It was there shown that the writer of the Pentateuch did not always speak of things and places by the names they bore in the times of which he was writing, but by the names best known to his contemporaries. God is thus said in the Pentateuch to have been

preached by the patriarchs under the name of Jehovah, not because such was
the name by which the patriarchs knew Him, but because this name was the
one most reverenced by the Jews. This point, I say, must necessarily be noticed, for in Exodus it is expressly stated that God was not known to the patriarchs by this name; and in chap. iii. 13, it is said that Moses desired to know
the name of God. Now, if this name had been already known it would have
been known to Moses. We must therefore draw the conclusion indicated,
namely, that the faithful patriarchs did not know this name of God, and that
the knowledge of God is bestowed and not commanded by the Deity.

It is now time to pass on to our second point, and show that God through
His prophets required from men no other knowledge of Himself than is contained in a knowledge of His justice and charity—that is, of attributes which
a certain manner of life will enable men to imitate. Jeremiah states this in so
many words (xxii. 15, 16): "Did not thy father eat, and drink, and do judgment and justice? and then it was well with him. He judged the cause of the
poor and needy; then it was well with him: was not this to know Me? saith
the Lord." The words in chap. ix. 24 of the same book are equally clear. "But
let him that glorieth glory in this, that he understandeth and knoweth Me, that
I am the Lord which exercise loving-kindness, judgment, and righteousness
in the earth; for in these things I delight, saith the Lord." The same doctrine
may be gathered from Exod. xxxiv. 6, where God revealed to Moses only
those of His attributes which display the Divine justice and charity. Lastly, we
may call attention to a passage in John which we shall discuss at more length
hereafter; the Apostle explains the nature of God (inasmuch as no one has beheld Him) through charity only, and concludes that he who possesses charity
possesses, and in very truth knows God.

We have thus seen that Moses, Jeremiah, and John sum up in a very short
compass the knowledge of God needful for all, and that they state it to consist
in exactly what we said, namely, that God is supremely just, and supremely
merciful—in other words, the one perfect pattern of the true life. We may add
that Scripture nowhere gives an express definition of God, and does not point
out any other of His attributes which should be apprehended save these, nor
does it in set terms praise any others. Wherefore we may draw the general
conclusion that an intellectual knowledge of God, which takes cognizance of
His nature in so far as it actually is, and which cannot by any manner of living be imitated by mankind or followed as an example, has no bearing whatever on true rules of conduct, on faith, or on revealed religion; consequently
that men may be in complete error on the subject without incurring the charge
of sinfulness. We need now no longer wonder that God adapted Himself to the
existing opinions and imaginations of the prophets, or that the faithful held
different ideas of God, as we showed in Chap. II.; or, again, that the sacred

books speak very inaccurately of God, attributing to Him hands, feet, eyes, ears, a mind, and motion from one place to another; or that they ascribe to Him emotions, such as jealousy, mercy, &c., or, lastly, that they describe Him as a Judge in heaven sitting on a royal throne with Christ on His right hand. Such expressions are adapted to the understanding of the multitude, it being the object of the Bible to make men not learned but obedient.

In spite of this the general run of theologians, when they come upon any of these phrases which they cannot rationally harmonize with the Divine nature, maintain that they should be interpreted metaphorically, passages they cannot understand they say should be interpreted literally. But if every expression of this kind in the Bible is necessarily to be interpreted and understood metaphorically, Scripture must have been written, not for the people and the unlearned masses, but chiefly for accomplished experts and philosophers.

If it were indeed a sin to hold piously and simply the ideas about God we have just quoted, the prophets ought to have been strictly on their guard against the use of such expressions, seeing the weak-mindedness of the people, and ought, on the other hand, to have set forth first of all, duly and clearly, those attributes of God which are needful to be understood.

This they have nowhere done; we cannot, therefore, think that opinions taken in themselves without respect to actions are either pious or impious, but must maintain that a man is pious or impious in his beliefs only in so far as he is thereby incited to obedience, or derives from them license to sin and rebel. If a man, by believing what is true, becomes rebellious, his creed is impious; if by believing what is false he becomes obedient, his creed is pious; for the true knowledge of God comes not by commandment, but by Divine gift. God has required nothing from man but a knowledge of His Divine justice and charity, and that not as necessary to scientific accuracy, but to obedience.

NOTES

1. Johann Koehler, *The Life of Benedict Spinoza*, translated and excerpted in Jacob Rader Marcus, ed., *The Jew in the Medieval World* (Cincinnati, Ohio: Hebrew Union College Press, 1990), 339–40.

2. Leo Strauss, *Persecution and the Art of Writing* (Chicago: University of Chicago Press, 1988).

3. Spinoza knew many languages, but seems fully at home in none of them. R. H. M. Elwes wrote: "A translator has special opportunities for observing the extent of Spinoza's knowledge of Latin. His sentences are grammatical and his meaning almost always clear. But his vocabulary is restricted; in fact, the niceties of scholarship are wanting. He reminds one of a clever workman who accomplishes much with simple tools."

4. Sephardic Jews are those whose ancestry can be traced back to the Jews of Iberia (Spain and Portugal). Ashkenazic Jews trace their ancestry to Northern and Central Europe, but migrated eastward as a result of the expulsions beginning in the late thirteenth century.

5. The terms *Marranos*, *conversos*, and *anusim* are usually used interchangeably to describe this population. *Marrano*, a word whose origins are obscure, initially had a pejorative connotation, but no longer does so. *Anusim*, Hebrew for "forced," is a good term, but unfamiliar to Western audiences. *Converso*, even for non-Spanish speakers, is self-explanatory.

6. Yirmiyahu Yovel, *Spinoza and Other Heretics* (Princeton, N.J.: Princeton University Press, 1989).

7. Isaac Deutscher, a Jewish Marxist, argued that even in his general philosophy Spinoza belongs to a special type that Deutscher termed "The Non-Jewish Jew."

8. It goes without saying that the TPT was listed by the Catholic Church in its index of forbidden books. Amsterdam's Jews were also prohibited by the Jewish community's ban of excommunication from reading anything Spinoza wrote or from having anything to do with him socially.

9. In my view, Spinoza both failed miserably and succeeded wonderfully with this statement. On the one hand, most people in the West continue to regard Jewish survival as "marvelous" (even if not desirable). On the other hand, Jewish historians for the last two hundred years have sought to explain Jewish survival along entirely secular (i.e., nonmiraculous) lines.

Chapter Two

Moses Mendelssohn's Defense of Judaism

Between Reason and Revelation

MENDELSSOHN'S LIFE AND TIMES (1729–1786)

I was born in the year 1729 (the twelfth of Elul, 5489, according to the Jewish calendar) in Dessau, where my father was a Torah scribe, or *sopher.* I studied Talmud with Rabbi Fraenkel, who was then the chief rabbi in Dessau. Around 1743, this learned rabbi, who had gained great fame among the Jewish people because of his commentary on the Jerusalem Talmud, was called to Berlin, where I followed him the same year. There, I developed a taste for the arts and sciences. . . . Eventually, I became first a tutor in the house of a rich Jew, later on his bookkeeper, and finally the manager of a silk factory, a position I am still holding. I was married in my thirty-third year and sired seven children, of whom five survive. I never attended a university, nor did I ever listen to an academic lecture.[1]

Reading between the lines of this autobiographical snippet, written to one of his many Christian admirers, we can imagine the struggle from poverty and parochialism, as well as the idealism and the ambition that made Mendelssohn the "patron saint" of German Jewry.[2] Discussions of modern Jewish thought that do not begin with Spinoza invariably begin with Moshe Mendelssohn. Mendelssohn was a heroic figure in many respects. Born to an obscure Torah scribe (son of mendel = mendels-sohn) in the town of Dessau, he followed his teacher to Berlin. While still a young man, Mendelssohn became the first Jew to achieve European-wide prominence as a thinker of the first rank. By his thirties, Mendelssohn kept some impressive company. Legend has it that he befriended the philosopher Gotthold Ephraim Lessing over a chess game. In 1763, Mendelssohn, a native Yiddish speaker, bested Immanuel Kant in an essay contest sponsored by the Prussian Royal Academy of Sciences.

Mendelssohn courted and then married Fromet Guggenheim in a decidedly modern fashion, writing her familiar letters, sending her unconventional prenuptial gifts, and recommending various philosophical classics for her leisure reading. Content as a businessman, philosopher, husband, and father, Mendelssohn's status as a living example that a Jew could be cultured and virtuous brought him much unwanted attention. In 1769, Johann Caspar Lavater, a Swiss clergyman and an admirer of Mendelssohn, dedicated his translation of a book "proving" the truth of Christianity to Mendelssohn. Lavater challenged Mendelssohn to either refute the author's proofs or do "what truth and honesty demand"; in other words, convert to Christianity. The whole affair, reminiscent of medieval religious disputation, disturbed Mendelssohn so much that he found himself permanently deflected from German philosophy into the arena of Jewish activism and education. Mendelssohn's answer to the question, why remain Jewish? would be given more fully in his *Jerusalem*. Nevertheless, he chided Lavater in true Enlightenment fashion:

> It is my good fortune to count among my friends many a man who is not of my faith. We love each other sincerely although both of us assume that we differ in matters of faith. We enjoy the pleasure of each other's company and feel enriched by it. But at no time has my heart whispered to me: what a pity that this beautiful soul should be lost. Only that man will be troubled by such regret who believes there is no salvation outside his church. It seems to me that anyone who leads man to virtue in this life cannot be damned in the next.[3]

While defending Judaism to the gentile world in public when necessary, Mendelssohn was active behind the scenes too. He encouraged Christian Wilhelm Dohm's influential treatise supporting Jewish emancipation, defended the "Aleinu" prayer against charges of anti-Christian animus, and lobbied for revision of the humiliating "Jewish Oath," required whenever a Jew gave testimony in a German court. Mendelssohn also fought for changes in the education and socialization of the Jews. He was willing to champion a three-day waiting period for Jewish burial in the face of hoary custom and in opposition to one of Germany's most prominent and polemical rabbis, Jacob Emden.

Mendelssohn also authored and/or edited a controversial Bible translation, which rendered the original Hebrew into polished German. (In fact, Rabbi Yehezkel Landau of Prague objected that the students would learn German, not Torah!)[4] Weaning Jews away from Yiddish to German was indeed one motive of the Bible translation, but Mendelssohn provided a slew of others in his letters. He took the education of his sons seriously; he found prior translations woefully inadequate; and he wished to stem the use of Christian

Bibles (containing the New Testament, apocryphal works, and Christological translations of key words and verses). Most importantly, in the realm of education, Mendelssohn represented the policy of the Jewish Enlightenment that the Bible, not the Talmud, ought to be the basis of the modern Jewish school curriculum. Mendelssohn's Bible commentary (in Hebrew) synthesized Jewish interpretive traditions with insights from contemporary philosophy and Bible scholarship. In its defense of the traditional Jewish text and in its agreement with rigorous medieval Jewish scholarship, the commentary presents a more conservative face than the translation. The Mendelssohn Bible is considered a crowning achievement of the Jewish Enlightenment, or *Haskalah.*

Mendelssohn's own religious views have been disputed. Some would "blame" Mendelssohn for the beginnings of Jewish religious reform, and point to the fact that four of six of his children converted to Christianity. But Mendelssohn himself remained from cradle to grave a halachically observant Jew, and the fact that his children waited until his demise to convert to Christianity only demonstrates how clearly they understood their father's commitment to Judaism. Mendelssohn threw down the gauntlet on the issue of trading religious reforms for political rights: "If civil union cannot be obtained under any condition other than our departing from the laws which we still consider binding on us, then we are sincerely sorry to find it necessary to declare that we must rather do without civil union."

Considering that Mendelssohn obtained permanent residential rights in Berlin only in 1762, long after achieving worldwide fame as a philosopher, this adamancy is little short of heroic. Mendelssohn paid the price for being a famous Jew. He suffered from scoliosis and other medical problem exacerbated by the Lavater affair. Like most Prussian Jews, he was subject to a variety of humiliating restrictions and distasteful obligations. Each year he was forced to purchase a given quantity of porcelain monkeys from the Prussian Royal ceramics factory—he wryly placed them on his mantelpiece to highlight the ridiculously feudal nature of this requirement. Once, on the holiday Shemini Atzeret, he was summoned to Frederick the Great's court at Potsdam and forced to violate the Sabbath by riding (he had the coach meet him outside the city limits lest he be seen as lax in this matter). Nor was Lavater's the last importuning challenge to defend Judaism. Mendelssohn's *Jerusalem* (1783), the first consciously modern statement of Jewish thought, began as a response to another—this time pseudonymous—challenge, to either vindicate Judaism or convert to Christianity. To attempt a noncontroversial generalization: Mendelssohn was committed to defending halachic Judaism against all comers, committed to moderate reform within the halachic framework, and committed to bringing German Jewry socially, culturally, linguistically, and intellectually into the modern era.

Previously, we used Spinoza to raise the question: What makes a thinker *Jewish*? I would like to use Mendelssohn to ask the even more difficult question: What makes a thinker *modern*? An enormous amount of scholarship has been devoted to explaining the complex phenomenon called *modernity*. In terms of economics, modernity implies a dynamic and capitalistic system. In terms of politics, modernity implies a quest, whether successful or not, for political equality. Socially, modernity accompanied a breaking down of the walls that separated various groups in medieval Europe. In religion, modernity has entailed both secular reformulations and a diminished level of practice. Yet defining sound criteria for the intellectual components of modernity proves difficult. I will suggest some features particular to the Jewish experience, but I acknowledge that the determination of modernity—for Jews as for non-Jews—is both tricky and debatable.

One feature of *Jewish* modernity, I would argue, is the mastery of an intellectual discipline outside Judaism. In Mendelssohn's case, this tradition was Enlightenment philosophy, especially in its Germanic form, which was, on the whole, less hostile to religion and less politically revolutionary than the French variety. It is said that until the end of his life Mendelssohn was always delighted to meet another follower of Christian Wolff, his philosophic mentor.[5] This criterion of modernity, however, is clearly not sufficient. Moshe Maimonides (1135–1204) wrote his most important legal work, the *Mishneh Torah*, in Hebrew; but his most important philosophic work, *The Guide of the Perplexed*, was in Arabic, and it evidences at every turn a mastery of both Greek and Arabic philosophy.

A related criterion for modernity emerges from Harry Wolfson's *From Philo to Spinoza*. In this book, Wolfson, a Harvard professor from Jewish Poland, argued that Spinoza's separation of reason and revelation (i.e., philosophical truth and Scriptural truth) marked the end of the medieval synthesis. To give a concrete example of post-Spinoza thinking: Mendelssohn claims that all human beings are able to obtain happiness and approval in God's eye simply by the exercise of their natural, God-given gifts. An aboriginal Australian does not need the Torah to lead a fulfilling life. Nor does a Native American require Christ to receive God's blessing. This attitude differs from the medieval. Maimonides, for instance, maintained that a pagan must not only follow the basic laws of humanity (called the Noahide Laws, and based on the laws given to Noah in Genesis 9), but must follow them out of a sense of God having commanded him to do so! In other words, for Maimonides, as for the medieval Christian thinker Thomas Aquinas, *salvation requires revelation*. For Mendelssohn, it does not.[6] God's greatest gift, human reason, is a universal endowment.

A famous rabbinic dictum contends, "Turn it and turn it again, for everything is contained within." Implicitly or explicitly, modern Jews reject this proposition. Most of us recognize that paleontology and archaeology have been able to establish that dinosaurs existed more than 5,760 years ago, the date since creation according to the Jewish calendar; we understand that their skeletons are not merely a clever ruse on God's part to test our faith. Science, in other words, is recognized as a valid discipline on its own terms. Very few educated Jews would be willing to discount the aesthetic contributions of Graeco-Roman culture, even if the values of that culture clash with those of Judaism. Most Jews obtain enrichment from Judaism in some areas of life, and instruction in other areas of life from other sources. Compartmentalization is the norm, not the exception.

Another rabbinic adage holds that there has been a "decline in the generations" (*yeridah b'dorot*) since Sinai. As in most traditional societies, the past was generally seen by Jews as both normative for and superior to the present. Here, too, our estimation differs from those of previous ages. Maimonides was a great physician; he did not do heart transplants. It ought to be emphasized here that Orthodoxy is perfectly compatible with this feature of modernity, though some forms of fundamentalism may not be. Joseph Soloveitchik's magnificent *The Lonely Man of Faith* begins by evoking the wonders of jet travel to suggest that, in many ways, moderns possess more human dignity than their predecessors. The recognition that any particular religious tradition provides some—but not all—of the answers to the challenges that modern life throws at us marks the modern Jewish thinker off from his (or her) medieval predecessor.

On the theme of modern Jewish thought, it should be noted that *being* modern need not entail an *approval* of modernity. Israel Salanter, the product of a relatively insular Jewish upbringing, understood that the modern world's emphasis on the individual and on rational calculations of personal advantage endangered the Jew's fear of God. But Salanter also realized that there was no "turning back the clock." The life of Torah would have to take place within the world of capitalism. Many scholars would see Salanter's advocacy of the guided study of rabbinic materials—as a means of correcting sharp business practices—as an anticipation of behavioralist models of human psychology. Not for Salanter any sermons on deathbed repentance: if one has not led a life of self-scrutiny (*teshuvah*), it is unlikely that at the last one will. Similarly, *Hasidism*, which many Jews (and presumably, many gentiles) would regard as a throwback to medievalism, displays a concern for the individualistic dimensions of prayer and performance, and for the cultivation of popular as well as elite religiosity, that is strikingly modern. In this respect, one may say the successors of the founder of Hasidism, Baal Shem Tov (1700–1760), were every bit as modern as their more famous German-Jewish contemporaries. Shimon Dubnov, very much a secular Jewish thinker whose intellectual world encompassed both traditionally Jewish and contemporary European thought, continually emphasized that modernity entailed a deplorable loss of Jewish autonomy.

To some extent, one can also recognize modernity by the level of concern with the phenomenon of the "marginal" Jew. In the medieval world one could be a sinful Jew, or even an apostate, but one could not maintain a detached posture regarding the norms of Jewish life. In our secularized atmosphere, however, this is a real challenge. One may be a Jew in name and little else. To state this reality more optimistically, we are all "Jews by choice." All of the Western European thinkers we will be discussing are aware of this phenomenon, and at a different level, so are Eastern European thinkers like Soloveitchik, Salanter, and Heschel. Mendelssohn recognized this and rejected the time-honored institution of *herem* (excommunication) as a means of maintaining communal discipline. If there were to be freedom from religious compulsion, as Mendelssohn and Spinoza both maintained, that freedom had to be across the board and had to include one's own religious tradition. Mendelssohn recognized that the social and communal modes of European Jewish life were changing dramatically. No wonder Mendelssohn emphasized that changing times do *not* alter the basic religious obligations of the Jew. His *Jerusalem* pronounces: "And even today, no wiser advice than this can be given to the House of Jacob. Adapt yourselves to the morals and the constitution of the land to which you have been removed; but hold fast to the religion of your father too. Bear both burdens as well as you can!"

Intentionally or not, in these words Mendelssohn anticipated a major problem for the modern Jew. As "morals and the constitution of the land" covered more and more areas of existence (dress, language, cultural tastes, leisure activities, political loyalties, educational issues), religion became increasingly compartmentalized and shunted off to the side. A true integration of the *Jewish* and the *modern* became a problem that Jewish thinkers at the turn of the nineteenth century would be forced to address. For Mendelssohn, this was not yet a pressing issue. He was wholly at home in his Judaism. Indeed, the willingness of Christianity to dictate creeds, where Judaism dictated only practices—the dogmatic assertion that only through belief in Jesus the Christ was salvation possible—quite convinced Mendelssohn that Judaism was both more tolerant and more reasonable than Christianity.

Alexander Altmann, a German Jew, Manchester rabbi, and Brandeis professor, wrote a monumental biography in the 1970s that seemed destined to be the final word on Mendelssohn. But important figures tend to provoke reconsideration, and I would like to mention briefly two recent works on Mendelssohn. David Sorkin's *Moses Mendelssohn and the Religious Enlightenment* warns against overemphasizing the modern flavor of Mendelssohn's contributions. Sorkin reminds his readers just how much of Mendelssohn's work was in Hebrew rather than German, and just how much he was influenced by medieval thinkers such as Nachmanides and Yehuda Halevy. Sorkin presents Mendelssohn as a transitional figure between medieval and modern Judaism, and like many transitional figures, one that was negotiating his way tentatively through uncharted terrain. Coming to a very different conclusion, Allan Arkush in *Moses Mendelssohn and the Enlightenment* agrees with Sorkin that *Jerusalem* is not meant as an all-inclusive statement of Mendelssohn's ideas. But Arkush argues that Mendelssohn's defense of Judaism was "more rhetorical than real," and was designed to confirm his credentials as an Orthodox Jew while giving him free rein "to transform his ancestral religion into something radically new and different." Mendelssohn knew exactly what he was doing: reforming Judaism for the socially acculturated, politically liberal world to come.[7]

So it seems that the debate over Mendelssohn is not finished. And all subsequent debates must interpret Mendelssohn's *Jerusalem. Jerusalem* probably was not intended to be a comprehensive philosophy of Judaism, but it nevertheless constitutes Mendelssohn's most complete presentation.[8] The book is divided into two parts. The first part, subtitled "On Religious Power," offers an Enlightenment-era discussion of freedom of religion. In some important ways, then, Mendelssohn is here following in the liberal footsteps of Spinoza's *Tractatus Theologico-Politicus*. The second part of *Jerusalem*, subtitled "On Judaism," also follows Spinoza to the extent that Mendelssohn agrees that the Commandments are the defining characteristic of Judaism, and that they regulate a far wider compass of life than, for instance, Christian dogma. Spinoza, however, contends that with the fall of the independent Jewish state, these Commandments lost their original purpose (and should be abandoned). Mendelssohn, on the contrary, considers them eternally binding on all Jews, for all times. While conceding that the Commandments are not necessary for human salvation, and while recognizing that the most important truths about the human condition are available through the exercise of reason, Mendelssohn argues that every Jew is bound by the Commandments on the basis of history and tradition. Mendelssohn also presents the Commandments as a supremely effective system of divine pedagogy, weaning Jews away from idolatry. Because Judaism's revelatory event (Sinai) enjoined behaviors, but no credal statement of belief, Jews were far less prone to be led astray in their quest for true worship of God. To reiterate: For Mendelssohn, Judaism teaches what one needs to do, *not* what one needs to believe.

I have reproduced the final pages of *Jerusalem*, which offer the most dramatic advice on how Jews should strive to be loyal to both their homeland and their ancestral religion.

QUESTIONS FOR MENDELSSOHN, *JERUSALEM*, 103–10

What was unique about the "Mosaic constitution" in ancient Israel?

Why does Mendelssohn cite (twice) Jesus's injunction, "To render unto Caesar . . . "? (I can think of at least three reasons.)

How does Mendelssohn present Jesus? As a Christian? As a Jew? Is this how you view Jesus?

Mendelssohn contrasts the mores and constitution of the country in which you find yourself with "the religion of your fathers." How neatly can these categories be divided? Which is the larger category? Is it difficult to be faithful to both categories?

Despite the alteration from ancient circumstances, Mendelssohn makes it clear that Jews remain obligated to the Commandments. Is the logic of his position clear to you? Is there anything particularly "modern" about Mendelssohn's rationale?

Mendelssohn argues that diversity is the obvious plan of Providence. What evidence does Mendelssohn adduce for this claim?

Mendelssohn concludes his work with a plea for tolerance. What does Mendelssohn mean by "tolerance"? Is there any discernible difference between Mendelssohn's understanding of this concept and our own?

Can you identify factors that make Mendelssohn part of the European Enlightenment? (To ask this question from another angle: Since Maimonides and Mendelssohn are indisputably *both* rationalists, why do their presentations of Judaism sound so different?)

Mendelssohn offers a response to Christian attempts to show the irrelevance of contemporary Judaism and also to Spinoza's attempts to impugn the sanctity of Scripture. With which challenge is Mendelssohn more concerned in these pages?

Why did God grant the Jews the Torah? Why didn't God grant the Torah to everyone, instead of giving it only to a numerically small, politically weak people like the Jews?

Elsewhere in *Jerusalem*, Mendelssohn suggests that Judaism commands actions but not beliefs. Is it plausible that a Jew uninfluenced by habitual practice of the Commandments or by social pressures would observe all the Commandments without some measure of belief in either their divine origin or tangible benefits?

Do you find Mendelssohn's presentation of modern Judaism in *Jerusalem* personally compelling?

STUDIES BY AND ABOUT MENDELSSOHN

The first part of *Jerusalem* requires a good background in eighteenth-century political philosophy but is worthwhile reading. More accessible to a student without this background are the excerpts of Mendelssohn's other writings found in Eva Jospe's *Moses Mendelssohn: Selections from His Writings* (New York: Viking Press, 1975). Unfortunately, Mendelssohn's Hebrew Bible commentary (*Biur*) has not yet been translated. Alexander Altmann's *Moses Mendelssohn: A Biographical Study* (Tuscaloosa: University of Alabama Press, 1973) will take you a long time to read, but by the end you will know a great deal about eighteenth-century German-Jewish life, the Jewish Enlightenment, and Mendelssohn's life and times. Steven Lowenstein, *The Jewish Community of Berlin* (New York: Oxford University Press, 1994), provides background on Mendelssohn's supporters, detractors, and environment. Every survey of modern Jewish thinkers discusses Mendelssohn. The opening chapter in Michael A. Meyer's *The Origins of the Modern Jew* (Detroit, Mich.: Wayne State Press, 1967) presents the issues well. Sorkin and Arkush, in the works discussed above, offer conflicting views of Mendelssohn's legacy. Edward Breuer in his *The Limits of Enlightenment: Jews, Germans and the Eighteenth-century Study of Scripture* (Cambridge, Mass.: Harvard University Center for Jewish Studies, 1995) masterfully places the Mendelssohn Bible in its historical context. Violating my own rule to cite only books (which are easier to find than articles), I must mention Arnold Eisen's "Divine Legislation as Ceremonial Script," *Association of Jewish Studies Review* 15, no. 2 (Fall 1990).

From *Jerusalem*

Moses Mendelssohn

I have said that the Mosaic constitution did not persist long in its original purity. Already by the time of the prophet Samuel, the edifice had developed a crack which continued to widen until the structure fell completely apart. The nation demanded a visible, bodily king for its ruler. Whether the reason was that the priesthood had already begun to abuse and lose the respect it had enjoyed among the people, as Scripture reports about the sons of the high priest

[I Sam. 2:12–17], or that the people's eyes were dazzled by the splendor of a neighboring court—whatever the reason, they demanded to have a king, as all other nations did. The prophet, angered, explained to them what it would mean to have a human king who has his own wants that he can satisfy and even expand at his pleasure. He also pointed out how difficult it would be to satisfy a weak mortal whom one has granted the prerogatives belonging only to God [I Sam. 8]. But in vain; the people persisted in their determination, got their wish, and experienced everything against which the prophet had warned them. In this way, the constitution was undermined, the unity of interests destroyed. State and religion were no longer the same, and a collision of duties was no longer impossible. Such a collision must, of course, have occurred only rarely as long as the king himself not only was one of the people but also obeyed the laws of the land.

But now, follow the course of our history through its varying fortunes and changes, through governments good or evil, god-fearing or godless, right down to the sorrowful period in which the founder of the Christian religion prudently counseled, "Render unto Caesar what is Caesar's, and unto God what is God's" [Mark 12:17], a palpable antithesis [setting the stage for] a conflict of duties. The state was under foreign rule, received its orders, as it were, from alien gods, while the indigenous religion persisted and continued to influence civil life at least in part. Here we have claim against claim, demand in conflict with demand. "To whom shall we give, whom shall we obey?" And the reply was "Bear both burdens as well as you can. Serve two masters with patience and resignation. Give to Caesar, but give to God too." To each his own, since the unity of interest had been destroyed.

And even today, no better advice than this can be given to the House of Jacob: Adopt the mores and constitution of the country in which you find yourself, but be steadfast in upholding the religion of your fathers, too. Bear both burdens as well as you can. True, on the one hand, people make it difficult for you to bear the burden of civil life because of the religion to which you remain faithful; and, on the other hand, the climate of our time makes the observance of your religious laws in some respects more burdensome than it need be. Persevere nevertheless; stand fast in the place which Providence has assigned to you; and submit to everything which may happen, as you were told to do by your Lawgiver long ago.

Indeed, I cannot see how those who were born into the household of Jacob can in good conscience exempt themselves from the observance of the law. We are permitted to reflect on the law, to search for its meaning, and occasionally, where the Lawgiver himself provides no reason [for a particular law], to surmise that it must perhaps be understood in terms of a particular time, place, and set of circumstances. Therefore, the law can perhaps also be changed according to the requirements of a particular time, place, and set of circumstances, but only if and when it pleases the supreme Lawgiver to let us recognize His will—to make it known to us just as openly, publicly, and beyond any possibility of doubt and uncertainty, as He did when He gave us the law itself. As long as this has not happened, as long as we can show no such authentic dispensation from the law, no sophistry of ours can free us from the strict obedience we owe to it. Reverence for God must draw a line between speculation and observance, beyond which no conscientious person may go.

Therefore, I repeat my previous assertion: Weak and nearsighted is the eye of man. Who can say, "I have entered God's sanctuary; I have comprehended the system of His intentions; and know how to determine their measure, goals, and limitations"? I may make conjectures but not decide or act in accordance with my conjectures. If I may not have, without authorization by the legislator or magistrate, the audacity in human affairs to contravene the law and to act on the basis of my own surmises and casuistry, how much less may I do this in divine affairs? To be sure, we are exempted today from those laws which were once, of necessity, connected with land ownership and certain civil institutions [in ancient Palestine]. Outside of Judea, without Temple and priesthood, there can be neither sacrifices nor laws of purification nor levies to support the priests, inasmuch as all these depend on our possession of that land. But personal commandments, duties imposed upon every son of Israel, which are unrelated to Temple service and land ownership in Palestine, must, as far as I can see, be strictly observed according to the words of the law until it will please the Most High to set our conscience at rest and to proclaim their abrogation clearly and publicly.

Here it seems obvious that "what God has joined together, man may not tear asunder" [Mark 10:9]. I cannot understand how any one of us, even if he were to convert to the Christian religion, could believe that he would thereby have appeased his conscience and freed himself from the yoke of the law. Jesus of Nazareth was never heard to declare that he had come to release the House of Jacob from the law. Indeed, he explicitly and emphatically said the opposite and, what is more, did the opposite himself [cf. Matt. 5:17ff.]. Jesus of Nazareth himself observed not only the law of Moses but also the ordinances of the rabbis; and whatever in his recorded speeches and actions seems to contradict this fact, actually only appears to do so at first glance. Carefully analyzed, all he said and did is in complete harmony with Scripture as well as with [rabbinic] tradition. If he came to put an end to the rampant hypocrisy and sanctimoniousness of that time, he would surely not have been the first to exemplify this very same sanctimoniousness by insisting, through personal example, on the observance of a law which had supposedly already been repealed and abrogated. On the contrary, his entire conduct as well as that of his early disciples is obviously guided and illumined by the rabbinic principle that anyone not born into the law need not bind himself to the law, but that anyone born into the law must live and die in accordance with it. If his followers, in later times, thought differently and believed they could exempt those Jews who accepted his teachings from obedience to the law, they certainly acted without his authorization.

And you, my brothers and fellowmen, who are followers of the teachings of Jesus, how can you blame us for doing what the founder of your religion himself has done and sanctioned by his authority? Can you seriously believe that you cannot reciprocate our love as citizens and associate yourselves with us for civic purposes as long as we are outwardly distinguished from you by our ceremonial law, do not eat with you, or do not marry you? As far as we can see, the founder of your religion himself would not have done these things or have permitted us to do them either.

If this should be and remain your true conviction—which one can hardly believe of truly Christian people—if we can be united with you as citizens only on the condition that we deviate from the law which we still consider binding, then we sincerely regret the necessity of declaring that we shall renounce our claim to civil [equality and] union with you. Everything the humanitarian von Dohm has written will in this case have been in vain, and everything will remain in the intolerable condition it is in now or into which your love of humanity may find it appropriate to put it. It is beyond our power to yield in this matter; but it is nevertheless also within our power, if we have integrity, to love you as our brothers and implore you as brothers to make our burdens as tolerable as you possibly can. Regard us, if not as brothers and fellow citizens, at least as fellowmen and coinhabitants of this country. Show us ways and provide us with means of becoming better fellow residents, and let us enjoy, together with you, the rights of humanity, as far as time and circumstances will permit. We cannot forsake the law in good conscience—and without a conscience of what use would fellow citizens be to you?

[You may ask], "But how, then, can the prophecy be fulfilled that some day there will be only one shepherd and one flock?"

Dear brothers, you are well-meaning. But do not let yourselves be deceived! To belong to this omnipresent shepherd, it is not necessary for the entire flock to graze on one pasture or to enter and leave the master's house through just one door. It would be neither in accord with the shepherd's wishes nor conducive to the growth of his flock. [Do you wonder why] some people deliberately turn these ideas upside down and purposely try to confuse them? They tell you that a union of religions is the shortest way to that brotherly love and tolerance you kindhearted people so earnestly desire. If all of us share the same faith, then—as some people try to make you believe—we shall no longer hate each other because of our different beliefs and convictions; religious hatred and persecution will be eradicated; the whip will be wrenched from the hand of hypocrisy, and the sword, from that of fanaticism. This, they say, will be the beginning of the happy days of which it is said that "the wolf will dwell with the lamb, the leopard with the kid," etc. [Isa. 11:6].

The gentle souls who propose such a union are ready to get started with the job right away. They want us to act as intermediaries in the humanitarian effort to negotiate an agreement among the faiths, bargaining about the truths and rights as if they were cheap merchandise. They want to demand, offer, haggle, threaten, implore, surprise, and outwit until the parties have shaken hands and a contract for the promotion of mankind's happiness can be written and signed. And many others, even though they reject such a scheme as chimerical and unfeasible, nevertheless speak of a union of religions as a very desirable state of affairs, and they are full of pity and sorrow for the human family because this pinnacle of happiness is not within man's reach.

But beware, you humanitarians, lest you listen to such notions without the most careful scrutiny! They may be snares laid by fanaticism (one that is currently powerless) in order to entrap freedom of conscience. You know that this enemy of the good appears in many shapes and forms: the lion's rage or the meekness of the lamb, the dove's simplicity or the cunning of the serpent—none of these postures is so alien to him that he could not adopt it, even if he did not [already] possess it, in order to realize his bloodthirsty designs. Since, as a result of your beneficial efforts, he can no longer openly resort to violence, he may possibly put on the mask of meekness in order to deceive you. Outwardly he may feign brotherly love and radiate a spirit of tolerance, while secretly he is already at work forging the chains with which he plans to shackle our reason so that, taking it by surprise, he can cast it back into the cesspool of barbarism from which you had just begun to pull it up.

Don't think this is merely an imaginary fear, a product of hypochondria. A union of faiths, if it were ever to come about, could have only the most disastrous consequences for reason and freedom of conscience. Suppose people were able to reach agreement concerning the doctrinal formulations they want to introduce as basic creed; suppose one could also manage to find symbols to which none of the religious groups now dominant in Europe could object—what would be gained by this? Would it mean that all of you had arrived at the same views about religious truths?

No one who has the slightest insight into human nature can possibly come to this conclusion. This would merely be agreement on words, on a formula. The unifiers of faith would simply be collaborating in pinching off a bit from some concepts here and there, in enlarging the texture of words elsewhere, until they become so vague and loose that any ideas, regardless of their inner

differences, can, if necessary, be squeezed in. Everybody would merely be at-
taching to the same words a different meaning, peculiarly his own. Therefore,
do you still want to boast that you have united mankind in faith, that you have
brought the flock under the care of its one shepherd? Alas, if the goal of this
universal delusion were to be realized, I am afraid man's barely liberated
mind would once again be confined behind bars. The shy animal would soon
have let itself be captured and put in harness again. Be as undemanding and
conciliatory as you may wish, as soon as you link faith to symbol, tie conviction to words, lay down unalterably your articles of faith, the unfortunate
wretch who arrives a day later and dares to find fault even with these inof-
fensive, purified words, will be in terrible trouble. He is a disturber of the
peace! Off to the stake with him!

Brothers, if you care for true godliness, let us not pretend that conformity
exists where diversity is obviously the plan and goal of Providence. Not one
among us thinks and feels exactly like his fellowman. Why, then, should we
deceive each other with lies? It is sad enough that we are doing this in our
daily relations, in conversations that are of no particular importance. But why
also in matters which concern our temporal and eternal welfare, our very destiny? Why should we use masks to make ourselves unrecognizable to each
other in the most important concerns of life, when God has given each of us
his own distinctive face for some good reason? Would this not mean that we
oppose Providence as far as we can; that we try, in fact, to frustrate the very
purpose of creation; and that we deliberately act contrary to our own vocation
and destiny in this life and the life to come?

Rulers of the earth! If an unimportant coinhabitant may be permitted to lift
his voice and to address you: Do not trust your counselors who, in smooth
phrases, seek to mislead you into such a harmful course of action. They are
either deluded themselves and cannot see the enemy of mankind lurking in
the background, or they deliberately try to deceive you. Our most precious
possession—the freedom to think—will be lost if you listen to their counsel.
For the sake of your happiness as well as ours, remember that *a union of
faiths is not tolerance.* It is the very opposite. For the sake of your happiness
and ours, do not use your powerful prestige to give the force of law to some
eternal truth that is immaterial to civic well-being; do not transform some religious doctrine to which the state should be indifferent into a statute of the
land! Concentrate on what men should or should not do; judge them wisely
by their actions; and let us retain the freedom of thought and speech with
which the Father of all mankind has endowed us as our inalienable heritage
and immutable right.

Should, however, the link between privilege and personal conviction have
become so solidified over the years, that the time has not yet come to abolish

it completely without serious damage, try at least to diminish its pernicious influence as much as you can and set wise limits to an obsolete prejudice.

At least prepare the way for your more fortunate descendants to [reach] that height of culture, that universal human tolerance for which reason is still sighing in vain. Reward and punish no doctrine; hold out no allurement or bribe to anyone for the adoption of a particular faith. Let every man who does not disturb the public welfare, who obeys the law, acts righteously toward you and his fellowmen be allowed to speak as he thinks, to pray to God after his own fashion or after the fashion of his fathers, and to seek eternal salvation where he thinks he may find it. Permit no one in your country to search someone else's heart or to judge someone else's thoughts. Let no one usurp a right which the Omniscient has reserved to Himself. If we render unto Caesar what is Caesar's, then let us also render unto God what is God's. Love truth! Love peace!

NOTES

1. Moses Mendelssohn, *Moses Mendelssohn: Selections from His Writings*, trans. and ed. Eva Jospe, with Alfred Jospe (New York: Viking Press, 1975), 52–53.

2. Alexander Altmann, "Moses Mendelssohn: The Archetypal German Jew," in *The Jewish Response to German Culture*, ed. Jehuda Reinharz and Walter Schatzberg (Hanover, N.H.: University of New England Press, 1985).

3. Mendelssohn, *Moses Mendelssohn: Selections from His Writings*, 18.

4. Alexander Altmann, *Moses Mendelssohn: A Biographical Study* (Tuscaloosa: University of Alabama Press, 1973).

5. Philosophically, Mendelssohn was behind the times, being unreceptive to the role of history as explained by his friend Lessing and unresponsive to Kant's critique of all revealed religions.

6. Rejecting Maimonides' position, Mendelssohn confided in a letter to Rabbi Jacob Emden: "These words are harder to me than flint. Are then, all dwellers on the earth except for us, doomed to perdition if they fail to believe in the Torah that was given as an inheritance only to the congregation of Jacob." Cited in commentary to Moses Mendelssohn, *Jerusalem: Or, On Religious Power and Judaism*, ed. Allan Arkush and Alexander Altmann (Hanover, N.H.: University of New England Press, 1983), 209n94.

7. David Sorkin, *Moses Mendelssohn and the Religious Enlightenment* (Berkeley: University of California Press, 1996); Allan Arkush, *Moses Mendelssohn and the Enlightenment* (Albany: State University of New York Press, 1994).

8. These cautions against overestimating the position of *Jerusalem* in Mendelssohn's works should not cloud the fact that the book represents a notable contribution to the Jewish intellectual tradition.

Chapter Three

Samson Raphael Hirsch's Defense of Judaism

The Reconciliation of Modernity and the Mitzvot

HIRSCH'S LIFE AND TIMES (1808–1888)

Samson Raphael Hirsch's *The Nineteen Letters on Judaism*, published in 1836 when he was but twenty-eight years old, established him as the premier spokesman for modern Orthodoxy, and as one of the most exciting Jewish thinkers of his day. So impressed was Heinrich Graetz, later the most influential Jewish historian of the nineteenth century, that he immediately apprenticed himself to Hirsch for a grueling three years of study that would have done in a less-devoted student. What Graetz saw in Hirsch is easy to understand. Graetz, who grew up in Xions, a rural hamlet of the Posen province (then Prussia, today Poland), lost his faith while watching the Yom Kippur *kapporah* ceremony (in which chickens are whirled overhead to atone for sins and then slaughtered). Here was Hirsch—the young, dynamic rabbi of Oldenburg, who went clean-shaven and at times bareheaded; who wore a handsome clerical robe; who wrote beautiful German; who quoted the German classics; and, who presented a modern and sophisticated image—a man who could never be mistaken for the traditionalists of Graetz's native Posen.[1]

But were that all that Graetz sought, he might have just as easily been drawn to Abraham Geiger, or any number of Hirsch's more radical opponents. This same Hirsch argued (beginning with *The Nineteen Letters*), that a system of Judaism must be built and be comprehensible from within. This same Hirsch devoted considerable energies to defending the smallest matter of religious observance (in *Horeb*). This modern rabbi proffered a systematic treatment of Torah Judaism as a religious philosophic system, yet he was a man of undoubted conviction and piety. Graetz recalls the effect as follows:

> How delighted I therefore was with a new book, *Iggerot tzafon* [the Hebrew title of *The Nineteen Letters*] anonymous, in which a view of Judaism I had never heard before or suspected was defended with convincing arguments. Judaism was represented as the best religion and as indispensable to the salvation of mankind. With avidity I devoured every word. Disloyal though I had been to the Talmud, this book reconciled me with it.[2]

The notion of a modern Orthodox Jew that so entranced Graetz is by now so commonplace that it hardly merits comment. Yet Hirsch really was somewhat novel in his day. Unlike Eastern European figures who received only a minimal exposure to secular subjects in *hedarim* (Jewish elementary schools), Hirsch attended public school and a Hamburg *Gymnasium* (German academic high school). An intellectually gifted traditionalist from Graetz's hometown would go to one of Lithuania's or Poland's famous *yeshivot* (colleges of advanced Jewish studies) to study Talmud and Codes. Hirsch, on the contrary, went to Bonn University, while receiving his advanced Jewish education from two great Orthodox figures (Jacob Ettlinger and Jacob Hacham Bernays, to whom the distinction of being the first German Jews who could be called both modern and Orthodox probably belongs).

In fact, by the standards of the Volozhin Yeshiva, Hirsch probably would have been considered a talmudic lightweight. During his brief, unhappy service as a rabbi in Moravia, Hirsch may have been "disrespected" on exactly these grounds, and this may also have been a factor in his decision not to seek the Posen rabbinate, for which an eager Graetz would have been happy to lobby. In Hirsch's day, the old school suspected the heretical impact of secular studies on youth. In Hungary, not so far from Moravia, an ultra-Orthodoxy was coming into existence that expressly rejected the inroads of modernity. The great figure in this Hungarian ultra-Orthodoxy, the Hatam Sofer, pronounced: "Everything new is forbidden by the Torah." These were not the words of a benighted man; they were an accurate sociological judgment regarding how difficult it would be to enter modernity yet maintain the same levels of Jewish commitment. Hirsch, following Mendelssohn in this regard, was willing to make a distinction between what the modern Jew needed to render unto Caesar and what he or she needed to render unto God. (This figure of speech is from the latter's *Jerusalem*.) In brief, Hirsch advocated cultural, political, and intellectual assimilation and strict observance of the *mitzvot*. The end product was to be, in Hirsch's words, "Mensch-Yisroel": the cultivated, integrated, modern, highly observant Jew.

Hirsch's entire adult life was spent in controversies, local and national. His most famous were those with the reform movements, and I would like to single out two of my favorite Hirschian screeds; he was a master polemicist and always outdid his opponents rhetorically. In "Religion in Alliance with Progress," which was written in response to the reform's successes in the 1840s and 1850s as community after community introduced new practices that violated Jewish law (*halachah*), Hirsch lampooned the bad faith of the reformers who, using the *Zeitgeist* (spirit of the times) as a justification, treated religion as a handmaiden of the values of the present day. Stressing the eternal values of "Torah Judaism" (another favorite Hirschianism), Hirsch sarcastically rejected *reform* and *prophetic* as valid Jewish adjectives. According to Hirsch, there is only one true dichotomy: good Jews and bad Jews! Judaism is eternal; the *Zeitgeist* must answer to it, not the other way around.

In "A Sermon on the Science of Judaism," Hirsch uses the setting of the Tisha B'Av holiday[3] to attack the historical investigations that threatened, in Hirsch's view, to undermine confidence in the transmission of Jewish tradition. Hirsch called attention to a modern Jewish tendency that replaced intimacy and identification with the past with historical facts and bits of information about that past. Hirsch concludes his sermon by rhetorically asking whether the Jewish martyrs of the Middle Ages would prefer their descendants to remember their names and forget their prayers; or be ignorant of the authors, but pray these prayers with devotion. At the heart of this sermon is Hirsch's skepticism toward the historical study of Judaism, which Hirsch feared would lead to an erosion of piety. Revealingly, one of Hirsch's main polemical targets was none other than the highly observant rabbi of Dresden (and grandfather of Conservative Judaism), Zacharias Fraenkel, whose book on the Mishnah proved that many Jewish laws (*halachot*) were very old but demonstrably post-Sinaitic. For Hirsch, this was heresy. It was simply not good enough that Fraenkel practiced Judaism as punctiliously as Hirsch did, and that he was clearly a man who both knew the authors' names *and* prayed their prayers. In Hirsch's eyes, not behavior alone, but also belief in the fundamentals, made one a "good Jew."[4] Ironically, Hirsch found Schilling and Hegel more palatable than Fraenkel and Graetz, and general culture a better vehicle to illuminate Judaism than the pioneers of the science of Judaism.

Hirsch energetically involved himself in communal and political life, especially after he settled in Frankfurt at the invitation of a group of observant laypeople who formed the Israelitische Religions Gesellschaft (IRG) in 1851. In Frankfurt, Hirsch established a modern Orthodox day school, gave tremendous sermons, and was virtually worshipped by his congregants. But Hirsch's political moment in the sun came in the 1870s when he led some of the IRG membership in seceding from the mainstream Jewish community.

This secession horrified mainstream Jewish leaders and also contravened the wishes of some respected rabbinic figures, including the revered Wurzburger Rav, Selig Bamberger. But Hirsch felt the Jewish mainstream's observances had deteriorated so badly that his community could no longer take part in them. He was no doubt aided in convincing some of his congregants by the fact that secession would exempt them from the communal tithe, which was due the Jewish community from each of its members by order of the Prussian Ministry of Religion. Robert Liberles's *Religious Conflict in Social Context* presents a fascinating description of Hirsch's gifted leadership of the IRG and his role in leading the secession.

Hirsch's fame as an original Jewish thinker rests primarily on *The Nineteen Letters on Judaism* and *Horeb*, two works that must be judged together. *The Nineteen Letters* offers a justification of Torah Judaism; *Horeb*, for its part, is a modern *Shulchan Aruch*. Just as the seventeenth-century *Shulchan Aruch* provided a useful handbook for legal observance in its day, Hirsch's *Horeb* was aimed at providing a detailed catalog of Jewish practice in a modern context. Ironically, *The Nineteen Letters* was written because Hirsch's publisher feared taking a financial loss on the publication of the massive *Horeb*. *The Nineteen Letters*, a much shorter, less-technical justification, proved very successful in the marketplace and encouraged the publisher to go ahead with *Horeb*. A systematic theology, which Hirsch went so far as to title *Moriah*, never appeared. Whether Hirsch decided he was simply not up to this Maimonidean task, or because it would contradict his goal of a self-constructed Judaism, is unclear. *Moriah* never appeared. But we do have these two books, which certainly merit the attention they have been given. I will address Hirsch's lovely description of Shabbat from *Horeb*, but will spend more time dissecting *The Nineteen Letters*, which may be divided as follows.

The opening nine essays set out the fundamentals of faith as Hirsch sees them. Especially noteworthy is the way in which Hirsch handles exile (*galut*) in letters 9 and 16. By emphasizing that "land and soil were never Israel's bond of union," Hirsch imagines a modern (versus medieval) exile in which Israel would be a light unto the nations and fully at home in the modern nation-state. While Hirsch remained convinced of the theological necessity of the Ingathering and return to Israel, his every word undermines the psychological dimension of exile. For medieval Jewry, exile was a painful reality. For Hirsch, exile becomes a positive means of spreading God's word throughout the world.[5]

Letters 10–15 classify the Commandments and hint at their contemporary justification and observance, which is fleshed out in *Horeb*. Letters 16–19 show Hirsch negotiating the uncharted ways of religious reforms, the new situation of the Jews as acculturating Germans (the process we call Emancipation), and the enduring claims of tradition. The presentation is masterful, and his soon-to-be rival Abrahm Geiger was only a little less impressed than Heinrich Graetz by the results.

Letter 18 deserves special mention. Here, Hirsch criticizes both Moses Maimonides and Moses Mendelssohn in similar language: "Maimonides sought to reconcile Judaism with the difficulties which confronted it from without instead of developing it creatively from within." In the case of Maimonides, Greek and Arabic philosophy were allowed to set the agenda; for Mendelssohn, it was set by the apologetic needs of responding to Christian hostility. Thus, the two Moshes produced explanations of the Commandments (*mitzvot*) that were, in Hirsch's opinion, reductionist, subjective, fallible, and Christianized. Hirsch explains:

> If, for instance, the sole purpose of the prohibition of labor on the Sabbath were to enable men to rest and recover from the toil of the week, if the Sabbath meant only the cessation of physical activity in order that the mind may come into play (and who could doubt it, since both the Moseses interpret it thus and the Christian Sunday agrees with their conception), who, then, would not consider it mere pettiness and pedantic absurdity to fill an entire folio with the investigation of the question of what particular activities are forbidden and what are permitted on the Sabbath Day?[6]

For Hirsch, the Torah ought to be the ultimate standard to which all other intellectual processes must respond. The question of whether or not Hirsch's criticism of the two Moshes is justified, and whether anyone could truly build up a system of Judaism exclusively from within (*aus sich selbst*), is something that I will leave to the reader to decide. In a major study of Hirsch, Noah Rosenbloom has contended that Hirsch's symbolic system owes much to the works of the German philosopher Hegel, although Rosenbloom's work has in turn elicited much criticism. Certainly on a conscious level, Hirsch attempted this *aus sich selbst* system of interpretation in both *The Nineteen Letters* and in *Horeb*. If we turn to Hirsch's elucidation of the Sabbath in *Horeb*, a very beautiful piece of writing indeed, we see his methodology in action. Typically, Hirsch reproduces the relevant Bible passages and then focuses on their exact wording to wrest the maximum symbolic meaning from the Commandment. The passage Hirsch explicates here is Exodus 31:12–17, and the reader would be well served by opening a Bible to the passage and following Hirsch's exegesis:

> Thus doing no work on the Sabbath is an *ot*, an expressive symbol for all time. The Sabbath expresses the truth the Only God is the Creator and Master . . . It is a *moed*, a time-institution, a day singled out from other days . . . It is *kodesh*, a holy time. . . . [T]he Sabbath comes to elevate him by directing him once again

toward the Creator . . . [I]t is a *brit*, a covenant the only contract and basis of every relationship between God and Jew, both as man and as Israelite . . . Finally it is a *berachah*, a blessing, if you thus renew your covenant with God every Sabbath God will give you renewed enlightenment of the spirit, enthusiasm and strength for the fulfillment of this great task.[7]

Hirsch's intense focus on the details of Sabbath worship must be understood in the context of the reform tendency to spiritualize very concrete proscriptions. As Harvard's Jay Harris has recently emphasized, Hirsch's view of the interrelationship between the Written Torah (the actual passages of the Hebrew Bible) and the Oral Torah (the way those passages have been applied to changing realities over the centuries) is innovative. Following the standard interpretations of Hirsch, I had always assumed that Hirsch regarded both the Written and Oral Torahs as divinely revealed, coeval, unified in their teaching, inseparable in practice, and eternally valid. Hirsch certainly defends every last iota of halachic Judaism as essential, denies any separation of "moral" versus "ceremonial" laws, and denies that the Oral Torah ever teaches something fundamentally at odds with the Written Torah. This is all true, but Harris notes that, in addition, Hirsch actually assigns a priority to the Oral Torah, seeing it as the "complete work" to which the Written Torah actually serves as a sort of *Cliffs Notes*. One can fake religious practice by reliance only on the *Cliffs Notes* version, but true practice relies on mastering and living the complete work. Conversely, for the person who has done the real work of study and observance, the reading of a *Cliffs Notes* summary serves to remind them of the highlights of that work. In other words, as a reminder the *Cliffs Notes* version is legitimate; as a substitute, it is not. Harris concludes, "[Hirsch] was thus led to a radical reformulation of the entire relationship between oral and written laws, one that preserved the divine authority of the entire body of Jewish law and vitiated any effort to historicize it."[8] Take a look at Hirsch's exegesis of the laws of the Hebrew slave (Exodus 21:2), and you will see his argument for the priority of Oral Torah in high relief.

Hirsch's commentary to the Pentateuch and Psalms was his last major contribution to the Jewish tradition. Hirsch's willingness to read into the Bible the polemical issues of his own day, and his modern sensibility, which inclines toward psychologizing biblical characters and injecting universalistic values where it may be doubted that any such values actually exist, make Hirsch very comprehensible and possibly very simpatico. Whatever his limitations as a talmudist, which are still being debated by scholars competent to judge the matter, there is no doubt that Hirsch was a careful and thoughtful reader of the Bible. For a taste of Hirsch as Bible commentator, take a look at this sermon of good parenting and gentile-Jewish relations, embedded in his discussion of Genesis 25:27.

Had Isaac and Rebecca studied Esau's nature and character early enough, and asked themselves how can even an Esau, how can all the strength and energy, agility and courage that lies slumbering in this child, be won over to the service of God . . . then Jacob and Esau, even with their totally different natures could still have remained twin brothers in spirit and life; quite early in life Esau's sword and Jacob's spirit could have worked hand in hand, and who can say what a different aspect the whole history of the ages might have presented.

To fully understand Hirsch's reading here, it is critical to know that Esau (or Edom) in Jewish tradition was taken as synonymous with Christianity, and Jacob (or Israel) with Judaism. Not surprisingly, rabbinic sources lavished blame on the older brother and praise on the latter, taking Esau's hatred for Jacob as an inexorable fact of life. Hirsch, however, laments that the two brothers, each with significant but different talents, did not join forces. Hirsch considered the centuries-long enmity between Esau and Jacob the result of bad parenting, not divine mandate. The political implications for his own day are apparent.

Without doubt, Hirsch represents an important example of a successful synthesis of tradition and modernity. With some overstatement, Hirsch may be considered the first modern Orthodox Jew. But we can ask: More than a hundred years after his death, and given that modern Orthodoxy is a reality, not just a wish, does reading Hirsch still pay benefits? Is he still important? For a number of reasons, I think the answer is yes. Hirsch dramatically draws our attention to Judaism's claim on us: we may be autonomous individuals, but we are also heirs to a religious tradition that commands and compels. Following from this, Hirsch consistently challenges us to consider what, *as Jews*, is our highest calling, or "read" on the purpose of life. Finally, Hirsch forces us to honestly confront our notion of proper Jewish practice and belief and to evaluate ourselves along those lines.

I trust that no further general introduction to *The Nineteen Letters* is needed. I have reproduced letter 16, "Emancipation," which nicely captures Hirsch's sense of the possibilities, parameters, and challenges of the new era he witnessed firsthand.

QUESTIONS FOR HIRSCH,
THE NINETEEN LETTERS ON JUDAISM, LETTER 16

Why did Hirsch feel that traditional Judaism needed defending in his day?

How does Hirsch understand *galut* (exile)? Is exile necessarily isolating? Is exile necessarily pejorative? What is Israel's role in exile? In the messianic era that ends exile?

Hirsch states: "Land and soil were never Israel's bond of union. That function was always fulfilled by the common task set by the Torah." Do you think most American Jews would accept that statement? Do you think most Israelis would?

Who determines "the common task set by the Torah"?

Are faith and progress reconcilable? How? Under what circumstances and conditions? What would "progress" in Judaism entail?

Is Hirsch a legitimate successor to Moses Mendelssohn? (After you read the next chapter on Abraham Geiger, come back to this question. Who is better able to claim the mantle of Mendelssohn?)

How does Hirsch understand Emancipation?

Does Hirsch favor Emancipation? Under what circumstances and conditions?

Hirsch disliked being characterized as an Orthodox Jew. He once wrote that "Orthodox Judaism does not know any varieties of Judaism. It does not know a Mosaic, Prophetic, and Rabbinic Judaism, nor Orthodox and Liberal Judaism. . . . It does indeed know conscientious and indifferent Jews, good Jews, bad Jews." How have our perceptions of Reform and Orthodox Judaism changed since Hirsch's day?

In *your* view, what makes a good or a bad Jew, or Christian, or Moslem?

STUDIES BY AND ABOUT HIRSCH

Most of Hirsch's voluminous writings have been translated in *The Collected Writings* (New York: Feldheim, 1984–1995). Some good scholarly discussions of Hirsch may be found in the following: Noah H. Rosenbloom, *Tradition in an Age of Reform* (Philadelphia: Jewish Publication Society of America, 1976); Arnold Eisen, *Galut: Modern Jewish Reflection on Homelessness and Homecoming* (Bloomington: Indiana University Press, 1986); and Robert Liberles, *Religious Conflict in Social Context* (Westport, Conn.: Greenwood, 1985). Dr. Isidore Grunfeld's long introductory essays to *Hirsch on the Pentateuch* and to *Horeb* and remarkably detailed and useful expositions are possibly of more use to the student already well grounded in Judaica. On the legacy of the Hirsch-Breuer family in America, I recommend Steve Lowenstein, *Frankfurt on the Hudson* (Detroit, Mich.: Wayne State University Press, 1989), or Allegra Goodman's novel, *Katerskill Falls* (New York: Delta, 1998).

From *The Nineteen Letters on Judaism*

Samson Raphael Hirsch

SIXTEENTH LETTER

Emancipation

You ask me for my opinion on the question which at present so greatly agitates the minds of men; namely emancipation. You wish to know whether I consider it feasible and desirable according to the spirit of Judaism. The new conception of Judaism which you have acquired, dear Benjamin, has rendered you so uncertain as to whether such ideas could be reconciled with the eternal ideals of our faith. You have begun to doubt whether the acceptance of these new relations is in harmony with the spirit of Judaism, inasmuch as it approximates to a close union with that which is different and alien, and a severance of the ties which bind us all to Israel's lot. You doubt its desirability, because, through too much intimacy with the non-Jew, Israel's own special characteristics might easily be obliterated. I respect your scruples, and will communicate to you my own opinion. Let us first examine whether it is in harmony with the spirit of Judaism.

When Israel began its great wandering through the ages and among the nations, Jeremiah proclaimed it as Israel's duty to:

> "Build houses and dwell therein; plant gardens and eat the fruit thereof; take wives unto yourselves, and beget sons and daughters, and take wives for your sons and give your daughters in marriage that they bear sons and daughters, and that you multiply *there*, and diminish not. *And seek the peace of the city whither I have exiled you, and pray for it to the Lord, for in its peace there will be unto you peace.*"

> (Jeremiah 29:5–7)

To be pushed back and limited upon the path of life is, therefore, not an essential condition of the *Galuth*, Israel's exile among the nations. On the contrary, it is our duty to join ourselves as closely as possible to the state which receives us into its midst, to promote its welfare and not to consider our own well-being as in any way separate from that of the state to which we belong.

This close connection with states everywhere is not at all in contradiction to the spirit of Judaism, for the independent national life of Israel was never

the essence or purpose of our existence as a nation, but only a means of fulfilling our spiritual mission.

Land and soil were never Israel's bond of union. That function was always fulfilled solely by the common task set by the Torah. Therefore the
people of Israel still forms a united body, though it is separated from a national soil. Nor does this unity lose any of its reality though Israel accept
everywhere the citizenship of the nations among which it is dispersed. This
spiritual unity (which may be designated by the Hebrew terms *am* and *goy*,
but not by the term "nation," unless we are able to separate from that word
the inherent concept of common territory and political power) is the only
communal bond we possess, or ever expect to possess, until that great day
shall arrive when the almighty shall see fit in His inscrutable wisdom to
unite again His scattered servants in one land, and the Torah shall be the
guiding principle of a state, a model of the meaning of Divine Revelation
and the mission of humanity.

For this future, which is promised us in the glorious predictions of the inspired prophets as a goal of the *Galuth*, we hope and pray, but actively to ac-
celerate its coming is prohibited to us. The entire purpose of the Messianic
age is that we may, in prosperity, exhibit to mankind a better example of "Israel" than did our ancestors the first time, while, hand in hand with us, the entire race will be joined in universal brotherhood through the recognition of
God, the All-One.

It is on account of this the purely spiritual nature of its national character
that Israel is capable of the most intimate union and states, with, perhaps, this
difference. While others seek in the state only the material benefits which it
secures, considering possessions and pleasures as the highest good, Israel can
regard it only as a means of fulfilling the mission of mankind.

Summon up before your mental vision the picture of such an Israel,
dwelling in freedom among the nations, and striving to attain to its ideal. Picture every son of Israel a respected and influential priest of righteousness and
love, disseminating among the nations not specific Judaism—for proselytism
is forbidden—but pure humanity. What a mighty impulse to progress, what a
luminary and staff in the gloomy days of the Middle Ages would Israel have
been then, if its own sin and the insanity of the nations had not rendered such
a *Galuth* impossible. How impressive, how sublime it would have been if, in
the midst of a race that adored only power, possessions and enjoyment, there
had lived quietly and publicly human beings of a different sort, who beheld
in material possessions only the means for practicing justice and love towards
all, a people whose minds, imbued with the wisdom and truth of the Law,
maintained simple, straightforward views, and emphasized them for themselves and others in expressive, vivid symbolic acts.

But it would seem as though Israel first had to be fitted, through the endurance of the harsh and cruel aspects of exile, for proper appreciation and utilization of the milder and gentler aspects of dispersion.

When *Galuth* will be understood and accepted as it should be, when, in suffering, the service of God and His Torah will be understood as the only task of life, when, even in misery, God will be served, and material abundance esteemed only as a means for this service, then, perhaps, Israel will be ready for the far greater temptations of prosperity and happiness in dispersion. Thus the answer to our question is quite obvious. Just as it is our duty to endeavor to obtain those material possessions which are the fundamental condition of life, so also is it the duty of every one to take advantage of every alleviation and improvement of his condition open to him in an honest way. For, the more means, the more opportunity is given to him to fulfill his mission in its broadest sense; and it is the duty of the community no less than that of the individual to obtain for all its members the opportunities and privileges of citizenship and liberty. Do I consider this desirable? I bless emancipation when I see how the excess of oppression drove Israel away from a normal life, limited the free development of its noble character, and compelled many individuals to enter, for the sake of self-preservation, upon paths which they were too weak to refuse to enter.

I bless emancipation when I notice that no spiritual principle, not even one of foolish fanaticism, stands in its way, but that it is opposed only by those passions which are degrading to humanity, namely, greed for gain and narrow selfishness. I rejoice when I perceive that in this concession of emancipation, regard for the natural rights of men to live as equals among equals is freely extended without force or compulsion, but purely through the power of their own inner truth. I welcome the sacrifice of the base passions wherever it is offered, as the dawn of reviving humanity in mankind, and as a preliminary step to the universal recognition of God as the sole Lord and Father, and of all human beings as the children of the All-One.

But for Israel I only bless it if, at the same time, there will awaken in Israel the true spirit which strives to fulfill the mission of Israel regardless of whether or not there is to be emancipation, to elevate and ennoble ourselves, to implant the spirit of Judaism in our souls, in order that it may generate a life in which that spirit shall be reflected and realized. I bless it, if Israel will regard emancipation not as the goal of its vocation, but only as a new condition of its mission, and as a new test, much severer than the trial of oppression. But I should grieve if Israel understood itself so little, and had so little comprehension of its own spirit that it would welcome emancipation as the end of the *Galuth*, and as the highest goal of its historic mission. If Israel should regard this glorious concession merely as a means of securing a greater degree of comfort in life, and greater opportunities for the acquisition of wealth and enjoyment, it would show that Israel had not comprehended the spirit of its own Law, nor learned anything from exile. And sorrowfully indeed would I mourn if Israel were so far to forget itself as to deem emancipation not too dearly purchased through capricious curtailment of the Torah, capricious abandonment of the chief element of our very being. We must become Jews, Jews in the true sense of the word, imbued with the spirit of the Law, accepting it as the fountain of spiritual and ethical life. Then Judaism will gladly welcome emancipation as affording a greater opportunity for the fulfillment of its task, the realization of a noble and ideal life.

NOTES

1. It is no accident that the subtitle to *Horeb*, Hirsch's modern legal code, carries the subtitle, "For Thinking Jewish Men and *Women*."

2. Philip Bloch's "Memoir," a mini-biography of Graetz, describes his apprenticeship to Hirsch. This may be found in Professor H. Graetz, *History of the Jews*, vol. 6 (Philadelphia: Jewish Publication Society of America, 1891–1898), 12–22. In Graetz's diary, a less favorable view of their relationship emerges.

3. Tisha B'Av (the ninth of the Hebrew month Av) commemorates the destruction of the two Jerusalem Temples.

4. It is a lovely piece of Jewish trivia that Hermann Cohen, a great Jewish philosopher, wrote Hirsch a letter ascertaining that his mentor, Rabbi Zacharias Fraenkel, could in no way be suspected of heresy on the basis of his high level of religious observance.

5. Arnold Eisen, *Galut: Modern Jewish Reflection on Homelessness and Homecoming* (Bloomington: Indiana University Press, 1986), brings this dimension of Hirsch's ideology out very clearly.

6. Samsom Raphael Hirsch, *The Nineteen Letters on Judaism*, ed. Bernard Drachman (New York: Feldheim, 1969), 124–25.

7. Samsom Raphael Hirsch, *Horeb* (London: Soncino Press, 1962), 63–64.

8. Jay Harris, *How Do We Know This?* (Albany: State University of New York Press, 1995), 227.

Chapter Four

Abraham Geiger's Defense of Judaism

Continuity and Change

GEIGER'S LIFE AND TIMES (1810–1874)

"The Bible is now and has always been an ever-living Word, not a dead letter."

"Though *Wissenschaft* may sometimes rage, life peacefully unites past and present."[1]

Abraham Geiger was the most articulate exponent of Reform Judaism in its formative decades. In the late 1830s, while serving as rabbi in Wiesbaden, he invited like-minded reformers to the first of several rabbinical assemblies that would meet under his tutelage. Geiger's leadership inaugurated a second round of reform efforts that far outstripped the largely aesthetic and stylistic (dress and decorum) changes of the 1810s, carried out in the wake of Napoleon's armies. His prayerbook revisions exerted an enormous influence on both Reform and Conservative prayerbooks in Germany and the United States. His theological presentation of prophetic Judaism was broad in scope and compelling in its conviction. Given the importance of Reform Judaism at this moment in time (it represents American Jewry's largest denomination), it is a pity that Geiger's life and works are not better known. Yet Geiger's scholarly contributions transcended denominational lines, even as they supported his theological position. Geiger's scholarly magnum opus, *The Original Text and Translations of the Bible*, "reclaim[ed] biblical studies as the legitimate concern of Jewish scholarship."[2] Geiger's *Das Judenthum und seine Geschichte (Judaism and Its History)*, though less widely read than Heinrich Graetz's histories, was equally impressive as a synoptic view of the Jewish past.

53

Geiger's early life seems in many ways the flip side of his rival, Samson Raphael Hirsch's early life. Not only did Geiger grow up in the Frankfurt Traditionalism that Hirsch would later wield into the first modern Orthodox community, but Geiger received his education in the old-fashioned manner. Ironically, Geiger received a far more traditional education than Hirsch. In a letter to Leopold Lipman Zunz, perhaps the greatest Judaica scholar of his day, Geiger recalled his early training:

> At this point I must make mention of my brother Salomon. Early in my youth he introduced me to Hebrew grammar and to the Bible; it was he who guided me through the Talmud too, along the straight path of healthy understanding, protecting my inquiring mind from the affectations of a hair-splitting *pilpulism* not founded on truth. I am grateful indeed that I may still benefit today from the youthful mental and spiritual vigor of him who has now reached a venerable old age.[3]

Michael Geiger, Abraham's father, died when the boy was only thirteen; Salomon, who remained a mainstay of the Orthodox community, clearly played a pivotal role in his younger half-brother's intellectual upbringing. In secular studies, a gentile was hired to provide young Geiger with his Latin, Greek, and mathematical background. Geiger seems to have been a typically precocious Jewish boy. At his bar mitzvah, he delivered a Hebrew discourse on the Talmud and a sermon in German. By the age of seventeen, Geiger began his first scholarly work, a study of the Mishnah that evidenced a sophisticated view of historical development: "It was already clear to me at that time, that just as the spirit of the Talmud is completely different from the spirit of the Bible, the two parts of the Talmud, Mishnah and *gemara*, are also very distant from each other."[4]

Michael Meyer has termed Geiger "the High Priest of *Wissenschaft*."[5] Geiger's commitment to rigorous scholarship was unqualified, and, more than that, Geiger expected scholarly inquiry to guide religious reforms. It is clear that his university days were formative ones in his intellectual development. Oscillating between philology and theology as a major, Geiger also moved from Heidelberg to Bonn University. At Bonn, Geiger and Hirsch formed a Jewish club devoted to sermons and to scholarship. While still in his early thirties, Geiger received rabbinical ordination and published his acclaimed doctoral dissertation, "What Did Mohammed Take from Judaism?" In these years, Geiger also began a long and controversial rabbinic career. Meyer has stressed the conflicting demands of being both a rabbi and scholar on Geiger's loyalties.

On the one hand, Geiger clearly thought *kashrut* was silly; circumcision, barbaric. He considered Hebrew less satisfactory than German for expressing one's deepest feelings, although he wrote Hebrew without difficulty. He considered most of the ceremonial aspects of Judaism expendable. Yet as communal rabbi (first in Wiesbaden and then in Breslau), Geiger observed the norms of Jewish practice. In sermons, Geiger relied on the rich legendary (midrashic) traditions that served so well in bringing the Bible to life. Yet intellectually, Geiger believed that these legends (*midrashim*) were fanciful and that many biblical incidents had little or no historical reality. Geiger wondered aloud in a letter to his friend Joseph Derenbourg:

> For the love of Heaven, how much longer can we continue this deceit, to expound the stories of the Bible from the pulpits over and over again as actual historical happenings, to accept as supernatural events of world importance stories which we ourselves have relegated to the realm of legend, and to derive teachings from them or, at least, to use them as the basis for sermons and texts?[6]

In Geiger's case, "how much longer?" was about forty years—not until the establishment of a Reform seminary in Berlin in 1871 did Geiger finally have a chance to relinquish the rabbinate. Three years later, Geiger died and was buried next to his wife Emilie, who had passed away in 1860 (her death fourteen years earlier had left Geiger emotionally distraught and solely responsible for the raising of their four children). Considering the nasty struggle that accompanied Geiger's first appointment to Breslau, his immediate family's continued adherence to Orthodoxy, his ambivalence regarding his rabbinic calling, the disappointment he suffered when Zacharias Fraenkel was awarded the chancellorship of the Jewish Theological Seminary despite Geiger's efforts in raising the funds and publicizing the project, and the hostile reception that his works on Judaism and Christianity received from gentile scholars, Geiger seems to have had enough disappointments for a couple of lifetimes. But he seems also to have been the sort of person for whom his work was important and satisfying enough that he continued to be a creative scholar until the very end.

Before turning to his creative theology, some assessment of Geiger's scholarly achievements seems in order. As a biblical scholar, Geiger mastered the techniques of Higher Criticism practiced in German theological faculties, a discipline that more conservative Jewish scholars eschewed. Geiger's knowledge of Hebrew philology and texts surpassed that of most Christian scholars. *The Original Text and Translations of the Bible* represented a tour de force in evaluating the process by which the Bible assumed its fixed, final form. In general, Geiger weighed the competition of various groups with Second Temple Judaism and the influence they exerted on the canonical form of the biblical text. Specifically, Geiger suggested that (1) many editions of the Hebrew Bible existed in the Late Second Temple period; (2) while later ages were punctilious about the exact words and punctuation of the traditional Hebrew text, earlier generations were far freer in copying and transmitting the text; and (3) the Samaritan Bible was not just a corrupt and late recension, but was in fact ancient and useful as a control on the traditional Hebrew text. All of these claims, as Nahum Sarna has noted, have turned out to be correct. Despite this line of analysis, which horrified traditionalists, Geiger took a most traditional position on the origins of monotheism. Rather than considering monotheism a very late development in the religion of Ancient Israel, as most nineteenth-century scholars did, Geiger considered revelation a spiritual reality characteristic of the entire nation and one that began with the first patriarchs.[7]

A similar tension between innovation and preservation existed in Geiger's rabbinic scholarship. On the one hand, Geiger boldly claimed that various works of the early rabbis deserved to be treated as discrete texts. That is, Geiger believed that the Talmud often misinterpreted the Mishnah, a conclusion that challenged the idea of a divinely determined law (*halachah*). Yet Geiger recognized that *halachah* clearly antedated the first rabbis—unlike some Reformers such as Samuel Holdheim, who considered all nonbiblical law irrelevant for the present, Geiger's evolutionary model accorded importance to all periods of Jewish history. One thing is certain: Geiger possessed tremendous scholarly skills and the ability to look at an old issue from a fresh perspective. To take the most dramatic instance: the order of the tractates of the Mishnah had long baffled Jewish scholars, who imagined all sorts of thematic possibilities, but Geiger concluded that the Mishnah was simply arranged *according to the number of chapters in each tractate in descending order*—a claim that has since won universal assent.[8]

Geiger's scholarship did not meet with a unanimously positive reception. In his own day, more conservative Jewish scholars, such as the historian Heinrich Graetz, Zacharias Fraenkel (the grandfather of Conservative Judaism), and the neo-Orthodox Hirsch, took him to task on many occasions. Christian scholars, who were entirely willing to accept Geiger's views regarding Islam's debt to Judaism, were far less willing to acknowledge the Jewish matrix of early Christianity, or his championing of the Pharisees, the principal "heavies" in the New Testament. Yet Geiger's sharpest critic was probably Gershom Scholem (1897–1982), the pioneering scholar of Jewish mysticism. Scholem considered Geiger the epitome of the destructive tendencies embodied by the first generation of scholarly investigators of Judaism (*Wissenschaft des Judentums*). For Scholem, the apologetic, politically driven, and self-censoring nature of much of this scholarship imparted a "ghostly" feel to the portrayal of Judaism that resulted. It is certainly true that Geiger, like other first-generation practitioners of *Wissenschaft*, emphasized the purely religious dimensions of Judaism at the expense of a more variegated portrayal of social, economic, and communal aspects. But compared to pure academics like Steinschneider or Zunz (at least later in Zunz's life), Geiger in his *Wissenschaft* always had one eye on a vigorous view of what Judaism should be in the modern age—though not, of course, a vision that the Zionist Scholem shared.

Recently, Susannah Heschel has reexamined Geiger as a historian and as a theologian. Her book *Rediscovering the Jewish Jesus: Abraham Geiger and the Christian Scholars* discredits the view, found among both Zionist and Orthodox critics, that Geiger was a diffident and would-be Protestant. Geiger presented a Jesus explicable only in a Jewish milieu, attributing most of what was best in Jesus to the religious background of Second Temple Judaism. Unlike his warmly received doctoral dissertation, published under the title "What Did Mohammed Take from Judaism?" Geiger's "Jesus book" provoked an angry reaction from Christian scholars.

Geiger's vision has justifiably been called "prophetic Judaism." Essentially, this meant that of all the eras in human history, the era of the prophets' social morality and universalizing view of God and God's world, set the standard for human behavior. The challenge of meeting this prophetic standard, rather than a ritually prescribed form of behavior, ought to guide Jews eternally. The means of meeting this prophetic standard was supplied by the "spirit of the times." The "spirit of the times," which Samson Raphael Hirsch regarded mainly as a challenge to traditional practices, Geiger embraced wholeheartedly and confidently applied to traditions he regarded as outmoded. What this meant in practice can be seen in Geiger's introduction to the Frankfurt Prayerbook of 1869:

> With all respectful retention of Judaism's historical elements, religious concepts which have had a temporal validity, but which have been displaced by a progressively purer conception, must not be retained in a one-sided and sharp accentuation. Rather must they be either totally removed or recast into a form which does not contradict the purer conception.
>
> Consequently,
>
> (1) Highly materialistic descriptions of the Deity, as they occur in the *piyutim*, must be removed;
> (2) The enumeration of the various angelic orders and the depiction of their activity cannot be admitted;
> (3) The belief in immortality must not content itself with the one-sided formulation of physical resurrection. It must, instead, be expressed in a manner which also includes the concept of spiritual continuity.[9]

This program sounds radical, yet the result was a prayerbook that most American Jews today would identify as "conservative." As a practicing rabbi, Geiger recognized the role played by local custom and traditional loyalties, including loyalty to a largely Hebrew prayerbook. Moreover, Geiger was no *Karaite*, a Jew who saw value only in the Bible, but not in the rabbinic traditions.[10] In all four eras of the history of Judaism (revelation, tradition, medievalism, scientific), there were some people willing to advance the progressive agenda embodied in the prophets. Geiger's Jewish heroes often reflect his self-conception. Witness this description of Hillel: "Hillel was a man who dared openly to oppose those who sought to make the Law more burdensome, and who was not at all afraid to be known as an advocate of leniency who sought to render the Law less difficult."[11]

Geiger shared the tendency of many German thinkers to pursue a system to the point of absurdity. Convinced that religious confession alone made one a Jew, he spoke with appalling lack of concern for Jews elsewhere in Europe and beyond, an attitude that earned him a special place in Zionism's rogues' gallery. On the other hand, his opposition to the dangerous mixing of church-state entanglements and Jewish nationalism makes for interesting reading in light of the sometimes unsympathetic attitude of Israel's chief rabbinate: "A Jerusalem with a mighty Jewish population would be the tyrant's strong castle of Judaism, the Jewish Rome." Geiger believed deeply in the ultimate victory of the forces of progress over the forces of reaction. He believed equally deeply that the eternal message of Judaism, not Christianity, embodied the universalistic ideas of humanity. In summary, no one before or since Geiger has enunciated the principles of Reform Judaism with such conviction and consistency.

In the 1860s, Geiger gave an important series of thirty-four lectures in Frankfurt and Berlin. They were lively, participatory talks given to the Jewish community and formed the nucleus of Geiger's synthetic presentation of Jewish history from the biblical era until the sixteenth century. Reflecting both its oral genesis and Geiger's mastery of the field, *Das Judenthum und seine Geschichte* quickly became his most popular work. The following selection relates to three central themes in *Judaism and Its History*: (1) Revelation and the Jewish Genius, (2) Judaism and Christianity, and (3) The Jewish State and Jewish Exile.

QUESTIONS FOR GEIGER, *JUDAISM AND ITS HISTORY*

What does Geiger mean by "genius"? "Religious genius"?

Does religious genius reside only in the prophets, or, is it the possession of the entire nation? In any case, how are the people and the prophets related in this matter?

Do the Jews still possess religious genius? Since there have been no prophets since Malachai (about 450 B.C.E.), how is this religious genius expressed in rabbinic, medieval, and modern Judaism?

Geiger cited both Judah Halevy and Moses Maimonides on the nature of revelation. To which view does Geiger seem to incline?

Does Geiger's portrayal of exile differ from Hirsch's? If so, how?

Geiger defines "tradition" as "that force of evolution that endures within Judaism as an invisible creative power." Is this what Hirsch would understand by tradition? What is your understanding of tradition, in a religious context?

What role does historical evolution play in Judaism and what impact does this have on Geiger's conception of revelation and (implicitly) the Torah?

Geiger portrays Hillel as a champion of reform. How does this interpretation serve Geiger's view of Judaism?

Geiger differentiates Judaism from Christianity in these pages on several accounts. How many divergences between Judaism and Christianity can you identify here? How important are these differences in your view? Would Hirsch agree with Geiger's list? Can you think of other differences that you would consider more central to explaining the difference between Judaism and Christianity?

What seems to be the purpose or "mission" of the Jews in human history? What is Jewish history really about? Would Hirsch differ from Geiger in terms of this mission, or only on the grounds of what the carrying out of the mission requires of actual Jews?

What, in your words, makes Geiger a "reform" thinker? What distinguishes Geiger's emphases from those of today's Reform Judaism?

STUDIES BY AND ABOUT GEIGER

Max Wiener, *Abraham Geiger and Liberal Judaism: The Challenge of the Nineteenth Century* (Philadelphia: Jewish Publication Society of America, 1962) contains a useful introduction and a helpful selection of Geiger's writings. Michael Meyer, *Response to Modernity* (New York: Oxford University Press, 1988), places Geiger in the context of nineteenth century religious reforms. *New Perspectives on Abraham Geiger*, ed. Jakob J. Petuchowski (Cincinnati, Ohio: Hebrew Union College-Jewish Institute of Religion, 1975) contains several useful scholarly articles. Susannah Heschel's *Rediscovering the Jewish Jesus: Abraham Geiger and the Christian Scholars* (Chicago: University of Chicago, 1998) offers an intellectually exciting view into Geiger's mind, Jewish-Christian polemics, and the world of nineteenth-century Bible scholarship.

From *Abraham Geiger and Liberal Judaism:*
The Challenge of the Nineteenth Century

There are phenomena of such overwhelming force that even the most reluctant of critical minds must accept them. One such phenomenon is the appearance of Judaism from out of the midst of a wilderness, like a strong root growing out of arid soil. . . . [*In the prophets*] we behold personalities of serene grandeur and simple dignity; these were men of fiery passion coupled with calm prudence; their boldness was coupled with profound humility and resignation. They impress us, and they make us sense the breath of a higher spirit within them. The teachers of old have already said it: no two prophets utter their prophecy in the same manner. Each prophet is a complete, well-rounded personality in his own right, with a distinct individuality of his own. Yet all the prophets have one common set of characteristics; they are all motivated by the one same great ideal . . . .

Generally speaking, we may distinguish in man two mental processes—a twofold attribute with which man has been favored: we differentiate between talent, on the one hand, and genius on the other. These two may touch at some points, yet they are forever essentially different and apart from one another. This difference is not simply one of degree, but of actual essence. Talent is the gift to comprehend ideas easily and quickly, to assimilate them and then skillfully and adeptly to communicate them. However, talent is based on that which is already in existence, on past achievements and on such riches as have already been acquired. It does not create anything original. Not so genius. Genius does not lean upon anything; genius is creative. It discovers truths which were previously hidden and reveals laws which have not heretofore been known. It is as if there were revealed before it in brilliant clarity, and in their context according to their orderly interplay, those forces which work deep within the core of nature. It is as if these forces were tangibly real, as if the spiritual impulses both within the individual and within mankind as a whole have unveiled themselves before genius, so that it may peer into the inmost recesses of the soul and from there single out the driving forces which motivate the human spirit. Talent may be cultivated; it may be acquired by effort and diligence. But genius is a free gift, a favor, a mark of consecration which is imprinted upon man; if it is not present in him, he can never acquire it on his own. . . .

The Greeks boasted of having been autochthons, of having been born in and of their own soil. Whether this claim is justified is a moot question. But another claim, which may perhaps reflect its deeper meaning, may surely be acknowledged, namely, the autochthonous nature of their mind, the originality of their particular national tendency. The Greeks had neither patterns nor teachers for their art and learning. They served as their own mentors and masters, and presently they shone forth with a perfection which made them the teachers of mankind in almost every age . . . .

Does not the Jewish people, too, have such a genius, a religious genius of this type? Was it not also an original force that enlightened its eyes so that it could look more deeply into the higher spheres of the spirit, that it could discern more clearly the close relationship between the spirit of man and the Universal Spirit, that it could grasp the higher challenge of human existence and perceive the profound ethical quality in man with greater clarity and intensity, expressing it as its unique insight? If this is indeed so, then this intimate contact of the spirit of the individual with the Universal Spirit, this illumination of individual minds by the all-encompassing force so that they could break through their finite barriers, is—let us not shy away from the word—revelation as manifested in the people as a whole.

Not all the Greeks were artists, they were not all Phidias or Praxiteles, and yet the Greek people as such had the gift of producing great masters. The same was true of Judaism. Certainly not all the Jews were prophets, and the verse *Would that all the people were prophets*! was no more than a pious wish. Another verse, *I shall pour My spirit over all flesh*, is a promise which never became reality. Nevertheless, the Jewish people is the people of the revelation which subsequently gave birth to the select instruments of that revelation. They were scattered sparks of light, as it were, which, gathered together by those chosen to proclaim the revelation, shone forth fused into one single bright flame. There is no reference to the God of Moses or to the God of the Prophets; our literature speaks only of the God of Abraham, Isaac and Jacob, of the God of the entire race, of its patriarchs who showed this same predisposition, that of introspective vision. This is the revelation which lay dormant in the people as a whole and then found a unifying focal point in certain individuals. It is a truism of profound significance that even the greatest prophet of them all left his work unfinished. He was not to stand out like Atlas who bore the world upon his shoulders, carrying out a task without participating in it—inspirer and executor at once . . . .

Truly, Judaism originated with the people of the revelation. Why, then, should we not be allowed to use this term when we speak of penetration to the deepest foundation, of an illumination emanating from the higher spirit, which cannot be explained and which, though subject to later evolution, was not evolutionary in its origin? . . .

We have no intention of limiting and narrowing the term in a dogmatic fashion. It may be interpreted in many ways; but its essence always remains the same—the contact of human reason with the First Cause of all things. Notwithstanding the high regard in which the teachers of old held the concept of revelation, they never sought to deny its relationship to human endowments. The Talmud teaches that the spirit of God will rest only upon a wise man, upon a man of mortal strength who is self-sufficient because he is content, having overcome all ambitions and lusts. Only a man of inner stature who senses the Divine within himself will be capable of absorbing the Divine. He must not be a mere mouthpiece through which the message is transmitted, through which the word is spoken without his being aware of it. He must be a man close to the Divine in the truest sense of the word, and therefore receptive to it. . . . Judah Halevy stresses that revelation is a tendency that was alive in the people as a whole. Israel, he says, is the religious heart of all mankind. As a group, Israel always maintained this higher susceptibility, and the great individuals who stood out in Israel's midst were the heart of that heart, as it were.

Maimonides said that revelation was to be viewed as a lightning-like flash of illumination; to some, he explained, such enlightenment is granted for a short while only; to others it comes more than once; and Moses had it at all times . . . .

VOL. I, PP. 27 FF.

The Exile and the Return: Tradition.

. . . Such nations as merely found states and maintain their existence for a period limited by the mandate of world history must break up as soon as they are cut loose from the states they have established. Their lives and their functions cease and they are doomed to extinction. But not so that nation which is only a means for the fulfillment of a higher purpose, the visible manifestation of a great idea that embraces all of mankind. True, the members of a nation such as this need time to dwell together so that they may become a united community within which that ideal may mature to its fullest expression. . . . But once this is achieved, that nation may cease to exist as a state without its inmost essence being broken up thereby. . . .

The Jews returned [*from Babylonian captivity*] and once again formed a new national entity. Why could they, of all peoples, have succeeded in this endeavor? The answer is that they were more than a nation; they were a brotherhood united by the bonds of a single common ideal. . . .

True, the actual, immediate creative force of revelation had come to an end. . . . [*Still*] the creative spirit had not entirely disappeared from the midst of Judaism. It had not come to a full stop, so that nothing new could have been produced or refined. The living spirit continued to pulsate through the ages. Despite the lamentation that *there is no longer a prophet in our midst*, that same holy, ennobling spirit still continued to make itself felt. Tradition is that force of evolution that endures within Judaism as an invisible creative power, as a certain undefinable something which never receives its final mold but which is continually at work just the same. Within Judaism, tradition is the soul that animates the body; it is the daughter of revelation, of the same high birth as the latter. It has never ceased, nor will it ever vanish from within Judaism; it is the fount which always fructifies the times anew, and which must give birth to new forms with every contact with the outside world, in accordance with new needs and situations. This was how the Jews succeeded in founding a new national and religious life.

If ever there should come a time—but this time will never come!—when the stream of tradition dries up; when Judaism is viewed as a completed, closed entity; when faces turn backward only, in contemplation of what the past has wrought, blindly seeking to preserve it—then, indeed, Judaism will be at an end. Or, if there should come a time when Jews see Judaism with romantic awe, with some sort of antiquarian affection, as a ruin which must be preserved in its decayed state, while others again pass by these ruins with haughty indifference, and no living force breaks forth from anywhere—then, indeed, the time will have come to dig a grave for Judaism. Then, truly, Judaism will be lifeless, spiritually dead, a walking skeleton which may still last for a time but is doomed to certain destruction in the end. But this is not Judaism. Judaism has an eternally procreative tradition—yes, let us pay due honor to this term. Tradition, like revelation, is a spiritual force that goes on forever. It is a higher force that springs, not from man, but from the Divine spirit; it is at work within the group as a whole; it selects those individuals who would serve as its bearers; it manifests itself in ever more mature and noble fruit and thereby remains a force, living and viable. . . .

VOL. I, PP. 68 FF.

Christianity as an Ecclesiastical World Power.
The Breakup of the Jewish Nation.

. . . Yes, Judaism has survived alongside Christianity, and in spite of it. It was fought not merely with earthly weapons, with fire and sword, with expulsion and oppression, but also with spiritual ammunition. Any good and noble trait that had been conceded to Judaism, before it had given birth to Christianity from within itself, was viewed simply as a preparation for Christianity, a

Christian quality that had come into being before Christianity itself. Nevertheless, Judaism has survived; it has preserved its eternal values and has not allowed them to become tarnished. It refused to allow its belief in God to be distorted or adulterated by alien elements. It has resisted every effort to graft onto it the concept of Original Sin, which others have attempted to read into its Scriptures. Judaism has not permitted its patent of human nobility and dignity to be destroyed. It has remained steadfast in its conviction that God has given to man the power of free self-determination and self-refinement; that, despite the animal lust which is part of his nature, man also has the strength to overcome it and, by dint of his own efforts, to refine and ennoble his personality. Moreover, since the belief in original sin and the corruption of human nature has remained alien to it, Judaism does not feel the need for a redemption accomplished from without to regain its purity. Judaism has not exchanged its own concept of a God of mercy for the God of that peculiar love which, in order to appease its wrath, requires a great vicarious sacrifice on behalf of the sinful masses. Judaism has not taken the development of all mankind to a higher goal to mean a denial of itself, and hence saw no need to fight against it. It never declared: "The time has already been fulfilled and the copingstone of the edifice was put into place eighteen centuries ago — the copingstone of the one world which was the cornerstone of another — and there is no other truth that can be added to the structure."

Christianity must of necessity look back upon that period as the most important in the history of the world; that era must forever be Christianity's heart and core, and the personality which brought it into being must forever represent its highest ideal. Even the most liberal among the Christians, who divest the founder of their religion of all supernatural qualities, if they are to preserve some tenuous bond with their faith, cannot escape the necessity of creating for themselves an artificial image of him, to which they then ascribe all the attributes of earthly perfection. This image, however, crumbles even more quickly before critical examination than the older, solid concept. Judaism, on the other hand, can dispense with personalities; it may give free rein to critical study as regards all of its great men, even if that critical study went so far as to eliminate the figure of Moses from Jewish history. Such an extreme step, of course, would constitute an excess of irresponsibility which we would perhaps deplore. But let us stop to consider: is it on Moses, or upon any other human participant in Jewish history that Judaism depends? There is a Torah; it is there that the faith of Judaism is imbedded, and there it will be preserved. Regardless of how the Torah came into Judaism, regardless of who gave it or what historical personality was its transmitter, whether it was a being free of sin or a mortal subject to human weaknesses — the fact remains that the Torah exists. This is why Judaism was able to preserve the character of its mission even later on; its history did not cease with the beginning of Christianity. . . .

VOL. I, PP. 145 FF.

NOTES

1. Michael Meyer, "Universalism and Jewish Unity in the Thought of Abraham Geiger," in *The Role of Religion in Modern Jewish History*, ed. Jacob Katz (Cambridge, Mass.: Association of Jewish Studies, 1975), 99.

2. Nahum Sarna, "Abraham Geiger and Biblical Scholarship," in *New Perspectives on Abraham Geiger*, ed. Jakob J. Petuchowski (Cincinnati, Ohio: Hebrew Union College-Jewish Institute of Religion, 1975), 27.

3. Max Wiener, *Abraham Geiger and Liberal Judaism: The Challenge of the Nineteenth Century* (Philadelphia: Jewish Publication Society of America, 1962), 141.

4. The Mishnah (ca. 200 CE) is the foundational text of rabbinic law, to which the *gemarah* provides commentary. Together, the Mishnah and *gemarah* form the Talmud.

5. *Wissenschaft* translates into English as either "science" or "scholarship." The best introduction for the nonspecialist to the important scholarly movement known as *Wissenschaft des Judentums* is to be found in Michael Meyer, *Origins of the Modern Jew* (Detroit, Mich.: Wayne State Press, 1967).

6. Susannah Heschel, *Abraham Geiger and the Jewish Jesus* (Chicago: University of Chicago Press, 1998), 33.

7. Sarna, "Abraham Geiger and Biblical Scholarship."

8. David Weiss Halivni, "Abraham Geiger and Talmudic Scholarship," in *New Perspectives on Abraham Geiger*, ed. Jakob J. Petuchowski (Cincinnati, Ohio: Hebrew Union College-Jewish Institute of Religion, 1975).

9. Jakob J. Petuchowski's *Prayerbook Reform in Europe*, (New York: World Union for Progressive Judaism, 1968), 165–66. I would also recommend this author's essay on Geiger and Holdheim, and their impact in America, which can be found in the *Leo Baeck Institute Yearbook* (1977).

10. The Karaites were initially a medieval Jewish sect that denied the validity of rabbinic traditions, including the Mishnah and Talmud. Karaite tendencies continued into modern times, including those of a friend and rival of Geiger's, the radical reformer Samuel Holdheim.

11. Weiner, *Abraham Geiger and Liberal Judaism*, 187.

Part Two

RECOVERING TRADITION FOR THE INDIVIDUAL AND THE COMMUNITY

INTRODUCTION

By the end of the nineteenth century, Jewish life in Western Europe and North America had been transformed. Political equality, the rise of the middle classes, nearly universal acquisition of European culture, and considerable social rapprochement with the Christian world made modern Jews radically different from their medieval and early modern predecessors. At midcentury, Geiger and Hirsch experienced this process as it was underway. By the end of the century, this process had played itself out with some unanticipated results. While the escape from the ghetto had opened vistas of opportunity for all Jews that were unimaginable except for a tiny minority in earlier times, Jewish learning had waned considerably. The last yeshiva in Germany closed its doors in 1824. English Jewry joined the majority of Englishmen in considering religious enthusiasm something for the mad or the déclassé. French and Italian Jewries settled for an untroubled mix of formal traditionalism and la dolce vita. Jewish spirituality, as we will see in the next section of this book, continued to flourish, but Jews were leaving the Pale of Settlement by the millions and even within the Pale, were migrating to cities such as Odessa, notorious for its religious laxity. Many Eastern European rabbis stigmatized America as an impure land (*trefye medina*) where Torah observance was a lost cause. The officials at Ellis Island managed to stay busy. All in all, secularization and bourgeois existence characterized the direction that Jews and Christians, especially in Western Europe, traveled together in the course of a century.

Although Mendelssohn would have been shocked by the results, Western Jewry had fully lived out his dictum, "Adapt yourselves to the morals and the constitution of the land to which you have been removed." The second part of Mendelssohn's charge, "Hold fast to the religion of your father too," had proven to be more problematic.[1] Religiosity, the primal, human desire for transcendence was woefully absent in late nineteenth-century Jewish religious life, argued Martin Buber in a series of essays. Jewish books, in Franz Rosenzweig's striking metaphor, occupied only a small part of the bookcase.[2] No wonder, Buber and Rosenzweig agreed, that the best Jewish youth found their intellectual homes beyond Jewry's rather narrow confines.

This alienation from Jewish life could be remedied, however, by the recovery of Jewish tradition and renewed involvement in the life of the Jewish community. Buber popularized Hasidism and propagandized for Zionism. Rosenzweig developed a center for adult Jewish learning and showed, through his own dramatic example, that even the most peripherally attached Jew could propel him- or herself toward the Jewish center. Together, they collaborated on a new translation of the Hebrew Scriptures. While Buber was a lifelong Zionist and Rosenzweig a continued adherent of the German-Jewish synthesis, both believed that only by being wholly a Jew could one become wholly human. The bifurcation Mendelssohn advocated worked for their parents and grandparents in the century-long struggle for Emancipation, but it did not work for them.

The picture of Jewish anomie that emerges from the writings of Buber, Rosenzweig, and many Zionists should not be taken at face value. The Jewish communities of Europe (though not America) also kept tabs on their members: registering their births, marrying them, collecting their tithes, and burying them. Although increasingly secularized, Jews in the modern world continued to marry each other, socialize primarily with other Jews, live in the same neighborhoods, work in a few chosen professions, and spend their leisure time together. Women often succeeded in preserving the home as an oasis of Jewishness, evoking through food and family something of a slower, quieter era. More than this, a Jewish press in both Jewish and vernacular languages, and secularized Jewish organizations like the Alliance Israelite Universelle, the Centralverein, and B'nai B'rith served to weld the Jews into something more than an informal, voluntary religious community. But these examples of modern Jewish creativity, however significant, did not impress Buber or Rosenzweig as vehicles of religion or spirituality.

Judaism no longer provided an all-encompassing framework of existence, but it still played an important role in the lives of many Jews. Friday night dinner, even if unaccompanied by blessings before and after the meal, remained a sacred time for family togetherness. Holidays were observed—or not observed—as a unit. Jewish humor remained a feature in many acculturated households (the Freuds are one example) and Yiddishisms spiced the speech of those who were not too embarrassed to use the quintessential Jewish language. Nevertheless, all this is somewhat irrelevant when trying to understand Buber and Rosenzweig, who spoke for a generation of young Jews unimpressed and uncommitted to the compromises of the preceding two or three generations. These writers addressed a generation in revolt from middle-class mores, nineteenth-century liberalism, and the Judaically *parve*.[3]

If Buber and Rosenzweig exerted great efforts creating Jewish individuals, the Zionist movement aimed at creating the conditions in which Jewry as a whole could flourish in radically changed circumstances. In Western Europe, where secularism had eroded the traditional religious patterns of life, remaining part of a generally disliked (and often discriminated-against minority) became increasingly a matter of loyalty, nostalgia, and comfort. A common Jewish fate remained long after a common Jewish faith had lost its importance. Theodor Herzl, the first figure to make Zionism a viable political movement, epitomized the ability to turn the awareness of a common fate into a program; specifically, a secular, nationalistic, and politically modern organization that would build a state for the Jewish people. Herzl did not want to recover religious tradition à la Buber and Rosenzweig (although he did recognize that his movement was a return to Judaism even before it was a return to Zion). Herzl did, however, share their goal of creating a superior basis for continued Jewish existence.

For Ahad Ha'am, the critical agenda item for modern Jews was to create a center of Jewish life that would radiate out to revivify a failing diaspora. Ahad Ha'am had an insatiable appetite for controversy, and a quick glance at his opponents will help us fix his own position. Against Theodor Herzl, who mainly wanted a safe haven for Jews suffering from persecution, Ahad Ha'am insisted that the problem was what form Judaism would take in a secularized world. Against his friend Simon Dubnov, who championed the cause of cultural and educational autonomy for Russia's Jews, Ahad Ha'am argued that Jews needed a center in the ancestral homeland (*Eretz Yisrael*) where Jews could develop *all* of their capacities.[4] Against radicals like Micha Yosef Berdichevski and Yosef Chaim Brenner, who were prepared to jettison large segments of the Jewish past, Ahad Ha'am contended that Jewish values were sacred and eternal even if their source was this-worldly—the Jewish people, rather than God.

Herzl and Ahad Ha'am do not represent the only important positions within the Jewish national movement. Many Eastern European Jews joined the BUND, a Jewish socialist party seeking democratic reform. The BUND drew its strength from the emerging industrial proletariat of the Pale. Since most of the Jewish workers spoke Yiddish and many remained respectful of Jewish traditions, the BUND gravitated to a more pronounced Jewish

agenda. The BUND moved closer to Dubnov on cultural issues and relations with the principal Russian socialist party—which rejected both religion and nationalism—grew tense. Dubnov, an autodidact who pioneered
the history of Eastern European Jewry, sought a synthesis between tradition
and modernity. Specifically, Dubnov wanted to preserve the Jewish people's ability to act as a collective organism (tradition) and the intellectual
and religious freedom ushered in by Emancipation (modernity). Other Jews,
most famously Rosa Luxembourg and Leo Trotsky, joined the Russian revolutionary parties, accepting Marx's view that the Jewish problem would be
solved by the elimination of class society in general. Aaron David Gordon
made a religion of labor, insisting that Jews working the land (in Palestine)
would effect a revolution of Jewish spirit. A wide variety of Socialist Zionists thought Herzl and Ahad Ha'am too indifferent to economic issues and
saw the cultivation of a Jewish labor movement as critical to the proper orientation of Zionism. Street names such as Nahman Syrkin and Ber Boro-
chov are found in every Israeli city, although contemporary Israel has abandoned much of its initial socialism.

In retrospect, the most important development for Jews at this time was the
emergence of religious Zionism in the first decade of the twentieth century.
Abraham Isaac Kook, who may be considered the most creative traditionalist
to emerge from early Zionism, will be discussed at greater length in part 3 of
this book. It should be noted that most of the Eastern European rabbinic establishment regarded Zionism as a heresy—God, not men, ought to decide
when the Ingathering and messianic redemption would occur. As early as
1902, a small group of Orthodox Jews, organized in a party called *Mizrachi*,
disagreed with this dichotomy. The Mizrachi, encouraged by Kook, Reines,
Bar-Ilan, and others, participated with the secular pioneers who drained
swamps, planted orchards, and established a new Jewish society. Kook regarded the traditionalists and the secular Zionists as working together for the
Redemption, to the benefit of both Jews and the entire world. By the time of
Kook's death in 1935, Zionism had progressed from a utopian dream to a
worldwide movement that had gained international recognition and developed the nucleus of what would become, in 1948, the first Jewish state since
the second and first centuries BCE.

Israel emerged as one of the two centers of twentieth-century Jewry. The
other, America, resulted from the mass flight from Czarist Russia in the years
between the first widespread pogroms (1881) and the passage of strict immi-
gration laws in the early 1920s. Over two million Jews, about 15 percent of
European Jewry, traveled by steamship to America. This exodus transformed
the community of 250,000 originally Central European, German-speaking,
but highly Americanized Jews, who both condescended to and substantially

aided the newcomers. Ultimately, the Yiddish-speaking "Russian" Jews were eager to Americanize and see their children achieve the levels of success typifying the "German" Jews and indeed, Americans at large. Coming from one of the most intensely Jewish cultures in Judaism's long history, the immigrant generation did not give overly much thought to the sort of Judaism that could flourish on American soil. They were too busy establishing a foothold in America, and Jewishness, at least for the first generation, was assumed to be a fact of life as natural as breathing. The Conservative movement's Jewish Theological Seminary was reorganized and both the (relatively established) Reform and (relatively new) Orthodox establishments reacted to this flood of immigrants. Nevertheless, the long-term implications of this encounter did not receive serious consideration. The most striking exception to this generalization—and there were others—was Mordecai Kaplan.

As early as the 1910s and 1920s, Kaplan realized that shoehorning American Jews into a denominational model of Reform–Conservative–Orthodox was to misrepresent the nature of Jewish life and in doing so, to guarantee apathy. For Jews, as Kaplan once put it, "God was in the background." The beauty of Jewish life was its ability to function as an organism. The tapestry of Jewish life expressed itself in a wide range of activities better characterized as a civilization than as a religion.[5] From this sociological perspective, Kaplan rejected the Mendelssohnian legacy as decisively as Buber and Rosenzweig rejected it from a religious-spiritual perspective. Kaplan insisted that American Jews should learn to inhabit both these civilizations—American and Jewish—and that all Jewish institutions should promote this highly desirable dialogue.

I have portrayed Buber and Rosenzweig as physicians for the Jewish individual, and Zionists such as Herzl, Ahad Ha'am, and Kaplan as technicians for the Jewish community. But of course, this dichotomy should not be overdrawn. Judaism deals with individuals and with a community; any serious Jewish thinker must pay heed to both. Let me simply highlight the underlying assumption of this section of the book: by the end of the nineteenth century, Emancipation, secularization, and modernization had introduced vastly expanded opportunities for individual Jews. These same factors had also introduced a new set of problems threatening the maintenance of Jewish identity on individual and on communal levels.

NOTES

1. Moses Mendelssohn, *Jerusalem* (Hanover, N.H.: University Press of New England, 1983), 133.

2. Franz Rosenzweig, "On Opening the Jewish Lehrhaus," in *On Jewish Learning*, ed. Nahum Glatzer (New York: Schocken, 1955), 95–98.

3. *Parve* means "neither meat nor milk." The English version is "neither fish nor fowl."

4. Ahad Ha'am supported a Jewish state, but he disagreed with political Zionists that this was the critical agenda item. Dubnov promoted Yiddish as the language of the masses; Ahad Ha'am, like most Zionists, regarded Hebrew as the sole legitimate *national* language.

5. Kaplan once described civilization as: "The accumulation of knowledge, skills, tools, arts, literatures, laws, religions, and philosophies which stand between man and external nature and which serves as a bulwark against the hostility of forces that would otherwise destroy him." Mordechai Kaplan, *Judaism as a Civilization* (New York: Macmillan, 1934), 179.

Chapter Five

Martin Buber

Restoring the Jewish Individual

BUBER'S LIFE AND TIMES (1878–1965)

Under the influence of [Buber's] biblical humanism and under the impact of the new Bible translation, the study of biblical sources became a major preoccupation of German Jewry, particularly of the youth. . . . Had the young generation of Jews that went through the Buber-Rosenzweig school of Bible reading been permitted to grow up, they would have become the most Bible-conscious Jews since the days before the ghetto walls had fallen.

—Ernest Wolf, "Martin Buber and German Jewry"

Wolf nicely captures the impact Buber had on German Jewry as a teacher and translator of Bible. But this reflects only a slight fraction of his influence. With only some exaggeration, it can be argued that liberal Judaism in the twentieth century centers around Martin Buber. His popularizing of Hasidism for Western audiences in the first decade of this century lies behind the turn to "spirituality" in recent years. His *dialogical philosophy*, expressed most eloquently in *Ich und Du* (*I and Thou*), champions individual experience and autonomy above dogma in all religions. Important contemporary liberal theologies, whether the *covenantal theology* of Eugene Borowitz, or Emil Fackenheim's "commanding voice of Auschwitz," bear the deep imprint of Buber's influence.

But Buber's influence extends beyond the realm of liberal Judaism. With the sole exception of A. J. Heschel, only Buber has exerted a distinct and acknowledged impact on the non-Jewish world. Christians and Jews have responded with equal seriousness to Buber, whose *I and Thou* remains the most widely assigned work by a Jew in college classes on contemporary religious thought. And, unlike almost all other non-Orthodox figures, including Heschel and Kaplan, only Buber has attracted the sustained attention (most of it critical and much of it implicit) of the Orthodox world. The reason is clear: Buber articulated a form of subjective religiosity clearly incompatible with *halachah* and possibly unworkable as the basis for a Jewish communal life. Yet Buber grew up in the household of a renowned Judaic scholar, drew his ideas from unimpeachably Jewish sources, and demonstrated an unshakable commitment to the Jewish people throughout his adult life. Among academics, Buber remains an unavoidable touchstone when assessing the message of Hasidism, translating and interpreting the Hebrew Bible, or evaluating the ideology of early Zionism. Even his severe critics, and there are many, need to grapple with his legacy.

Born in Vienna, Buber was three when his parents divorced. His first memory was unhappy but illuminating. Standing by the Danube River, his baby-sitter spoke about his mother, "No, she will never come back." Buber recalled, "I know that I remained silent, but also that I cherished no doubt of the truth of the spoken words." Buber would see her again only once more, after a hiatus of twenty years.[1] Buber lived briefly with his father, Carl, who soon sent the boy to live with his grandparents in Lemberg, Austria-Hungary (now Lvov, Poland). We are accustomed to dividing nineteenth-century Jewry into two models: the highly Westernized, assimilated model and the highly traditional, parochially Jewish, Czarist-Russian model. But the Jewry of the Austro-Hungarian Empire displayed both characteristics. In Lemberg, Buber was surrounded by a linguistic hodgepodge. The language of instruction in the public schools was Polish; the everyday language of the Jews was Yiddish; and his grandfather Solomon, an important scholar of Jewish lore (midrash), worked mainly in Hebrew. The decisive influence, however, came from his grandmother Adele, whose mastery of German language and literature inspired Martin Buber's amazing facility with languages. This background helps to explain Buber's ability to move from culture to culture effortlessly. This talent would prove essential in his single-handed success in bringing the generally despised hasidic culture to the attention of Westernized, assimilated Jews as a model of Jewish religiosity and as a vehicle for spiritual inspiration.

This ability to relate to the two Jewish cultures of nineteenth-century Europe also goes a long way in explaining his importance in adapting the cultural Zionism of Ahad Ha'am to German Jewry, which initially adhered to the purely political Zionism of Theodor Herzl. In 1896, the year Herzl published his important tract *Der Judenstaat*,[2] Buber returned to his hometown and enrolled in the University of Vienna. Until Herzl's death in 1904, Vienna was the center of Zionist activity and Buber found himself editing the movement's journal (*Die Welt*). He also joined a group of Eastern Europeans (the Democratic Faction) who rebelled against what they considered Herzl's narrow political conception of Zionism and his authoritarian tendencies. In a thinly veiled comparison of Herzl and Ha'am, Buber wrote: "Leading without teaching attains success: Only what one attains is at times a caricature of what, in the ground of one's soul, one wanted to attain. Unhappy certainly, is the people that has no leader, but three times as unhappy is the people whose leader has no teaching."

Herzl thought a political state was the necessary condition to alleviate Jewish suffering. Buber inclined more to the view that Zionism needed to create a people before it created a state. Through youth movements, journals, and artistic and physical training, Buber wished to reacquaint Western Jews with their culture, language, and *religion*. This activity, called "work-for-the-present-day," Herzl regarded as a waste of time. In fact, Buber was neither a "Herzlian" nor an Ahad Ha-Amist, for the latter was an agnostic, while Buber believed deeply in God, and considered religion as essential a means of binding Jews together as culture. (His granddaughter recalls: "When we grew older and Buber learned that we both [Judith and her sister, Barbara] did not believe in God, I think it was difficult for him.")[3] In 1904, the twenty-six-year-old Buber "retired" from Zionist activity: It would be the first of several occasions in which Buber oscillated between high levels of this-worldly activism and a more withdrawn scholarly existence.

Buber's publication of the *Tales of Rabbi Nachman* (1906), the first of dozens of hasidic tales rendered by Buber into German, marks an important turning point in the cultural history of Western Jewry. Previous scholarly treatments of the Jewish mystical tradition, and Hasidism in particular, were marked by unconcealed animosity. Heinrich Graetz, the most widely read Jewish historian of the nineteenth century, described Hasidism as a "hideous parasite" and a "poisonous flower." Buber, on the contrary, "made plausible the thesis that Hasidism would necessarily play a role in Jewish renaissance" (Robert Weltsch). In his moving autobiographical essay, "My Way to Hasidism," Buber explained that in Hasidism he found true community and true leadership—so absent from the alienated, industrialized, manipulative world of fin-de-siècle Europe. For all of its medieval excesses, the spirit of Hasidism called out to modern Jews, offering them a spiritual treasure far more meaningful than the tepid, bourgeois forms of religion to which they had been exposed. Rather than portraying Hasidism as a late-medieval perversion of normative Judaism, Buber lauded it: "Nowhere in the last centuries has the soul force of Judaism so manifested itself as in Hasidism. . . . Still bound to the medieval in its outward appearance, hasidic Judaism is already open to regeneration in its inner truth."[4]

These words notwithstanding, Buber did not become a Hasid. He differed with many of Hasidism's theological premises and was far too much of a European to return to an exclusively Jewish setting. As Buber himself put it, to become a Hasid "would have been an impermissible masquerading." Rather, through his Zionist activism and his immersion in hasidic literature, Buber found his way back to involvement with the Jewish world and with Judaic sources. Buber had ceased practicing traditional Judaism as a teenager and had even married a Catholic-born fellow university student and author named Paula Winkler. Intermarriage was still unusual in this period: in Austria, it was only legal after 1895. Their relationship, which Buber hid from his grandparents and which earned him the disapproval of some of his Zionist collaborators, proved to be Buber's most passionate and productive. Paula Buber subsequently converted to Judaism, wrote some moving defenses of Zionism, and accompanied her husband to Palestine. Her death in 1958 was undoubtedly his greatest personal loss since his mother's abandonment.

Buber's hasidic tales won many admiring readers, a few skeptics (including Josef Berdichevski and Nahum Glatzer), and one persistent critic: Gershom Scholem (1897–1982). Scholem, almost twenty years younger than Buber, troubled himself to learn Hebrew and eventually charged Buber with misrepresenting Hasidism, rendering it more existentialist, universalistic, and subjectivist than it actually was. To Scholem, Buber seriously underplayed the complex mystical (kabbalistic) underpinnings of Hasidism and failed to adequately indicate that Hasidism accepted valid Jewish practice only within the normative, halachic framework. Over Hasidism, these two brilliant thinkers experienced a distinct failure of communication. According to Scholem, Buber at one point threw up his hands and exclaimed, "If you are right Herr Scholem, then I have been studying Hasidism for fifty years in vain." The Buber-Scholem debate continues today, with Buber's defenders pointing to the right of a creative thinker to read texts in light of the needs of the moment, and his critics replying that Buber ought to have made it clear that he was adapting, not analyzing, Hasidism. With a measure of justice on both sides, it may be asserted that no figure deserves more credit than Buber for bringing Hasidism to the serious, respectful attention of assimilated Jews.[5]

The years before the outbreak of the First World War found a reactivated Buber preaching to Zionist youth movements in Western and Central Europe. A series of addresses given in Prague became the booklet *Three Addresses on Judaism*, whose great influence even Scholem was quick to concede. The First World War did not prove to be the cataclysmic event for Buber that it was for so many European youth, perhaps because Buber was already thirty-six years old when the war erupted. Scholem, for instance, who opposed the war on Zionist grounds, was thrown out of his parents' home. Franz Rosenzweig used his time as a German soldier on the Macedonian front to draft his theological classic, *The Star of Redemption*. Nevertheless, the immediate postwar turmoil led to failed revolutions and the brutal murder of Gustav Landauer, a close friend of the Bubers.

The years from 1916–1922 led to a new conception: the dialogical philosophy, illustrated by Buber's most famous book, *I and Thou*. In a revealing autobiographical snippet, Buber tells of a young man who solicited his guidance. Buber recalls having been listening to the young man with only partial attention and thus having missed the note of desperation in the young man's voice. This young man later committed suicide, and Buber was shaken by his sin of omission. He had failed to be a full partner in dialogue, failed to respond not only to the words but to the person who uttered them. This proved to be a pivotal encounter. "Since then I have given up the religious which is nothing but the exception, extraction, exaltation, ecstasy; or it has given me up. I possess nothing but the everyday out of which I am never taken . . . I do not know much more. If that is religion then it is just everything, simply all that is lived in its possibility of dialogue."[6]

This insight sealed Buber's renunciation of any sort of religious experience (*Erlebnis*) that led to a mystic, solipsistic retreat from the world. Meaning, for Buber, would henceforth be found in the encounter, in the reciprocal, transient moment of meeting "the other" not as wife, as boss, as obstacle, or as means, but as end, the confronted, the intimate one, the noumenal "other."[7] Buber recognized that most of the time we exist in an I-IT mode, in which we do not achieve this level of relationship. But at our most human, the I-THOU mode is achieved. Buber concludes the first of three parts of *I and Thou* as follows: "And in all the seriousness of truth, listen: without IT a human being cannot live. But whoever lives only with that [IT] is not human."[8]

Part 1 of *I and Thou* explains the dichotomy of I-IT and I-THOU. Part 2 chronicles the tyranny of I-IT in the world, leading to alienation from each other and from God. In part 3, Buber extended this I-IT and I-THOU duality of relation to the divine. Although we can never truly relate to God as an IT, since we cannot delimit God as we can a tree, humans have all too frequently related to their own poor projections and definitions of God instead of encountering God in relationship. But it is possible to relate to God in an I-THOU manner. What we receive in this encounter is critical to understanding Buber's break with tradition; or, in some people's opinion, his religious anarchism:

> Man receives and what he receives is not a content but a presence, a presence as strength. This presence and strength include three elements that are not separate but may nevertheless be contemplated as three. First, the whole abundance of actual reciprocity, of being admitted of being associated while one is altogether

unable to indicate what that is like with which one is associated nor does association make life any easier for us—it makes life heavier but heavy with meaning. And this is second: the inexpressible confirmation of meaning. It is guaranteed. Nothing, nothing can henceforth be meaningless . . . This comes third: it is
not the meaning of "another life" but that of this our life, not that of a "beyond"
but of this our world and it wants to be demonstrated by us in this life and this
world. . . . The meaning we receive can be put to the proof in action only by each
person in the uniqueness of his being and the uniqueness of his life. No prescription can lead us to the encounter, and none leads from it.[9]

Buber's reading of God's threefold presence as strength, as confirmation of
meaning, and as a model for other relationships is very radical and very far
from the traditional Jewish view of revelation. Yet for Buber, as for tradition,
revelation ultimately leads to redemption. The last sentence of *I and Thou*
pronounces: "But the God-side of the event whose world-side is called return
is called redemption" (168). However radical Buber's views, *I and Thou* has
been, for many, moving and even convincing. *I and Thou* is a difficult, elusive, sometimes maddeningly quasi-prophetic work. Every translation into
English must, in addition, overcome the lack of distinction between the German formal *Sie* and the informal *Du*. The title *Ich und Du*, which is meant to
highlight intimacy, and is translated as *I and Thou*, inspired by the Quaker use
of Thou," sounds quite formal. At times, scholars have read too much systematic theology into what seem like passages that aim at being mostly
evocative. Much has been written about *I and Thou* and some of these works
certainly deserve to be read. But we can say without hesitation that from the
early 1920s onward, the dialogical philosophy embodied in *I and Thou* would
be the prism through which Buber would view the world and which would
drive his creative intellectual works.

In 1925, Martin and Paula were happily ensconced in a Frankfurt suburb
named Heppenheim, when Buber agreed to an initiative from the Christian
publisher Lambert Schneider to undertake a translation of the Hebrew Bible.
Buber agreed on condition that Franz Rosenzweig, already living in Frankfurt
and suffering from amyotrophic lateral sclerosis (ALS), which would claim
his life in 1929, would serve as a collaborator. The fruit of this tragically brief
collaboration was a startling translation of the Five Books of Moses (Buber
ultimately completed the entire Tanach translation by himself in the early
1960s). Legend has it that Rosenzweig initially argued that they must base
their new translation on the Luther Bible, an acknowledged German classic.
Rosenzweig gave Genesis 1 a try, and concluded that Buber was right; they
needed to begin with a clean slate.

The translation method they employed has been described by Everett Fox,
whose own recent translation of the Bible owes a deep debt to the Buber-

Rosenzweig Bible.[10] Assuming that the Bible was meant to be heard aloud, not read in silence, Buber-Rosenzweig broke up the lines to approximate natural pauses of breath, stripping chapter and verse notations (not to mention commentary!) down to a minimum. Additionally, they Hebraized their German translation to capture the syntax and cadence of Hebrew, a much more concrete language than German. Luther's Bible, much like the King James in English, is an artful literary creation. But Buber and Rosenzweig wanted the reader to be constantly aware that Hebrew was the language of the original. Keeping the Hebrew names (Moshe, not Moses; Yosef, not Joseph) also served to remind the readers that the etymologies of these names were an integral part of the characters' identities. Finally, the repetitive nature of the Hebrew, usually covered up in translation, was deliberately preserved by Buber and Rosenzweig. Buber argued that the repetition of certain lead-words (*Leitworten*) served as means of highlighting a key thought, theme, or characteristic. The two men generated this unique translation, significant correspondence on how to relate to the Hebrew Bible, and a series of essays on individual passages and themes that are classics of modern Bible commentary. I have chosen to reproduce the beginning of one of these essays, Buber's "People Today and the Jewish Bible," at the end of this introduction.

Before turning to "People Today and the Jewish Bible," some words on Buber's later years are in order. Buber's most creative period coincided, in my opinion, with the application of the dialogical philosophy of *I and Thou* to the Bible and to the later versions of hasidic tales during the 1920s, during the period of cultural flowering associated with the Weimar Republic. But without doubt, Buber's most heroic period coincided with the Nazi seizure of power in 1933 and his role as a teacher, leader, and comforter of a community under assault.

Forced to relinquish his position at the University of Frankfurt (within a year the Nazis had purged their universities of all Jews), Buber worked to shore up the morale of German Jewry until his emigration to Israel in 1938. Long interested in Jewish-Christian dialogue, Buber watched helplessly as large segments of Christian Germany collapsed before the Nazi regime. In the course of the five years between the Nazi seizure of power (1933) and his own emigration (1938), Buber challenged the calumnies launched against the Jews, including those of former university colleagues such as Gerhard Kittel. Kittel, a Protestant-Nazi theologian, justified the reghettoization of Jews by invoking the image of Ahasveros, the Wandering Jew. Kittel regarded Ahasveros as a fit symbol for diaspora Jewry that ought to be reduced to the status of "resident aliens." Buber responded that Ahasveros, like so many Nazi caricatures, was an anti-Semitic, not a Jewish creation. Buber further attacked Kittel's attempt to employ biblical concepts to impose a subservient condition, without any of the responsibility attendant on hearkening to God's primal message: "Love thy neighbor as thyself" (Lev. 19:18). No fewer than thirty-six Commandments address themselves to protecting the status of the "resident alien," as Buber pointed out. The Nazis finally banned Buber from speaking in public, and he certainly ran some high personal risks in his advocacy of German Jewry. As Ernst Simon said, "Anyone who did not see Buber in these years has not seen true civic courage."

Buber spent almost thirty years in Israel (1938–1965), yet to my mind he remains a European figure. Despite his superb Judaic training, Buber needed to master contemporary, spoken Hebrew. Politically, Buber was on the far left, supporting a binational solution in which Jews and Arabs would be autonomous partners within a single state. Jews and Arabs would have their own languages, schools, and internal self-governance. While a similar arrangement succeeded, more or less, after 1867 in Austria-Hungary, both the German-speaking Austrians and the Magyar-speaking Hungarians had good reasons for making it work. In British-controlled Palestine, this was not the case; and Buber, along with Scholem and the chancellor of the Hebrew University, Judah Magnes, was politically marginalized. Although a position was created for Buber at the Hebrew University, he spent quite a bit of time lecturing abroad. I find it symbolically appropriate that one of his more interesting later works, *Two Types of Faith* (1950), analyzes the different spiritual stands of Judaism and Christianity, hardly a burning issue in the world's only majority Jewish society!

Buber was honored and awarded in the wider world more than in Israel. He lectured frequently abroad, and accepted Germany's highest award, the Goethe Prize, which naturally sparked some controversy. Even in Israel, Buber managed to attract a small but devoted following. His death in Jerusalem at age eighty-seven was marked in a manner appropriate to the world's most famous Jewish thinker.

QUESTIONS FOR BUBER, "PEOPLE TODAY AND THE JEWISH BIBLE"

Please note: Tanach, the Jewish Bible, contains fewer books, a different order of books, a different division of parts, and sometimes very different manuscript traditions from the Old Testament used by the Christian world. Although Buber was well aware of these differences, they are *not* the key to understanding what Buber means by the phrase "Jewish Bible."

Buber's title could have read "People Today and the Bible." What does the world *Jewish* add? In terms of the function of the Bible in a living community? In terms of a national possession? In terms of the role of generational responses? In terms of theology?

What are the prerequisites for an authentic approach to the Bible? Since the Bible has been the same for centuries, why does an authentic approach in the modern era pose special problems for so many of Buber's contemporaries?

What should we bring (and not bring) to the Bible as readers and as religious individuals?

Buber loves to develop a third way and does so in many essays, including this one. (See also "The Words on the Tablets," in Buber, *On the Bible*, for a further illustration.) What is the way of metaphor and myth? What is the way of supernaturalism? Why does Buber reject both of these ways as fitting for "people today"?

What is the third way that Buber proposes? How does this third way disarm the seemingly paralyzing question that Buber raises: "Do we still believe it? Can we still believe it?"

Buber criticizes Christianity's "fusing" of revelation and redemption. Do you see what Buber means by this problematic Christian reading of the Bible? Is this a Christian misreading of the Bible, or is it simply a reading of the *Christian* Bible? Can there be an ecumenical reading of the Bible, in Buber's view? In your view?

What does Buber mean by the word *decision*?

Having read my introduction and the Buber passages, can you explain what Buber meant by his dialogical philosophy? Can you distinguish this dialogical philosophy from existentialism—whether secular or religious?

Can you see any practical application of Buber's essay to your own relationship with the Bible?

STUDIES BY AND ABOUT BUBER

There are numerous works both by and about Martin Buber. The most accessible works by Buber remain the two collections *On Judaism* and *On the Bible*. Buber's essays in *Hasidism and Modern Man* and *The Origins and Meaning of Hasidism* are captivating, even when they tell us more about Buber than about Hasidism. Everett Fox and Lawrence Rosenwald have collected, translated, and commented on a series of Buber-Rosenzweig essays about the Bible in *Scripture and Translation* (Bloomington: Indiana University Press 1994), from which the following selection is drawn.

The secondary scholarship on Buber is overwhelming. Pamela Vermes and Maurice Friedman have both written lovely one-volume books on his life and works. For those primarily interested in the biographical aspects, Hayim Gordon, *The Other Martin Buber* (Athens: Ohio University Press, 1988); Paul Schilpp, ed., *The Philosophy of Martin Buber* (La Salle, Ill.: Open Court, 1967); and Nahum Glatzer and Paul Mendes-Flohr, eds., *The Letters of Martin Buber* (New York: Schocken, 1991) remain the best places to start. Graete Schaeder's *The Hebrew Humanism of Martin Buber* (Detroit, Mich.: Wayne State University Press, 1973) and Rivka Horwitz's *Buber's Way to I and Thou* (Philadelphia: Jewish Publication Society, 1988) are challenging but worthwhile.

From "People Today and the Jewish Bible"[11]

Martin Buber

"The Bible," i.e., *biblia*, i.e., "books": such is the name of a book that is a book of books.[12] But it is in reality One Book. All its stories and songs, all its sayings and prophecies are united by one fundamental theme: the encounter of a group of people with the Nameless Being whom they, hearing his speech and speaking to him in turn, ventured to name; their encounter with him in history, in the course of earthly events. The stories are either explicitly or implicitly accounts of encounters. The songs are laments over exclusion from the grace of encounter, pleas for the return of it, thanksgivings for the gift of it. The prophecies exhort those who have gone astray to return to the place of encounter, and promise the restoration of the bond torn asunder. When we hear cries of doubt in this book, we hear the doubt fated for those who experience distance after closeness, and who learn from distance what it alone can teach. When love songs are found here, we must understand that to see God's love for his world as revealed in the profundities of human love is not a late reinterpretation of the biblical text, but an insight originating with the first development of "biblical" consciousness.

This book has since its beginning encountered one generation after another. Confrontation and reconciliation with it have taken place in every generation. Sometimes it is met with obedience and offered dominion; sometimes with offense and rebellion. But each generation engages it vitally, and faces it in the realm of reality. Even where people have said "no" to it, that "no" has only validated the book's claim upon them—they have borne witness to it even in refusing themselves to it.

It is otherwise with people today. By "people today" I mean "intellectuals," people to whom it seems important that there be intellectual goods and values; people who admit, or even themselves declare, that the reality of these goods and values is bound up with their realization through us; but people also who when probed in inmost truth, where people are ordinarily not probed at all, must then admit that this feeling that *Geist*[13] has obligations is itself for them only an intellectual matter. The intellect's freedom from real obligation is the signature of our time. We proclaim the rights of intellect, we formulate its laws; yet these rights and laws enter not into life but only into books and conversations. They hover in the air above our heads, and do not walk among us on the earth; everything, it seems, is *Geist* except the actual lives we lead. Here we meet with a false idealism, erecting above our life a blue firmament, in the unconstrainingly edifying contemplation of which one recovers from the aridity of earth; there a false realism, which understands *Geist* only as a function of life and dissolves its absolute unconditionality into mere psychological or sociological conditions. In either case a false relation between *Geist* and life is put in place of a real connection between them: in place of a marriage.

People today have, to be sure, noted the disintegrative effects of such a separation of inter-related things—noted, that is, a disintegration that must touch deeper and deeper layers, until the entirely disempowered *Geist* is reduced to the willing and complacent servant of any powers that be. These people have, moreover, had thoughts on how this decline is to be rectified; and they have appealed to religion as the only authority now capable of introducing a new covenant between *Geist* and world. But what is today called "religion" is not capable of that. "Religion" today is itself a thing of unattached *Geist*—one of its departments, a clearly privileged department of the superstructure of life, an especially impressive chamber among the upper rooms. It is not a life-encompassing whole, and cannot on the basis of its present status become one; it cannot lead us to unity, because it has itself fallen into disunity, has accommodated itself to this dichotomy of our existence. Religion would itself have to return to reality before it could have a real effect on people today. But religion has always been reality only when it has been fearless—when it has taken upon itself the whole concreteness of reality, has signed nothing away as belonging by right to some other agent, has embodied *Geist* and at the same time consecrated the quotidian.

The chief document of this reality, however, is Scripture, the so-called Old Testament. This is distinguished from the great books of the other religions of the world by two linked traits. One is that in it, event and word take place entirely within the people, within history, within the world. Nothing happens in the isolated space between God and the individual man; rather the word goes by way of the man to the people, which then must hear and realize it. Events are not raised above the history of the people; rather they are precisely the secret of the people's history made manifest. But the people is in consequence positioned against any national centeredness, against any cult of the group, against the "breath of universal history." Rather it must establish the community of God's own as a model for the numerous and diverse peoples of the earth; the historical continuity in "seed" and "land" is bound to the "blessing" (Gen. 12:7ff.), and the blessing is bound to the charge. Holiness enters into history without disenfranchising it.

The other trait of this book is that in it a law speaks that concerns the natural life of human beings. Eating meat and sacrificing animals are linked; marital purity is consecrated monthly in the sanctuary; people in their drives and passions are accepted as they are and included in holiness, lest their drives and passions become obsessions. The desire to possess land is not prohibited, and renunciation of it is not commanded; but the owner of the land is God, and man is merely "a sojourner and settler" with him. God the owner introduces the rhythm of property compensation, so that the growing inequity will not shatter the community existing among its fellows. Holiness enters into nature without raping it.

The living spirit seeks both to spiritualize and to animate; to have *Geist* and life find one another, to have *Geist* shape itself into life and life clarify itself by *Geist*. It seeks to have creation complete itself from itself. The "Old Testament" seeks to bear witness to this striving, and to the command to serve *Geist* in its bond with life. If we take the book as "religious writing," belonging to some department of *Geist* in isolation, then it fails; and we must deny ourselves to it.[14] If we take it as the impression of a life-encompassing reality, then we grasp it; and it grasps us. People today, however, are hardly capable of this. When they still "take an interest" in Scripture at all, it is precisely a "religious" interest—and for the most part the interest is not even that, but is rather "historical" or "cultural" or "aesthetic," or whatever. In any case the interest is that of the detached *Geist*, distributed into independent subjects. People do not in the manner of earlier generations stand before the biblical word in order to hear it or to take offense at it; they do not any longer confront their lives with the word. Rather they store the word in one of the numerous secular warehouses, and rest contented. They thus cripple the power that of all existing powers would most likely suffice to deliver them.[15]

Before, however, I describe more clearly the guiding power of Scripture for people today, and demonstrate that power by means of a few examples, I must deal with the fundamental question that the reflective reader is now posing. Suppose that this reader—suppose that we, in fact—managed to approach with our whole self the totality of this book that you are talking about; would there not, even then, be missing the one thing absolutely indispensable to such an encounter? Would we, that is, be able to *believe* the book? Would we be able to believe *it*? Can we do more than believe that such a belief as this book reports and proclaims once existed?

People today have little access to sure belief, and cannot be given such access. When they are in earnest, they know this and do not let themselves be deceived. But an openness to belief is not denied them. They too can, precisely when they are in earnest, open themselves up to this book and let themselves be struck by its rays wherever they may strike; they can, without anticipation and without reservation, yield themselves and let themselves come to the test; they can receive the text, receive it with all their strength, and await what may happen to them, wait to see whether in connection with this or that passage in the book a new openness will develop in them. For this, of course, they must take up Scripture as if they had never seen it, had never encountered it in school or afterwards in the light of "religious" or "scientific" certainties; as if they had not learned all their lives all sorts of sham concepts and sham propositions claiming to be based on it. They must place themselves anew before the renewed book, hold back nothing of themselves, let everything happen between themselves and it, whatever may happen. They do not know what speech, what image in the book will take hold of them and recast them, from what place the spirit will surge up and pass into them, so as to embody itself anew in their lives; but they are open. They believe nothing *a priori*; they disbelieve nothing *a priori*. They read aloud what is there, they hear the word they speak, and it comes to them; nothing has yet been judged, the river of time flows on, and the contemporaneity of these people becomes itself a receiving vessel.

If, however, we wish to understand rightly what is at issue here, we have to visualize clearly the abyss that lies between Scripture and people today.

The claim with which Scripture has approached and still approaches every generation is the claim to be acknowledged as a document of the true history of the world—of the history, that is, in which the world has an origin and a goal. Scripture demands of the human being to embed his or her own life in this true history, so that I may find my origin in the origin of the world and my goal in the world's goal. At the midpoint between origin and goal, however, Scripture puts not something that happened once and in the past; rather it sets there, as a moving, circling, indeterminate center, the moment in which I, the reader, the hearer, the human person, perceive through Scripture the voice that speaks from the origin toward the goal—this moment, my moment, mortal and eternal at once. Creation is the origin, redemption is the goal; but revelation is not a datable, determinate point poised between them. The center is not the revelation at Sinai but the continual possibility of receiving it. *That* is why a psalm or a prophecy is no less "Torah," teaching, than is the story of the exodus from Egypt. The history of the people—accepting and refusing together—points to the history of humanity; but the secret conversation heard in psalm and prophecy points to my own secret.

Scripture as a document in the history of a world hovering between creation and redemption, of a world that in its history encounters revelation— a revelation that encounters me *if I am there*:[16] with this notion in mind we can understand the resistance of people today as a resistance of their innermost being.

People today stand in two relations to history. In the relation *ad libitum*, they accept (and join with) history in the backwards and forwards movement of events, in the rise and fall of struggles for power; history is a muddle, an indiscriminate sequence of processes: the deeds of peoples, the death of peoples, seizings and losings, triumph and misery—a bustle in itself meaningless, to which a sham meaning, unfounded and unstable, can be attributed only by persons themselves. In the dogmatic relation, people determine laws from sequences of events and predict sequences to come, as if the great lines of things were written on a scroll that was just now being unrolled, as if history were not time, time constantly becoming, time constantly and vitally being determined, time into which my time and my decision stream in all force, but a rigid, already present, inescapable space. Both relations are misunderstandings of destiny. Destiny is neither accident nor fate; it is nothing that happens and nothing that is there before. In biblical perspective, destiny is the secret reciprocity of the lived moment, the coinciding of over here and over there, the resolution of all time in this particular time. Where there is knowledge of origin and goal, there is no chaos; we are sustained by a meaning that we cannot ourselves devise. We do not, however, receive this meaning to formulate it but to live it; and it is lived in the fearful and magnificent full decisiveness of the moment—of the historical moment, which in its actualities is everywhere a moment of biography, yours and mine no less than Alexander's or Caesar's, but not your moment of yourself but of your encounter. People today know of no beginning— history eddies toward their feet from the whole of cosmically unchronicled time; they know of no ending—history foams past them into cosmically unchronicled time. And what lies between has become so violent and trivial an interval! People no longer know of origins or goals because they no longer wish to know of the midpoint—the midpoint to which they must give themselves in order to perceive it. Only as seen from the presentness of revelation are creation and redemption true. People today resist Scripture because they cannot abide revelation. To abide revelation means to sustain the full decisiveness of the moment, to respond to the moment, to be responsible for it. People today resist Scripture because they are no longer responsive or responsible. They claim to venture much; but the one true venture, the venture of responsibility, they industriously avoid.

NOTES

1. Martin Buber, "Autobiographical Fragments," in *The Philosophy of Martin Buber*, ed. Paul Schilpp (La Salle, Ill.: Open Court Press, 1967), 2–3.

2. The title of Herzl's *Der Judenstaat* may be translated into English in two ways: "The Jews' State" or "The Jewish State." Although the latter has been more frequently used, the former better represents Herzl's tract, for there is nothing culturally, spiritually, or intellectually Jewish about Herzl's vision.

3. Judith Agassi-Buber, in *The Other Martin Buber*, ed. Haim Gordon (Athens: Ohio University Press, 1988), 7.

4. Martin Buber, "My Way to Hasidism," in *Hasidism and Modern Man*, ed. Maurice Friedman (New York: Harper Torchbooks, 1958), 48.

5. Jon D. Levenson, "The Hermeneutical Defense of Buber's Hasidism: A Critique and Counterstatement," *Modern Judaism* 11 (1991).

6. Buber, "Autobiographical Fragments," 27–28.

7. I hope that most of these terms are clear. By *noumenal* I mean the "self" itself, not as simply the sum of the descriptions of that self or other. The humanistic presumption that the whole is greater than the sum of its parts, beginning with Kant, leads to the distinction between noumenal and phenomenal.

8. Martin Buber, *I and Thou*, trans. Ronald Gregor Smith (New York: Charles Scribner's Sons, 1970), 85.

9. Buber, *I and Thou*, 159.

10. Everett Fox, *The Five Books of Moses* (New York: Schocken, 1996).

11. *Der Mensch von heute* is rendered as "People Today" rather than, with Olga Marx in her translation of the first part of this essay (in *Israel and the World* [New York: Schocken, 1963]), "The Man of Today," because the German *Mensch* refers equally to men and women, and English "man" does not. We have not in this translation wanted to obscure sexist terminology in the original, but equally we have not wanted to add to it.—This note from editors, Everett Fox and Laurence Rosenwald, *Scripture and Translation*. (Bloomington: Indiana University Press, 1994).

12. The Greek *biblia*, from which English "bible" and German *Bibel* both come, means "books."—This note from Eds. Fox and Rosenwald, *Scripture and Translation*.

13. German *Geist* means both "intellect" and "spirit." It has two adjectives attached to it, one of which means "intellectual" (as in the first sentence of the present paragraph) and the other of which means "spiritual" (or even sometimes "clerical"). Buber's use of these terms is sometimes crucial to his argument; accordingly, the translation sometimes retains the German terms, and sometimes footnotes passages where his manipulation of the complex of terms is especially intricate. In general, all words referring to "spirit," "intellect," and "mind" in this essay are translations of the complex of terms centered around *Geist*.—This note from Eds. Fox and Rosenwald, *Scripture and Translation*.

14. "Fails" and "deny" render various uses of the same German word, *versagen*.—This note from Eds. Fox and Rosenwald, *Scripture and Translation*.

15. This was said nine years ago. Today, Scripture is once again something that people take offense at; and that seems to me a first step toward taking it seriously.

16. Buber may be alluding to the divine name, which he understands as meaning "I will be there"; see below, "The Eternal."—This note from Eds. Fox and Rosenwald, *Scripture and Translation*.

Chapter Six

Franz Rosenzweig

From Alienated Existentialist to Ba'al Teshuvah

ROSENZWEIG'S LIFE AND TIMES (1886–1929)

Franz Rosenzweig: we can only think of him with love and stand before his memory in awe—the great Jewish soul who found home to brighten the sky over German Jewry as the lights were about to go out. And yet, intellectually he was unable to liberate himself from the net of an arrogant civilization that claimed to be the world.

With these words, Eliezer Berkovits, a maverick in the world of contemporary Orthodox thought, a rabbi whose life was uprooted and whose synagogue was destroyed during Kristallnacht, concluded his critique of Rosenzweig.[1] Subsequent thinkers have frequently responded to Rosenzweig with this mixture of veneration and rejection. Franz Rosenzweig was a promising historian and a wide-ranging philosopher. Most of all, Rosenzweig was a model *ba'al teshuvah*,[2] an assimilated Jew who reclaimed his heritage through extraordinary and heroic efforts.

Born Christmas Day 1886 to Georg and Adele Rosenzweig, Franz grew up in Kassel, a child of typical German-Jewish parents: solid middle-class citizens who readily combined German patriotism with communal loyalty to Jews and low levels of religious observance. Like so many Western Jews who grew up in comfortable circumstances, Rosenzweig found the previous generation's synthesis of Jewishness and modernism unsatisfactory. In his teens and early twenties, Rosenzweig watched several of his relatives convert to Christianity. Given the pragmatic benefits of being a Christian in an anti-Semitic society, the poor repute of Judaism in late-nineteenth-century European intellectual circles, and the attraction of full participation in a European culture, the apostasy of several thousand Jews comes as no surprise.

In a letter to his mother, with whom Franz shared a close relationship, he defended the baptism of his cousin in 1909 as follows:

> About Hans we simply don't see eye to eye. What you say about the three visits to a Jewish theologian won't hold water. Not even three hundred visits would have changed matters. We are Christian in everything. We live in a Christian state, attend Christian schools, read Christian books, in short, our whole "culture" rests entirely on a Christian foundation; consequently a man who has nothing holding him back needs only a very slight push . . . to make him accept Christianity. In Germany today the Jewish religion cannot be "accepted," it has to be grafted on by circumcision, dietary observances and Bar Mitzvah. Christianity has a tremendous advantage over Judaism: it would have been entirely out of the question for Hans to become a Jew; a Christian, however, he can become.[3]

Despite Rosenzweig's sense of Christianity's superiority, he tarried four years before determining to take the same step as Hans Ehrenberg. After Rosh Hashanah 1913, Franz confided to his mother his plans to have himself baptized. Adele's strong reaction must have shocked him. She told Franz that their synagogue had no room for apostates and that she would have him turned away on Yom Kippur. Franz's response was to board the train for Berlin, where he attended Rabbi Marcus Petuchowski's Orthodox services on Potsdammerbruecke Street. That day, Rosenzweig became a believing Jew, and for the remainder of his tragically brief life he pursued Jewish learning with a fanatical devotion that astounded everyone who had contact with him. During the years between Rosenzweig's 1913 Yom Kippur "conversion" and the outbreak of the First World War, Franz abandoned an incredibly impressive early career as an academic historian. (While still a graduate student, he discovered a manuscript enabling him to prove that Schelling, not Hegel, was the first formulator of German idealism. This would be akin to discovering that John Adams, not Thomas Jefferson, had drafted the Declaration of Independence.) He also studied with the aged but vibrant Hermann Cohen, one of Germany's most prominent philosophers, a longtime spokesman for German Jewry, and something of a *ba'al teshuvah* himself.

When war broke out, Rosenzweig joined the German army and spent 1916–1918 on the Macedonian front. There, on German army postcards sent home one by one, Rosenzweig drafted his theological magnum opus, *Der Stern der Erloesung* (*The Star Of Redemption*). We will investigate this work together at the end of this chapter; what needs to be noted now is that this was Rosenzweig's first and last systematic book of theology. Rosenzweig decided to dedicate himself to Jewish education, not Jewish philosophy. He wrote that the task of the time was *not* the creation of more Jewish books, but the cultivation of more Jewish people. Fittingly, the closing words of *The Star* were "Into Life." Already in 1917, Rosenzweig had penned "*Zeit Ist's*" (It Is Time), a call for a new program of Jewish education. The research institution that emerged from this initiative proved a disappointment to Rosenzweig, but by 1920 he had settled in Frankfurt, had married Edith Hahn, and had been instrumental in raising the funds and in organizing his chosen vehicle for adult Jewish education, the Free Jewish Lehrhaus in Frankurt. Rosenzweig gave a typically frank and programmatic statement of the Lehrhaus's goals:

> There is no one today who is not alienated, or does not contain within himself some small fraction of alienation. All of us to whom Judaism, to whom being a Jew, has again become the pivot of our lives—and I know that in saying this here I am not speaking for myself alone—we all know that in being Jews we must not give up anything, not renounce anything, but lead everything back to Judaism. From the periphery back to the center; from the outside in.[4]

In practice, this meant that the Lehrhaus teachers were also students. Mathematicians would be instructors in Bible classes; lawyers would teach elementary Hebrew. (Rosenzweig adopted as his personal motto: "Not a day without a line of Hebrew.") Every area of Judaic learning would be considered fair game as long as there were students and teachers willing to explore it. Participants with no Jewish background and those with substantial background were equally welcome. The Lehrhaus upheld no specified level of observance as normative, because Rosenzweig recognized that the journey from periphery to center must proceed *according to where on the periphery one started*. All were engaged in a journey whose destination was a matter of trust, rather than of dogma. Rosenzweig did not want Jews to "give up" their love for German culture, art, music, hobbies, and so forth. For Rosenzweig, becoming an authentic Jew could not be purchased at the price of self-falsification. To be an authentic Jew, one must be an authentic human being.

The Frankurt Lehrhaus drew from the German adult education movement and from the traditional Jewish house of study (*beit midrash*) and achieved an impressive success: in Frankfurt, a city with a Jewish population of only twenty-seven thousand, over one thousand Jews per semester came through the doors to "learn."[5] The Frankfurt Lehrhaus also sparked similar institutions in other German cities, a story well told by Michael Brenner's book, *The Renaissance of Jewish Culture in Weimar Germany* (New Haven, Conn.: Yale University Press, 1996). Only the Nazi seizure of power in 1933 decisively ended the Lehrhaus experiment. One might add that every Jewish adult education institution, from New York's 92nd Street Y to the Cleveland College of Jewish Studies, where I teach, owes at least something to the Frankfurt original.[6]

We have already discussed the extraordinary collaboration between Buber and Rosenzweig that took place in the mid-1920s over their Bible translation (see chapter 5). This collaboration took place despite some very serious philosophical differences between the two men, best exemplified by Buber's essay "Herut: On Youth and Religion"; Rosenzweig's response to this essay, "The Builders"; and some probing letters the two men exchanged fleshing out their positions.[7] A little background to this interchange may be helpful. Like so many turn-of-the-century European thinkers, Buber and Rosenzweig rebelled against earlier philosophical systems. Rosenzweig's *The Star of Redemption*, for instance, includes a very long prologue in which he guns down a series of philosophical syntheses in favor of an individualistic-existentialist starting point for any system ("The truth must be truth *to someone*"). In this particular correspondence, the main target is Immanuel Kant (1724–1804), the great philosopher from Koenigsberg who equated all legitimate religious impulses with ethics. For Kant, any religious practice unrelated to the cultivation of ethical behavior (including, for instance, most rituals and all ceremonial laws), was nonsense. Kant exemplified Enlightenment thinking with respect to religion: he was antimystical and lacking in what we today would term "spirituality." Post-Enlightenment thinkers criticized Kant's view of religion as narrow and constricting. From a Jewish point of view, the God of the patriarchs and matriarchs was far more personally involved with us than Kant's God, defined by Kant as "the postulate of practical reason."

Buber's "Herut" argued forcefully that immersion in the "teachings" of Judaism, especially its mystical ones, developed a spiritual potential far transcending (note: transcending, not contradicting) the ethical. Moreover, Buber legitimated engagement with a particular nation as an integral part of a person's religious development. Full religious development of Jewish youth entailed the immersion in Jewish culture. Thus, Buber wrote in this essay: "Our religious literature must become the object of reverent and unbiased knowledge. Similarly, the Jewish masses and all their beliefs and customs must also become the object of reverent and unbiased understanding."

Rosenzweig praised Buber for his declaration of independence: "You have removed us from the danger of making our spiritual Judaism depend on whether or not it was possible for us to be followers of Kant." Only personal involvement in Judaism could validate (or invalidate) the meaning of a particular practice or teaching. But Buber, in Rosenzweig's view, didn't go far enough. If there was an existential imperative to immerse oneself in all dimensions of Judaism, why did Buber exclude immersion in the *halachah*? Observance of the *halachah* had undoubtedly played a large role in Jewish life. Was not immersion in the *halachah* also called for by the logic of Buber's position? Buber, Rosenzweig believed, had been far too quick to concede to Kant's view that the *halachah* ordained practices imposed from without, impersonally legislated and therefore destructive of human autonomy.

For Rosenzweig, the *halachah* was sometimes only Law (*Gesetz*), but was always capable of being transformed into a personal imperative that proceeded from within, that is, a Commandment (*Gebot*).[8] When asked if he were laying phylacteries (*tefillin*), Rosenzweig gave the oft-quoted response "Not yet." What Rosenzweig meant was: I have not yet experienced the donning of *tefillin* in such a way as I feel it Commanded me in the same way as "Thou shalt love the Lord thy God" is Commanded me, but someday, I might. Thus Rosenzweig's "The Builders" lays out a pathway back to observance without violating the integrity and authenticity of the individual *ba'al teshuvah*, what Rosenzweig calls "a hygiene of return." Rosenzweig, who grew up in a religiously lax household, and Buber, who grew up in a traditionalist household, passed each other in the opposite direction. By the end of his life, insofar as his physical disability allowed, Rosenzweig had become an observant Jew. Incapacitated by illness, Rosenzweig managed, with his wife's aid, to translate not only the Bible, but also parts of the yearly liturgy that, he held, tied the individual Jew to the community.

We now return to *Der Stern der Erloesung*, a difficult and highly original work that combines philosophy, theology, poetry, and mystical-messianic speculation. Rosenzweig begins on an existentialist tack, savaging the Western philosophical tradition culminating in Hegel[9] as fundamentally unresponsive to the individual. Rosenzweig then devotes the longest section of *The Star* to explaining the basic categories explicable by philosophy: Man, God, World, and their theological correlates: Creation, Revelation, and Redemption. Drawing these two triangles of categories superimposed, the latter on the former, makes the six-pointed Star of David. The star was no mere metaphor or marketing device, but rather a divinely encoded symbol of the All, that culminates in the messianic realization: redemption.

The vehicle for realizing redemption, Rosenzweig maintains, is the interplay between Judaism and Christianity, a completely original theological innovation on his part that blatantly responds to Rosenzweig's own youthful dilemma. For Rosenzweig, Judaism is eternal; it is the very star that blazes in the metaphysical center. Christianity, the rays of that star, goes out into the world and conquers it. Yet Christianity, represented by the "Man on the Cross," always faces the danger of being overcome by "Siegfried," the pagan root onto which Christianity's essentially Jewish mission is grafted. The "dangers" that Christianity runs in carrying out its messianic mission, "spiritualization of God, apotheosis of man, pantheification of the world," are real dangers, corresponding to the three major forms of Christianity: Eastern Orthodoxy, Protestantism, and Catholicism.[10] The "dangers" Judaism runs are less serious, as self-involved retreat cannot lead to self-falsification. Jewry can descend no further than impotence and parochialism. Rosenzweig expands these Jewish-Christian dichotomies at considerable length. Nevertheless, these two modes of revelation will meet and together usher in the messianic era. How and when that will occur is beyond human ability to discern.

Much of Rosenzweig's *Star* makes for painful reading today. Misrepresenting Islam, one of the world's largest religions, certainly points to a serious problem in Rosenzweig's picture of Judaism and Christianity as necessary and sufficient partners in the messianic drama. Rosenzweig's language about the importance of Jewish blood sounds awful after the Nazis' use of this vocabulary. His picture of Judaism as static and beyond history, coupled with his personal indifference to Zionism, seems untrue to the dynamism of recent Jewish political history in Israel and even in America. Berkovits's criticism that Rosenzweig was unable to liberate himself intellectually from the net of his particular place and time is well taken. But this is partly true of all thinkers and all works. Who today would endorse the sexism of an Aristotle or a Maimonides? The issue really is: What questions does a thinker raise that continue to challenge us? Rosenzweig ponders the (European) Jewish relationship with Christianity and argues that it is far more than a historical accident, that Judaism has a theological relationship with Christianity, and that the troubled history of Jewish-Christian relations fits into the divine plan. *The Star* presents a theological view of Jewish survival well worth considering; Rosenzweig played out the implications of placing "Israel" before "Torah" in a more serious manner than anyone had since the days of Yehuda Halevy, a medieval philosopher for whom Rosenzweig felt a great affinity.[11]

Reviewing the 1930 edition of *The Star of Redemption*, Gershom Scholem held that only when the personally inspiring image of Rosenzweig faded, could his *Star* be evaluated objectively. Over sixty years later, the man and the work remain as inseparable as the dancer and the dance; *The Star* continues to shine.

QUESTIONS FOR ROSENZWEIG,
THE STAR OF REDEMPTION, 413–17

How does Rosenzweig explain Christian anti-Semitism? What do you think of this explanation? Compared to Herzl's explanation of anti-Semitism, do you find Rosenzweig's explanation more or less persuasive? How would Rosenzweig explain anti-Semitism in a non-Christian society?

What does Rosenzweig mean by the word *verification*?

When Rosenzweig talks about the fire of the star (Judaism) and the rays of the star (Christianity) what category of language is this? Instructive metaphor, poetry, mysticism, metaphysics?

What roles do Judaism and Christianity play, respectively, in bringing on the messianic era?

Why is Judaism's relationship to Christianity so central an issue for Rosenzweig?

Theologically, does Rosenzweig explain Christianity in terms of Judaism or Judaism in terms of Christianity?

If Rosenzweig were alive today, do you think his views on the relationship between Judaism and Christianity would be substantially different? Specifically, does the Holocaust (or *Shoah*) make Rosenzweig's view of Jewish-Christian relations more or less compelling?

Quite a few Jewish thinkers (Eliezer Berkovits, for example) find Rosenzweig's position on this issue wholly objectionable. Can you critique Rosenzweig's view from a Jewish theological point of view? Why might Christians also find Rosenzweig's view problematic?

Rosenzweig is sometimes called the model *ba'al teshuvah*. (A *ba'al teshuvah* originally meant a penitent; in modern times, it is anyone who reclaims Jewish identity after profound alienation from it.) What is the ideal *ba'al teshuvah*? Must a *ba'al teshuvah* be Orthodox? On the way to becoming Orthodox?

STUDIES BY AND ABOUT ROSENZWEIG

Rosenzweig's more accessible writings have been excerpted and translated in Nahum N. Glatzer, ed., *On Jewish Learning* (New York: Schocken, 1955) and Nahum N. Glatzer, ed., *Franz Rosenzweig: His Life and His Thought* (New York: Schocken, 1953). The latter also contains a biographical sketch. Regrettably, most scholarship on Rosenzweig is highly academic. Paul Mendes-Flohr has edited a series of essays, *The Philosophy of Franz Rosenzweig* (Hanover, N.H.: University Press of New England, 1988), but Mendes-Flohr's articles on Rosenzweig in *Divided Passions* (Detroit, Mich.: Wayne State University Press, 1991) strike me as more readable for a general audience. Despite its title, Norbert Samuelson's *A User's Guide to Franz Rosenzweig's Star of Redemption* (Surrey, UK: Curzon Press, 1999) seems to me less accessible than Stephane Moses's *System and Revelation: The Philosophy of Franz Rosenzweig* (Detroit, Mich.: Wayne State University Press,

1992). Rosenzweig has enjoyed a recent renaissance, especially as a philosopher of language. Alan Udoff and Barbara Galli, trans. and eds., *Franz Rosenzweig's "The New Thinking,"* (Syracuse, N.Y.: Syracuse University Press, 1999); Barbara Galli, trans. and ed., *Cultural Writings of Franz Rosenzweig* (Syracuse, N.Y.: Syracuse University Press, 2000); and Rosenzweig's *Understanding the Sick and the Healthy: A View of World, Man, and God*, ed. Nahum Norbert Glatzer (Cambridge, Mass.: Harvard University Press, 1999) all supplement Glatzer's collections and William Hallo's translation of *The Star of Redemption*, 2nd. ed. (New York: Holt, Rinehart and Winston, 1971).

From *The Star of Redemption*

Franz Rosenzweig

THE LAW OF VERIFICATION: TELEOLOGY

The Meaning of Bifurcation

And withal: the Jew does it. Not with words, for what would words still avail in this realm of vision! But with his existence, his silent existence. This existence of the Jew constantly subjects Christianity to the idea that it is not attaining the goal, the truth, that it ever remains—on the way. That is the profoundest reason for the Christian hatred of the Jew, which is heir to the pagan hatred of the Jew. In the final analysis it is only self-hate, directed to the objectionable mute admonisher, for all that he but admonishes by his existence; it is hatred of one's own imperfection, one's own not-yet. By his inner unity, by the fact that in the narrowest confines of his Jewishness the Star of Redemption nonetheless still burns, the Jew involuntarily shames the Christian, who is driven outwards and onwards, to the utter dissipation of the original fire, into the outermost reaches of emotion, an emotion which no longer knows of a whole in which it might find itself at one with every other emotion to a truth beyond all feeling, but rather an emotion which itself was already blissful. The uttermost in Christianity is this complete losing oneself in the individual emotion, this immersion, be it in the divine spirit, the divine man, the divine world. No current of action any longer runs between these emotions; they themselves already stand beyond all action. True, that attenuation of emotion is essential, just as its constriction is in Judaism. But whereas the latter finds its resolution in Jewish life itself, in the world-redemptive meaning of a life-in-the-law, the former, the attenuation, no longer finds its resolution in any life, since it itself is already an uttermost experience.

The Eternal Protest of the Jew

If, therefore, the Christian did not have the Jew at his back he would lose his way wherever he was, just as the three Churches, which, after all, are none other than the earthly domiciles of those ultimate three emotions, experience their affinity on the Jew; without him they might at most know it but not feel it. The Jew forces on Christianity the knowledge that that emotional satisfaction remains denied to it. The Jew sanctified his flesh and blood under the yoke of the law, and thereby lives constantly in the reality of the heavenly kingdom; the Christian's constantly profane flesh and blood sets itself in opposition to redemption, and he learns that he himself is not permitted to anticipate redemption emotionally. By anticipating redemption, the Jew purchases the possession of truth with the loss of the unredeemed world; he gives the lie to the Christian who, on his march of conquest into the unredeemed world, has to purchase his every forward step with illusion.

The Two Testaments

Christianity is well aware of this relationship, of the dependence of its own development on the existence—and no more than the existence—of Judaism. It was always the hidden enemies of Christianity, from the Gnostics to the present day, who wanted to deprive it of its "Old Testament." A God who was only spirit, and no longer the Creator who gave his law to the Jews, a Christ who was only Christ and no longer Jesus, a world which was only All and its center no longer the Holy Land—though it would no longer offer the slightest resistance to deification and divinization, there would be nothing left in them to recall the soul from the dream of this deification into unredeemed life; the soul would not just get lost, it would remain lost. And the mere Book would not render this service to Christianity, or rather: it renders this service only because it is not mere book, because our life is living testimony that it is more than a mere book. The historical Jesus must always pull out from under the feet of the ideal Christ the pedestal on which his philosophic or nationalistic worshipers would like to set him. For an "idea" can after all be united with any theory or self-conceit to lend it its own halo. But the historical Jesus, that is precisely Jesus Christ in the dogmatic sense, does not stand on a pedestal; he really walks the streets of life and forces life to submit at his glance. It is exactly the same with the "spiritual" God in whom all those believe gladly and easily who hesitate to believe in Him, "who created the world that he might reign over it." In his spirituality, that spiritual God is a very agreeable partner who leaves us entirely free to dispose of a world which is

98 Chapter Six

not "purely spiritual" and thus not his but consequently presumably the devil's. And this world itself—how gladly one would like to regard it as All, and oneself as the gloriously irresponsible "speck of dust in the All," rather than as its responsible center about which everything rotates or as the pillar on whose stability the world rests.

The Eternal Hatred for the Jew

It is always the same. And as that ever-present struggle of the Gnostics shows, it is the Old Testament which enables Christianity to withstand this its own danger, and the Old Testament only because it is more than mere book. A mere book would easily fall victim to the arts of allegorical exegesis. Had the Jews of the Old Testament disappeared from the earth like Christ, they would [now] denote the idea of the People, and Zion the idea of the Center of the World, just as Christ denotes the idea of Man. But the stalwart, undeniable vitality of the Jewish people, attested in the very hatred of the Jews, resists such "idealizing." Whether Christ is more than an idea—no Christian can know it. But that Israel is more than an idea, that he knows, that he sees. For we live. We are eternal, not as an idea may be eternal: if we are eternal, it is in full reality. For the Christian we are thus the really indubitable. The pastor who was asked for the proof of Christianity by Frederick the Great argued conclusively when he answered: "Your majesty, the Jews!" The Christians can have no doubts about us. Our existence stands surety for their truth. That is why, from the Christian point of view, it follows logically that Paul should let the Jews remain to the end—till "the fullness of the peoples shall have come in,"[12] that is, to that moment when the Son shall return the dominion to the Father. The theologism from the beginnings of Christian theology enunciates what we have here explained: that Judaism, by its eternal endurance through all time, the Judaism attested in the "Old" Testament and itself attesting livingly to it, that this is the One Nucleus whose glow provides invisible nourishment to the rays which, in Christianity, burst visibly and divisibly into the night of the pagan proto- and hypocosmos.

The Meaning of Verification

Before God, then, Jew and Christian both labor at the same task. He cannot dispense with either. He has set enmity between the two for all time, and withal has most intimately bound each to each. To us [Jews] he gave eternal life by kindling the fire of the Star of his truth in our hearts. Them [the Christians] he set on the eternal way by causing them to pursue the rays of that Star of his truth for all time unto the eternal end. We [Jews] thus espy in our hearts the true image of the truth, yet on the other hand we turn our backs on temporal life, and the life of the times turns away from us. They [the Christians], for their part, run after the current of time, but the truth remains at their back; though led by it, since they follow its rays, they do not see it with their eyes. The truth, the whole truth, thus belongs neither to them nor to us. For we too, though we bear it within us, must for that very reason first immerse our glance into our own interior if we would see it, and there, while we see the Star, we do not see—the rays. And the whole truth would demand not only seeing its light but also what was illuminated by it. They [the Christians], however, are in any event already destined for all time to see what is illuminated, and not the light.

And thus we both have but a part of the whole truth. But we know that it is in the nature of truth to be imparted, and that a truth in which no one had a part would be no truth. The "whole" truth, too, is truth only because it is God's part. Thus it does not detract from the truth, nor from us, that it is only partially ours. A direct view of the whole truth is granted only to him who sees it in God. That, however, is a view beyond life. A living view of the truth, a view that is at the same time life, can become ours too only from the immersion into our own Jewish heart and even there only in image and likeness. As for the Christians, they are denied a living view altogether for the sake of a living effectiveness of the truth. Thus both of us, they as much as we, we as much as they, are creatures precisely for the reason that we do not see the whole truth. Just for this we remain within the boundaries of mortality. Just for this we—remain. And remain we would. We want to live. God does for us what we want for so long as we want it. As long as we cling to life, he gives us life. Of the truth he gives us only what we, as living creatures, can bear, that is our portion. Were he to give us more, to give us his portion, the whole truth, he would be hoisting us beyond the boundaries of humanity. But precisely as long as he does not do this, just so long too we harbor no desire for it. We cling to our creatureliness. We do not gladly relinquish it. And our creatureliness is determined by the fact that we only take part, only are part. Life had celebrated the ultimate triumph over death in the Truly with which it verifies the personally vouchsafed truth imparted to it as its portion in eternal truth. With this Truly, the creature fastens itself to its portion which was imparted to it. In this Truly, it is creature. This Truly passes as a mute mystery through the whole chain of beings; it acquires speech in man. And in the Star it flares up into visible, self-illuminating existence. But it remains ever within the boundaries of creatureliness. Truth itself still says Truly when it steps before God. But God himself no longer says Truly. He is beyond all that can be imparted, he is above even the whole, for this too is but a part with him; even above the Whole, he is the One.

The Truth of Eternity

Thus the Truly, and even the highest Truly, the Yea and Amen jointly recited, by those redeemed for eternal life and on the eternal way, in a chorus in sight of the Star of Redemption, is still the sign of creatureliness, and the realm of nature has not yet ended, not even in the eternity-become-structure of the redeemed hypercosmos; but then the end submerges back into the beginning. That God created, this premonitory first word of Scripture does not lose its power till all be fulfilled. Till then, God will not recall back into his lap this first word to emanate from him. We had already seen the eternal truth sinking back into the revelation of divine love: redemption was altogether none other than the eternal working out of the beginning ever newly posited in revealing love. In love, the concealed had become manifest. Now this ever-renewed beginning sinks back into the secret, ever-enduring beginning of creation. The manifest becomes the concealed. And with revelation, redemption too now merges back into creation. The ultimate truth is itself only—created truth. God is truly the Lord. As such he revealed himself in the power of his creativity. If we call on him thus in the light of eternal truth—it is the Creator from the beginning, it is He who first called "Let there be light" whom we call upon thus. The midnight which, behind the existence of creation, always glitters for our blinded eyes in eternal stellar clarity—it is the same as that which spent the night in God's bosom prior to all existence. He is in truth "the first and the last." "Before the mountains were born and the earth was delivered—from eternity to eternity thou wast God." And thou wast from eternity what thou shalt be unto eternity: Truth.

NOTES

1. Eliezer Berkovits, *Major Themes in Modern Philosophies of Judaism* (New York: Ktav, 1974), 67.

2. A *ba'al teshuvah* ("master of return" or "he/she who returns") originally meant a sinning Jew who repented. In modern times, it more often means an alienated Jew who returns to observant Jewish life.

3. Nahum Norbert Glatzer, *Franz Rosenzweig: His Life and His Thought* (New York: Schocken, 1953), 19.

4. Glatzer, *Franz Rosenzweig*, 231.

5. Rosenzweig began his address "On the Opening of the Jewish Lehrhaus" (cited above) by discussing the Yiddish connotation of the verb *lernen*. The German verb means simply "to learn," but in Yiddish, it connoted the study of the Torah, a sacred, intimate, and existential activity.

6. The Orthodox adult-education "kollel" system owes something to the Lehrhaus, but much more to Eastern European models pioneered by the musar movement.

7. Martin Buber, "Herut: On Youth and Religion," in *On Judaism*, ed. Nahum N. Glatzer (New York: Schocken, 1967), 149–74; Franz Rosenzweig, "The Builders," in *On Jewish Learning*, ed. Nahum N. Glatzer (New York: Schocken, 1955), 72–92.

8. This distinction between Law (*Gesetz*) and Commandment (*Gebot*) drew directly from Kant and heavily influenced both Buber and Rosenzweig. It may well represent a distinction that is not nearly so sharp from a Judaic perspective.

9. Georg Friedrich Wilhelm Hegel (1770–1831), a prominent German philosopher, influenced Rosenzweig deeply. Rosenzweig ultimately rejected Hegel's "historicism," lampooning that complacent view of history as ignoring the manifold episodes of "murder and manslaughter."

10. Norbert Samuelson, *An Introduction to Modern Jewish Philosophy* (Albany: State University of New York Press, 1989), 212–66.

11. Rosenzweig once whimsically described himself as Yehuda Halevy's "pint-sized reincarnation."

12. Romans 11:25.

Chapter Seven

Theodor Herzl

A Jewish Modernist from Western Europe

HERZL'S LIFE AND TIMES (1860–1904)

For some time past I have been occupied with a work of infinite grandeur.
. . . At the moment I do not know whether I shall carry it through. It looks
like a mighty dream. But for days and weeks it has possessed me.

—Theodor Herzl

I was in my second year in Berlin when, in 1896, Theodor Herzl published
his tract, now a classic of Zionism, *Der Judenstaat*. It was an utterance
which came like a bolt from the blue. We had never heard the name Herzl
before; or perhaps it had come to our attention only to be lost among those
of other journalists. . . . Fundamentally, *Der Judenstaat* contained not a
single new idea for us; that which so startled the Jewish bourgeoisie, and
called down the resentment of the Western Rabbis, had long been the substance of our Zionist tradition. . . . Yet the effect produced by *Der Judenstaat* was profound. Not the ideas, but the personality which stood behind
them appealed to us.

—Chaim Weizmann

On my bookshelf, there is a handsome volume, published on the 100th anniversary of Herzl's birth. The book is a richly illustrated edition of his 1902
novel *Altneuland* (*Oldnewland*), in which Herzl tried to imagine the emerging
society in Palestine. At first, this novel did not win many accolades. Most
Western Jews considered it foolish and dangerous utopianism. Many Zionists
considered *Altneuland* symptomatic of the Judaic shallowness at the core of
Herzl's Zionism. The initial reception of *Altneuland* makes the volume on my
bookshelf all the more perplexing, because the illustrations (Haifa's factories,

pictures of sporting events, the Hebrew University, lots of healthy-looking Israeli youth) point to the fact that Herzl's imaginings—more or less—came true.

Whatever opposition Herzl faced from within the Zionist ranks when he was alive, his premature death at forty-three clinched his role as the movement's icon. As the historian David Vital once noted, early Zionism had only one hero. The picture of that hero—the only one that hangs over the Israeli Knesset—is Theodor Herzl's. Like that of many heroes, Herzl's public image, cultivated even in his own lifetime, served a variety of interests and does not always accord with historical reality. In Herzl's case, the reality only makes the hero more intriguing and more enigmatic.

Theodor (Dori, for short) was born in Budapest, the child of comfortable, very nonobservant Jews who nevertheless, like most Central European Jewry, lived in a Jewish neighborhood, had mainly Jewish friends, and, so far as I can tell, entirely Jewish relatives. Herzl is often regarded as a quintessential denizen of Vienna, where he spent most of his adult life and wrote for the prestigious, liberal, highbrow newspaper the *Neue Freie Presse*.[1] Herzl's ability to galvanize the Jewish masses into a nationalistic program has been likened, controversially, with other Viennese politicians, including a couple of anti-Semites. German nationalism, as well as anti-Semitism, flourished in Vienna and fired youthful imaginations. Germany's success at nation building made a great impression on Herzl, who wished that he had been born a Prussian nobleman (*Junker*). He wrote Otto von Bismarck near the beginning of his Zionist period, attempting to interest the Iron Chancellor in his plans (Herzl received no reply). Herzl is also associated with Paris, where, as a *Neue Freie Presse* reporter, he covered the Dreyfus Affair, a cause célèbre in France from 1894 to 1906.[2] Herzl spoke excellent French, in addition to German and Magyar (Hungarian), and admired France as the land of political progressivism.

Nevertheless, the impact of his Hungarian background should not be underestimated. Herzl spent his first eighteen years in Budapest, receiving his education in that city's public schools. He witnessed firsthand the Magyars' struggle for national self-determination; in 1867, Hungary won special status within the Hapsburg Empire. Herzl may well have been aware of Gyozo Istoczy, one of the first anti-Semitic demagogues to succeed in parliamentary politics. Even if Andrew Handler cannot document his claim that Herzl got his first Zionist "impulse" from Istoczy's demand that Jews be exiled to their original homeland (many anti-Semites, after all, wanted to exile the Jews), Herzl was deeply preoccupied by anti-Semitism from an early age.[3]

Still, anti-Semitism probably represented nothing more than a dark undercurrent in Herzl's youth. It is a common misconception among American Jews that European Jews in the nineteenth century were constantly barraged by anti-Semitism. While this may have been somewhat true in Czarist Russia, Western and Central European Jews were generally able to go about their lives unmolested. Even in Germany and Austria-Hungary, where anti-Semitic sentiment ran high, the governments of the kaiser and the emperor kept anti-Semites in line. Most Jews, not surprisingly, chose neighborhoods, friends, and careers where contact with Jew-haters could be kept to a minimum. One could choose to confront anti-Semitism politically: throughout Europe, Jews formed and joined anti-anti-Semitic organizations. One could also (consciously and unconsciously) absorb many anti-Jewish prejudices from the general environment. Herzl himself said some things about the Jews that certainly qualify as Jewish self-hatred. Most Jews, however, compartmentalized anti-Semitism as an unpleasant but bearable fact about the world in which they lived and on the whole, thrived.

I stress this because even though it is a myth that Herzl never gave Jewishness a thought before the Dreyfus Affair, neither did he grow up consciously agonizing over the future of world Jewry. Like so many boys of his age who grew up in comfortable circumstances, he was fascinated by achievements in science and technology, and interested in military matters and school productions. Interestingly, for a well-to-do Jewish boy, Herzl spent time in both the purely academic high school (*Gymnasium*) and the more technically oriented *Realschule*. A mediocre student, Herzl was fortunate to pass his final exams, a necessity for entering the university.

The tragic death of Herzl's sister, Pauline, and the family's move to Vienna coincided with Herzl's entry into that city's prestigious university. Herzl studied law and belonged to a university fraternity (Albia). He later resigned from Albia, protesting its decision to admit no more Jewish members. German-speaking universities were hotbeds of anti-Semitism at the end of the nineteenth century. One debate, ridiculous in our eyes, was over whether "Aryans" ought to do "Semites" the honor of dueling with them. (Having been a bad undergraduate saber-fencer myself, I can only rue that my opponents were always eager to give me "satisfaction.") Fin-de-siècle Aryans were less accommodating, and many Jewish youths had to do without the cheek-slashed scars that signified honor. Honor (*Ehre*) preoccupied Herzl greatly. He was an immaculate dresser, carefully coiffed, proud of his wit, and highly conscious of his role as a German man of culture. It irked Herzl that Jews were regarded, on the whole, as a people conspicuously lacking in both culture and honor.

At twenty-nine, Herzl married Julie Naschauer, a beautiful, rich young woman also of Hungarian descent. The couple had three children but were often unhappy together, especially after Herzl turned to Zionism. Professionally, Herzl had quickly abandoned law for journalism and the theater. He was a respected cultural critic for the *Neue Freie Presse* but had failed to gain the sort of acclaim for his plays that he thought they deserved. Herzl exchanged his works and letters with another Viennese Jew—Arthur Schnitzler. Schnitzler, one of the greatest writers of the era, encouraged Herzl's efforts, but in retrospect it is clear that Herzl's genius was not literary.[4] (Later, Herzl would also correspond with an even more famous Viennese Jew—Sigmund Freud.) In any event, Herzl found himself in his early thirties vaguely successful and vaguely dissatisfied.

By the early 1890s, Herzl was becoming increasingly despondent about the chances of anti-Semitism fading away, as liberal ideology assumed it must. Herzl was a firsthand witness to discouraging events in Austria and France. The liberal party was trounced in the 1891 Austrian elections. And Karl Lueger, who would become Vienna's mayor in 1895, the first democratically elected, avowedly anti-Semitic mayor of a major European city, had already embarked on his rise to power. In France, the disastrous mismanagement of the Panama Canal project fueled a populist anti-Semitism disseminated by journalists such as Alphonse Toussenel and Edouard Drumont. Jews and well-meaning Christians took countermeasures. Viennese liberals established an Austrian branch of a Society to Combat Anti-Semitism, founded in Berlin a few years earlier. Herzl, writing to Bertha von Suttner, a pioneer in the peace movement and a subsequent supporter of Herzl's Zionist efforts, described the society as a "noble error."

Herzl's mounting frustration comes through loud and clear in his last pre-Zionist play, *The New Ghetto* (1904). Herzl's hero, partly a self-portrait and partly a portrait of a friend who had committed suicide after financial setbacks, gives up on the possibility of a Jew living a dignified existence. The historian Jacques Kornberg has argued persuasively that the Dreyfus Affair has been simplistically considered the sole incident that spurred Herzl to reconsider the Jewish Problem. In fact, Herzl had long been preoccupied by this problem, and worked his way to a solution more slowly than is usually presented in Hebrew schools. Nevertheless, the months from 1894 to 1895 that led to the composition of *Der Judenstaat* (1896) were dramatic ones. Herzl obsessively penned four different drafts of the classic, frequenting the opera to hear Richard Wagner's *Tannhauser* for inspiration. Before returning to the ideas contained in *Der Judenstaat*, a brief discussion of Herzl's meteoric but short career as the leader of modern Zionism is in order.

Having been disappointed by the Jewish plutocrats' lack of support for his plans, Herzl turned to the Jewish masses. He did so brilliantly. The First Zionist Congress was billed—with little exaggeration—as the first sovereign assembly of the Jewish people since the Maccabees. Without any military power, without much money, without any experience in modern self-governance, and faced with the hostile opposition of most Western and Central European Jews, Herzl needed to pull a rabbit out of the hat. He did.

Frightened by imputations of dual loyalty, German rabbis of all denominations forced the congress to switch venues from Munich to Basle, Switzerland. The Swiss welcomed the business, and in August 1897, 208 Zionist delegates from sixteen nations met with considerable fanfare. Herzl, of course, chaired most sessions. Probably more importantly, he stage-managed the press coverage, the impressive location of the congress, the dress of the delegates, and the tone of the speeches. Herzl wanted to project an organized, dignified national movement, not "an army of schnorrers," as he occasionally referred to his opponents.[5] The Basle Congress ended with an emotional singing of "Hatikva," now Israel's national anthem, and a bold program designed to anchor and direct Zionism as a movement. As the Israeli journalist Amos Elon notes in his biography *Herzl*, the playwright finally had his moment in the sun.

The annual congresses, under Herzl's leadership, succeeded in establishing Zionism as a democratic movement responsible to its membership. At the time of Herzl's death (1904), Zionism had established the treasury that would purchase many of the lands settled by Jews in the twentieth century. Throughout Europe, Jews contributed a token "shekel" for membership and filled little blue-and-white metal boxes with spare change to purchase lands in Palestine. By 1904, Zionism had organized student movements and press organs in every nation with a substantial Jewish population, and mostly as a result of Herzl's own activities, had projected itself as a viable representative of a segment of the Jewish community. A mere twenty years separated the adoption of the Basle Program (1897) from the issuing of the Balfour Declaration (1917) in which the British Empire promised to carve out a Jewish homeland.

Herzl worked tirelessly from 1897 until his death in July 1904, trying to get a legal charter for Jewish settlement from the Ottoman Turks through the intervention of a variety of European monarchs. He expended much of his family's wealth, embittered his wife further with his monomania, and ruined his health in the cause. His novel *Altneuland*, as noted above, got a very mixed reception. More divisive still, Herzl seriously considered a British Foreign Office proposal for a colonial territory in British East Africa (known forever after as the Uganda Plan, although the territory corresponded more closely to present-day Kenya). Given the atrocious pogroms in Russia, and himself devoid of any religious-emotional attachment to the land of Israel, Herzl wanted to pursue the African option, if only as a temporary asylum (*Nachtasyl*). At the Sixth Zionist Congress, when he broached the Uganda Plan, the movement's only hero was nearly dethroned. A coalition of mainly, but not exclusively, Eastern European Zionists held firm: Israel or nowhere! Herzl had badly misjudged their commitment to Zion.[6]

In some ways Herzl's error was understandable. After all, these Eastern European Zionists had largely broken from the traditional Judaism of their parents. Eastern, not Western, Jews suffered from pogroms. But the Easterners were also committed to an "authentic" Jewish culture (which included Israel—Zion—as its sole homeland) that was foreign to Herzl. The rank and file had also tired of Herzl's failed attempts to throw a diplomatic touchdown and of his relative lack of interest in patiently cultivating a Zionist culture in Europe. Herzl's last months were spent recuperating from the blow dealt him at the Sixth Zionist Congress, but all was forgiven at his death. Thousands of wailing mourners attended his funeral.

Der Judenstaat represents Herzl's greatest claim as a Jewish thinker, which, in some people's opinion, is not saying very much. Chaim Weizmann, Israel's first president, averred that *Der Judenstaat* contained "not a single new idea." Admittedly, Herzl did not even know of a number of Zionist tracts that preceded his own. Ahad Ha'am and Martin Buber found him a shallow, inauthentic Jew. The Budapest boy who may or may not have had a bar mitzvah needed to be coached to say the simplest prayers when Zionist proprieties forced him to appear in synagogue. But all these objections, however true, simply miss the point. Relying on the work of two scholars, Arthur Hertzberg and Steven Beller, I will suggest why Herzl indeed ought to be considered a modern Jewish thinker—in fact, one of the first rank.

By 1895, Herzl had arrived at both an analysis of and a solution to the "Jewish Question." The problem, in Herzl's view, was that Jews had become middle class in the ghetto and that their incorporation into Europe inevitably led to economic competition and hostility with the bourgeoisie, exactly the class that mattered in the nineteenth century. It did no good at all to pretend that Jews were just individuals who happened to go to synagogues rather than churches. The Jews were a people, one people, bound together less by a common faith than by a common fate. No *individual* solution would therefore solve a *national* problem. In fact, as long as Jews were in Europe, anti-Semitism was inevitable, incurable, and unavoidable. However, and this is Arthur Hertzberg's great insight into Herzl's thinking, anti-Semitism could be channeled to the Jews' benefit. Since all national leaders wanted to solve anti-Semitism (which represented a force of destabilization), they could, should, and would aid Zionists in using anti-Semitism to move the Jews from Europe to Asia.

From Herzl's perspective, harnessing the power of anti-Semitism would benefit all concerned parties. Everybody would win: European merchants would have less business competition from a group that became middle class in the ghettos; European rulers would have more stable regimes, free from the disruptive forces of anti-Semitic agitators; and Jews would be able to lead proud and productive lives, freed from a savage circle of occupational segregation and the resulting hostility. Herzl realized that many Jews in Western Europe were quite content to remain where they were. He realized that the Jews of Czarist Russia would be the initial rank and file of Zionist settlers. But in the end, most European Jews would recognize the truth of his analysis. In early diary entries, Herzl had imagined solving the Jewish Problem through conversion and/or intermarriage, in other words, the assimilationist solution. That solution would still obtain for those (few) Jews who refused to emigrate to their *Judenstaat*—these remaining Jews would succeed in disappearing into their respective European nations. But the Jewish future would be in Palestine.

What would be the tangible goals of Zionism, above and beyond providing the venue for Jewish honor? To realize the goals of Emancipation, but in Palestine, not Europe. Jews would become, in Steven Beller's words: "The worthy citizens of a liberal state. . . . The integration of Jews into the modern world will be effected, not by them as individuals, but by them as a nation."[7] A new type of Jew would embody the best of Western civilization. The *Judenstaat* would be truly tolerant, allowing freedom of religion. It would have enlightened social policies, including a seven-hour working day. It would be technologically adept, bringing advantages to the entire population, Jewish and Arab alike. It would need no huge armies; a professional soldiery armed with up-to-date equipment would be adequate for self-defense. The *Judenstaat* would be run by an idealistic meritocracy. In a word, Jews would be normalized, but normalized to the best rather than to the worst of what fin-de-siècle Europe had to offer.

Both Herzl's analysis and his solution to the Jewish Problem have been attacked, in his own day and down to the present, as simplistic and naïve. Dozens of objections can be lodged, and I hope the readers of this book have already been busy lodging them as they read the last couple of paragraphs. Let me say two things in Herzl's defense. One, although anti-Semitism was not as easily managed as Herzl thought (e.g., the Holocaust), it *has* been the motor that drove the bulk of the Israeli population to its present location. Two, however threadbare Herzl's visions for the Jewish future were on Judaistic grounds, many Israelis would be happy to live in an updated version of Herzl's paradise. Would not many Israelis trade obsessive press coverage, debates over "Who is a Jew?" and the unending battles between secular and religious Jews for a government no more influenced by organized Judaism than England is by organized Anglicanism?

I have avoided translating the title of Herzl's *Der Judenstaat* until now deliberately (but see chapter 5, 7n). For *Der Judenstaat* can be translated into English in two different ways. The "Jewish State," the most common rendering, implies something necessarily and qualitatively Jewish or even Judaic about the place. Many Zionists insisted on this; Herzl did not. What Herzl had in mind is better conveyed by "A Jew's State" or, as Beller suggests, "A State of Jews." Herzl looked not to the Jewish past, but to a yet-to-be-developed future. The Jews would become a normal people, even if their children would all be above average.

In many respects, Herzl's vision of the Jewish future did not materialize. One can call Israel many things, but certainly not ordinary. Yet, as the book on my bookshelf suggests, in some fundamental ways, Herzl got what he wanted. Even skeptics in the academic world cannot say very much when confronted by Herzl's famous diary entry, penned during the heady first days of the First Zionist Congress in Basle:

> Were I to sum up the Basle Congress in a word—which I shall guard against pronouncing publicly—it would be this: At Basle I founded the Jewish State. If I said this out loud today, I would be answered by universal laughter. Perhaps in five years and certainly in fifty, everyone will know it.[8]

Herzl was off—by eight months.

QUESTIONS FOR HERZL, *THE JEWISH STATE*

Herzl claims that Jews are "one people." Why does Herzl think this assertion will stir up the wrath of anti-Semites and the fear of European Jews?

Supposing that you wanted to use a different term to describe Jewry than *peoplehood*—would you choose *nation*, *race*, or *religion*? Do you think Herzl's definition is a good one? What make "a people"? In Herzl's view? In your own?

How much of Herzl's explanation for anti-Semitism turns on the Jews' unusual economic status? Do you think this makes sense? Does Herzl consider the history of Jewish-Christian rivalry sufficiently? (Compare Herzl to Rosenzweig on this point.)

What were the previous attempts at solving the Jewish Problem, as Herzl sees it? In Herzl's view, why didn't they work? Is there any logical reason that they should not work?

Do you think that Herzl preferred Palestine or Argentina as a homeland when he wrote *Der Judenstaat* in 1895–1896? Is it clear why Herzl eventually accepted Palestine as the only possible site for the Jewish homeland?

Can you imagine organizing a state out of thin air? Supposing that you were Herzl's lieutenant, what would be your list of priorities in order to achieve the goal of a Jewish homeland?

In Herzl's view, what benefits will the Jews' state yield to the world? To the Jews themselves?

What are the most serious obstacles to the formation of a Jewish homeland? How does Herzl plan on overcoming these obstacles?

STUDIES BY AND ABOUT HERZL

Herzl's major works are all available, though many of his essays and plays remain untranslated. For insight into Herzl's character, I would recommend perusing his revealing diaries. The Zionist writing I most enjoy is his novel *Altneuland*, a piece of utopian fiction (*Old New Land*, trans. and ed. Lotta Levensohn, with an introduction by Jacques Kornberg [New York: M. Wiener-Herzl Press, 1987]). Of the many Herzl biographies, I prefer Amos Elon's nonacademic *Herzl* (New York: Schocken, 1986). Andrew Handler's *Dori: The Life and Times of Theodor Herzl in Budapest (1860–1878)* (Tuscaloosa: University of Alabama Press, 1983) is indispensable for Herzl's Hungarian period. Jacques Kornberg's *Herzl: From Assimilation to Jewish Nationalism* (Bloomington: Indiana University Press, 1993) meticulously reconstructs Herzl's emergence as a Zionist in the mid-1890s. For those who relish psychobiography, Ernst Pawel's *The Labyrinth of Exile: A Life of Theodor Herzl* (New York: Farrar, Straus and Giroux, 1989) will be enjoyable.

From *The Jewish State*

Theodor Herzl

No one can deny the gravity of the Jewish situation. Wherever they live in appreciable number, Jews are persecuted in greater or lesser measure. Their equality before the law, granted by statue, has become practically a dead letter. They are debarred from filling even moderately high offices in the army, or in any public or private institutions. And attempts are being made to thrust them out of business also: "Don't buy from Jews!"

Attacks in parliaments, in assemblies, in the press, in the pulpit, in the street, on journeys—for example, their exclusion from certain hotels—even in places of recreation are increasing from day to day. The forms of persecutions vary according to country and social circle. In Russia, special taxes are levied on Jewish villages; in Romania, a few persons are put to death; in Germany, they get a good beating occasionally; in Austria, anti-Semites exercise their terrorism over all public life; in Algeria, there are traveling agitators; in Paris, the Jews are shut out of the so-called best social circles and excluded from clubs. The varieties of anti-Jewish expression are innumerable. But this is not the occasion to attempt the sorry catalogue of Jewish hardships. We shall not dwell on particular cases, however painful.

I do not aim to arouse sympathy on our behalf. All that is nonsense, as futile as it is dishonorable. I shall content myself with putting the following questions to the Jews: Is it not true that, in countries where we live in appreciable numbers, the position of Jewish lawyers, doctors, technicians, teachers, and employees of every description becomes daily more intolerable? Is it not true that the Jewish middle classes are seriously threatened? Is it not true that the passions of the mob are incited against our wealthy? Is it not true that our poor endure greater suffering than any other proletariat? I think that this pressure is everywhere present. In our upper economic classes it causes discomfort, in our middle classes utter despair.

The fact of the matter is, everything tends to one and the same conclusion, which is expressed in the classic Berlin cry: "*Juden 'raus!*" ("Out with the Jews!").

I shall now put the question in the briefest possible form: Shouldn't we "get out" at once, and if so, whither?

Or, may we remain, and if so, how long?

Let us first settle the point of remaining. Can we hope for better days, can we possess our souls in patience, can we wait in pious resignation till the princes and peoples of this earth are more mercifully disposed toward us? I say that we cannot hope for the current to shift. And why not? Even if we were as near to the hearts of princes as are their other subjects, they could not protect us. They would only incur popular hatred by showing us too much favor. And this "too much" implies less than is claimed as a right by any ordinary citizen or ethnic group. The nations in whose midst Jews live are all covertly or openly anti-Semitic.

The common people have not, and indeed cannot have, any comprehension of history. They do not know that the sins of the Middle Ages are now being visited on the nations of Europe. We are what the ghetto made us. We have without a doubt attained pre-eminence in finance because medieval conditions drove us to it. The same process is now being repeated. We are again being forced into money-lending—now named stock exchange—by being kept out of other occupations. But once on the stock exchange, we are again objects of contempt. At the same time we continue to produce an abundance of mediocre intellectuals who find no outlet, and this endangers our social position as much as does our increasing wealth. Educated Jews without means are now rapidly becoming socialists. Hence we are certain to suffer acutely in the struggle between the classes, because we stand in the most exposed position in both the capitalist and the socialist camps.

Previous Attempts at a Solution

The artificial methods heretofore employed to remedy the plight of the Jews have been either too petty, such as attempts at colonization, or falsely conceived, such as attempts to convert the Jews into peasants in their present homes.

What is achieved by transporting a few thousand Jews to another country? Either they come to grief at once, or, if they prosper, their prosperity gives rise to anti-Semitism. We have already discussed these attempts to channel poor Jews to new regions. This diversion is clearly inadequate and useless, if not actually harmful, for it merely postpones and drags out if not actually hinders the solution.

But those who would attempt to convert Jews into peasants are committing a truly astonishing error. For the peasant is a creature of the past, as seen by his style of dress, which in most countries is centuries old, and by his tools, which are identical with those used by his earliest forebears. His plow is unchanged; he sows his seed from the apron, mows with the time-honored scythe, and threshes with the flail. But we know that all this can now be done by machinery. The agrarian question is only a question of machinery. America must conquer Europe, in the same way as large landed possessions absorb small ones. The peasant is, consequently, a type which is on the way to extinction. Wherever he is preserved by special measures, there are involved political interests who hope to gain his support. To create new peasants on the old pattern is an absurd and impossible undertaking. No one is wealthy or powerful enough to make civilization take a single step backward. The mere preservation of obsolete institutions is a task vast enough to strain the capacities of even an autocratic state.

Will anyone, then, suggest to Jews, who know what they are about, that they become peasants of the old cast? That would be like saying to the Jew: "Here is a crossbow; now go to war!" What? With a crossbow, while others have small arms and Krupp cannon? Under these circumstances the Jews would be perfectly right in remaining unmoved when people try to place them on the farm. The crossbow is a pretty piece of armament, which inspires a lyrical mood in me whenever I can spare the time. But its proper place is the museum.

Now, there certainly are regions where desperate Jews go out, or at any rate are willing to go out, and till the soil. And a little observation shows that these areas, such as the enclave of Hesse in Germany and some provinces in Russia—these areas are the very hotbeds of anti-Semitism.

For the do-gooders of the world who send the Jews to the plow forget a very important person, who has a great deal to say in the matter. That person is the peasant. And the peasant is absolutely in the right. For the tax on the land, the risks attached to crops, the pressure of large proprietors who produce at cheaper rates, not to mention American competition, all combine to make life difficult enough for him. Besides, the duties on corn cannot go on increasing indefinitely. For the factory worker cannot be allowed to starve, either; his political influence is, in fact, in the ascendant, and he must therefore be treated with ever-increasing respect.

All these difficulties are well known; therefore I refer to them only cursorily. I merely wanted to indicate clearly how futile have been past attempts—most of them well intentioned—to solve the Jewish question. Neither a diversion of the stream nor an artificial depression of the intellectual level of our proletariat will avail. And we have already dealt with the panacea of assimilation.

We cannot overcome anti-Semitism by any of these methods. It cannot be eliminated until its causes are eradicated. But are they eradicable?

Causes of Anti-Semitism

We now no longer discuss the irrational causes, prejudice and narrow-mindedness, but the political and economic causes. Modern anti-Semitism is not to be confused with the persecution of the Jews in former times, though it does still have a religious aspect in some countries. The main current of Jew-hatred is today a different one. In the principal centers of anti-Semitism, it is an outgrowth of the emancipation of the Jews. When civilized nations awoke to the inhumanity of discriminatory legislation and enfranchised us, our enfranchisement came too late. Legislation alone no longer sufficed to emancipate us in our old homes. For in the ghetto we had remarkably developed into a bourgeois people and we emerged from the ghetto a prodigious rival to the middle class. Thus we found ourselves thrust, upon emancipation, into this bourgeois circle, where we have a double pressure to sustain, from within and from without. The Christian bourgeoisie would indeed not be loath to cast us as a peace offering to socialism, little though that would avail them.

At the same time, the equal rights of Jews before the law cannot be rescinded where they have once been granted. Not only because their recision would be contrary to the spirit of our age, but also because it would immediately drive all Jews, rich and poor alike, into the ranks of the revolutionary parties. No serious harm can really be done us. In olden days our jewels were taken from us. How is our movable property to be seized now? It consists of printed papers which are locked up somewhere or other in the world, perhaps in the strongboxes of Christians. It is, of course, possible to get at railway shares and debentures, banks and industrial undertakings of all descriptions, by taxation; and where the progressive income tax is in force all our movable property can eventually be laid hold of. But all these efforts cannot be directed against Jews alone, and wherever they might nevertheless be made, their upshot would be immediate economic crises, which would by no means be confined to the Jews as the first affected. The very impossibility of getting at the Jews nourishes and deepens hatred of them. Anti-Semitism increases day by day and hour by hour among the nations; indeed, it is bound to increase, because the causes of its growth continue to exist and are ineradicable. Its remote cause is the loss of our assimilability during the Middle Ages; its immediate cause is our excessive production of mediocre intellectuals, who have no outlet downward or upward—or rather, no wholesome outlet in either direction. When we sink, we become a revolutionary proletariat, the corporals of every revolutionary party; and when we rise, there rises also our terrifying financial power.

Effects of Anti-Semitism

The pressure applied to us does not improve us, for we are no different from ordinary people. It is true enough that we do not love our enemies; but he alone who has quite mastered himself dares throw that up to us. Oppression naturally creates hostility against oppressors, and our hostility in turn increases the pressure. It is impossible to escape this vicious circle.

"No!" some softhearted visionaries will say. "No! It *is* possible! Possible by means of the perfectibility of man."

Is it really necessary for me, at this late stage, to show what sentimental drivel this is? He who would peg the improvement of conditions on the goodness of all mankind would indeed be writing a *Utopia!*

I referred previously to our "assimilation." I do not for a moment wish to imply that I desire such an end. Our national character is too glorious in history and, in spite of every degradation, too noble to make its annihilation desirable. Though perhaps we *could* succeed in vanishing without a trace into the surrounding peoples if they would let us be for just two generations. But they will not let us be. After brief periods of toleration, their hostility erupts again and again. When we prosper, it seems to be unbearably irritating, for the world has for many centuries been accustomed to regarding us as the most degraded of the poor. Thus out of ignorance or ill will they have failed to observe that prosperity weakens us as Jews and wipes away our differences. Only pressure drives us back to our own; only hostility stamps us ever again as strangers.

Thus we are now, and shall remain, whether we would nor not, a group of unmistakable cohesiveness.

We are one people—our enemies have made us one whether we will or not, as has repeatedly happened in history. Affliction binds us together, and thus united, we suddenly discover our strength. Yes, we are strong enough to form a State, and, indeed, a model State. We possess all the requisite human and material resources.

This would, accordingly, be the appropriate place to give an account of what has been somewhat crudely termed our "human material." But it would not be appreciated till the broad outlines of the plan, on which everything depends, have first been marked out.

NOTES

The first epigraph to this chapter is taken from Theodor Herzl, "Of the Jewish Cause, Begun in Paris, Around Pentecost, 1895," in *The Complete Diaries of Theodor Herzl*, ed., Raphael Patai, vol. 5 (New York: Herzl Press-Thomas Yoseloff, 1960), 3.

The second epigraph is taken from Chaim Weizmann, *Trial and Error* (New York: Harper and Brothers, 1949), 43.

1. The *New York Times* is the obvious equivalent to Vienna's *New Free Press*. Herzl wrote wide-ranging cultural reviews (*feuilletons*) and was well known in his day.

2. The Dreyfus Affair began with the bogus conviction on the charge of treason of a Jewish captain in the French army, Alfred Dreyfus. This case became a cause célèbre for several years, dividing the Third Republic into "Dreyfusards and anti-Dreyfusards." In the end, Dreyfus was exonerated and returned to his commission.

3. Andrew Handler, *Dori: The Life and Times of Theodor Herzl* (Tuscaloosa: University of Alabama Press, 1983), 106–18.

4. Amos Elon, *Herzl* (New York: Schocken, 1986), 109–11.

5. A schnorrer is somebody who solicits funds.

6. Israel Zangwill, a British Jew who coined the term *melting pot* in a play of the same name, pressed the idea of a territory other than Palestine at the Seventh Zionist Congress and beyond. "Territorialism" became one of the several fringe movements on the edges of mainstream Zionism.

7. Steven Beller, *Herzl* (New York: Grove Press, 1991), 58.

8. Raphael Patai, ed., *The Complete Diaries of Theodor Herzl*, vol. 5 (New York: Herzl Press-Thomas Yoseloff, 1960), 581.

Chapter Eight

Ahad Ha'am (Asher Zvi Ginzberg)

A Jewish Modernist from Eastern Europe

AHAD HA'AM'S LIFE AND TIMES (1856–1927)

Ahad Ha'am is the symbol of the great culture that will be built by the community of Jews in the Land of Israel and will unify all segments of Jewry throughout the world.

—Chaim Nachman Bialik

The praises of the poet Bialik notwithstanding, Ahad Ha'am has not been a lucky winner in the Jewish History Sweepstakes. Forever in the shadow of Theodor Herzl, Ahad Ha'am is known to few American Jews, although a host of better-known figures including Martin Buber, Chaim Weizmann, and Mordechai Kaplan were proud to name him as their teacher.[1] For a brief period, Ahad Ha'am epitomized the rich possibilities of creating a modern, secular, yet authentically Jewish culture.

Bialik's "optimistic" estimation of Ahad Ha'am stands in contrast with the latter's personal demeanor and leadership style. Armed with a needle-sharp pen, Ahad Ha'am inclined more to criticism than to constructive leadership. He expressed contempt for other leaders (on Herzl: "He was lucky in life, he was lucky in death") and for moments that swept other people away (on the First Zionist Congress: "I felt like a mourner at a wedding"). His first published essay, "This Is Not The Way" (1888), highlighted the failings of the early Zionist movement (Hovevei Zion—"the Lovers of Zion").[2] He spoke almost prophetically about the challenge of dealing with the Palestinian Arabs.[3] He savagely noted the moral and intellectual self-censorship of Western Jews.[4] He recognized, though never solved, the dilemma of defining a culture that was truly Jewish, yet without its traditional theological premises. Who was the individual behind the pen name that translates as "one of the people"?

Born Asher Zvi Ginzberg in a small Ukrainian town in 1856, his family thrived economically and lived extremely pious lives. If there were a Jewish "aristocracy" in the Pale of Settlement,[5] then Ahad Ha'am belonged to it.[6] The family paid its religious loyalties to the Sadagora rebbe, leader of an important hasidic dynasty. Martin Buber, while visiting his father's farm in Bukovina, used to visit the court of the Sadagora rebbe. In his autobiographical "My Way To Hasidism," Buber found Sadagora's *hasidim* an exemplary community and the rebbe an exemplary leader. Ahad Ha'am, on the contrary, broke with this pietistic form of Judaism while still a teenager, without experiencing the alienation from Judaism so typical of Western Jews. He became, in Arthur Hertzberg's paradoxical but appropriate language, "the Agnostic Rabbi" of Zionism.

Contemporary child psychologists would probably consider his upbringing abusive. He had virtually no friends, living as he did from age twelve in a remote, rural hamlet. His father Isaiah beat him, and his pedagogic method involved making Asher feel as inadequate as humanly possible. The "bright side" of this upbringing intellectually, if not emotionally, was that the young man became an autodidact of impressive proportions. That Asher *spoke* Yiddish and Russian was a given. But he also taught himself to *read* Russian by deciphering street signs. Before he left for Odessa to begin his mission at age twenty-nine, he had also mastered German and Latin. In time, he would pick up English and French, too.

Ahad Ha'am's relationship to Hebrew merits a whole book, but at least we can give it a few sentences. As Benjamin Harshav's *Language in Time of Revolution* (Berkeley: University of California Press, 1993) makes clear, Hebrew was never really a dead language. Every Yiddish speaker used plenty of Hebrew words, every observant Jew knew the Psalms of the Prayerbook by heart, and in many cases, the weekly portions of the Torah as well. It is true that Hebrew had not been used as a colloquial language for centuries, but yeshiva students would be able to quote large blocks of the Bible and Mishnah (also written in Hebrew) in the course of their deliberations. Hebrew writing, in the form of rabbinic decisions, commentaries, and even poetry, had never ceased.

Having noted that modern Hebrew was not simply invented out of thin air by Eliezer ben Yehuda (which remains the Sunday-school version of the story), the transformation of Hebrew into a usable tongue really is remarkable, and Ahad Ha'am played a notable part in its development. Any reader of his Hebrew essays (he wrote no poetry or novels) will testify that Ahad Ha'am is a model of clarity, without all the stuffing (endless quotes, allusions, convolutions) that accompanied traditional rabbinic prose. His strong editorial hand at the Hebrew monthly *Ha-Shilo'ah* can best be likened to the modernizing impact of Yitzhak Leib Peretz on the fledgling Yiddish writers of the Pale. Both men were thoroughly Jewish culturally and imbued with a deep love for the entire nation, but both had broken decisively from their religious upbringings. Both forged new paths in terms of bringing European sensibilities to the use of a Jewish language (for Peretz, Yiddish; for Ahad Ha'am, Hebrew). Both led by example as essayists in their own right and as figures around whom aspiring writers congregated. (By way of contrast, Peretz was a wide-ranging writer of short stories, poems, and plays, while Ahad Ha'am concentrated mainly on political prose.)

Ultimately, it is Ahad Ha'am's critique of Zionism that earns him his place in the story of modern Jewish thought. His rise to prominence occurred in the wake of his move in 1884 to Odessa, the Black Sea port city in which he spent his most creative years. Without much fear of exaggeration, Zionism's practical accomplishments before the advent of Herzl were meager indeed. The Hovevei Zion raised very little money, supported a few settlements in Palestine, had a very modest structure within the Pale of Settlement, and enjoyed no reputation on the world stage. The Lovers of Zion generally conducted their affairs in the furtive, semi-conspiratorial style so typical of underground movements in Czarist Russia. But what bothered Ahad Ha'am, who also tended to the furtive and conspiratorial, was that enthusiasm over the modest Palestine settlements threatened to overrun the evolutionary cultivation of a Jewishly committed, Hebrew-speaking elite in the Pale as well as in Palestine. Only this elite, he held, could develop the nucleus of a modern Jewish nation.

This criticism of Hovevei Zion, seemingly picayune, incorporates some of Ahad Ha'am's key ideas: (1) a new Jewish nation must precede a new Jewish state; (2) the process of nation and state building is evolutionary; no international fiat can make a Jewish people fit for the twentieth century; (3) culture is more important than politics; and (4) the slow, patient work of cultivating Zionism where the vast majority of Jews reside (i.e., the Pale) is as important to the Jewish future as what a few thousand Palestinian settlers are doing in the land of Israel. Surrounding himself with an impressive cadre of admirers, Ahad Ha'am became the titular head of B'nei Moshe, a movement dedicated to carrying out these ideals.[7]

In many respects, Ahad Ha'am stuck to these principles even after 1897, when Herzl and his allies demonstrated that a broad-based, public, well-publicized movement with diplomatically oriented goals could galvanize Jewish nationalist sentiment in a far more effective manner than Hovevei Zion. From 1897 to 1904, Herzl dominated the fortunes of Zionism, with gradually mounting opposition from the Eastern European Jews who objected to his high-handed tactics and his Judaic shallowness.

Behind this opposition (organized into a group called the Democratic Faction) stood Ahad Ha'am, already regarded as the moral weathervane for the Zionist cause.

Ahad Ha'am's opposition to Herzl contained a mix of serious criticisms and jealous sniping; it is rarely easy to disentangle the two. For example, Ahad Ha'am savagely attacked Herzl's 1902 utopian novel *Altneuland* (*Oldnewland*) because the culture portrayed in it was Western European and without any trace of Jewishness. Even earlier, in the "The Jewish State and the Jewish Problem" (1897), Ahad Ha'am had warned Herzl that Zionism's true goal must be to create a state that is truly Jewish and not just a state for Jews. Without doubt, Herzl was not interested in the "Jewishness" of the Jewish state. Herzl struggled to establish a modern, secular Jewish state as a feasible *political* goal; no mean achievement at the time. Herzl's *Altneuland*, after all, was only a novel, and hardly precluded other views of the Zionist future.[8] Herzl's contribution to Zionism was necessary if not sufficient. Even some of Ahad Ha'am's most ardent supporters expected him to be more charitable to Zionism's first hero. Martin Buber, a member of the Democratic Faction, conceded that a nation needed not only a teacher (Ahad Ha'am), but also a leader (Herzl). Shmaryahu Levin, active as a Zionist and in Russian politics, went further, contending that Ahad Ha'am offered only criticism, whereas Herzl offered a positive program of nation building.

Beneath this critique of Herzl lurked a serious problem for Ahad Ha'am— in my view, the most serious. Herzl wanted (minimally) a refuge for Jews from anti-Semitism, and (maximally) a hypermodern Switzerland with liberal-democratic politics and enlightened social policies. He did not care if the resulting state exemplified Jewish values. Ahad Ha'am cared deeply about this, but was pressed by critics to define what he meant by Jewish values. Maimonides (1135–1204) would have had no trouble defining a Jewish state. It would be a state regulated by God-commanded Torah laws; in short, a theocracy. Of course, for a religious rebel such as Ahad Ha'am, a theocracy was anathema. The very beauty of Zionism was that it offered a home for Jews on a national and secular, rather than on a religious, basis.

But how to instill and define "Jewishness" in an otherwise modern setting? And how to determine which Jewish values truly represented the nation? In practice, Ahad Ha'am championed institutions like the Hebrew University and the Herziliya Gymnasium that were secular, humanistic, and still decisively Jewish. In principle, Ahad Ha'am resorted to theories of cultural nationalism that spoke of a *Volksgeist*, a spirit-of-the-people, that existed as a guiding force in Jewish history.[9] He considered the Hebrew language, prophetic ethics, and a non-halachic version of Shabbat to be desiderata ordained by this *Volksgeist*. But more radical figures like Berdichevski felt that only the biblical (and not the rabbinic) past ought to be a guide, and still more radical figures wished to access pre-Sinaitic Judaism for their cultural models.

Even for the religious reformers of the West who believed in revelation, serious disagreements emerged over which were essential and which were inessential components of that tradition. But once the divine source of Judaism was jettisoned, as Ahad Ha'am and his more radical antagonists were prepared to do, the issue of defining the essentially Jewish became harder still. Moreover, how could Ahad Ha'am continue to assert the universal validity, and even superiority of Jewish ethics, the doctrine of Chosenness, without belief in a chooser? What was to prevent the Jewish state from becoming a second-class banana republic with second-class values? In this matter, Ahad Ha'am's confidence in the Jewish nation, his true religious belief, outran his vaunted logic.

A devout secularist, Ahad Ha'am attributed no mystical properties to the land of Israel. Unlike the traditionalist Abraham Isaac Kook and also unlike the modern, Tolstoyan figure Aharon David Gordon, Ahad Ha'am did not have confidence that combining the Jew and the land would inevitably lead to a marvelous new creation. He did not think, as Kook and Gordon did, that there was some mystical, spiritual potential that would be unlocked when the settlers got off the boat in Haifa. Unlike Herzl, Klatzkin, and others, Ahad Ha'am did not harbor particularly rosy expectations about the benefits a state would yield. He certainly did not share Herzl's romantic (and colonialist) idea that this state would be a bridge linking Europe and Asia. So it might be asked: what makes Ahad Ha'am a Zionist? The answer, I think, is his innate pessimism about the diaspora.[10] If creating the ideal conditions for a modern Jewish culture was difficult in the ancestral homeland, elsewhere it would be impossible.

In Western Europe, the nations would not permit Jews to cultivate their own national properties. They would insist, inevitably, thought Ahad Ha'am, that emancipated Jews join the French, English, or German nation wholeheartedly and without reservation. In "Slavery in the Midst of Freedom," Ahad Ha'am charged that Western Jews would respond by dropping their Jewish loyalties and conforming to national expectations. Elsewhere, Ahad Ha'am caricatured the Western Zionists who would solve their inferiority complex and find a nice outlet for Jewish activism in Zionist meetings and committees, but would be unable or unwilling to participate fully in the building of a new Jewish culture. Whether the assimilation was volitional or inadvertent, only a slow withering away could be expected from Western Jews left to their own devices.

In Eastern Europe, where Yiddish remained the mother tongue of the Jewish majority, the desire to be just like Polish or Russian peasants was negligible. Charging assimilationism, therefore, was an inadequate rebuttal to those

like the BUND (the Jewish Socialist Party) or to cultural autonomists like
Shimon Dubnov, who argued that in the Pale of Settlement, Jews could carve
out a meaningful modern existence. Against Dubnov, whose views were often very close to his own,[11] Ahad Ha'am reiterated his own view that the lib-
eralization of Russia that Dubnov counted on would not occur. Secondarily,
he adopted a somewhat Herzlian view and argued that without a state, or at
least something very close to it, the Jewish people would not be able to develop in an organic and holistic manner all their potential. Ahad Ha'am supported the autonomist struggle for improved Jewish conditions in the diaspora. He agreed that Jewish survival in the modern world could not be made
contingent on the realization of that state and the liquidation of the diaspora.
But, Ahad Ha'am contended, diaspora existence alone and unaided by a spiritual center would never amount to more than half a loaf.

Zionism, then, offered the best though far from perfect formula for developing a Jewish culture in a modern context. Zionism also offered a means by
which the diaspora, which Ahad Ha'am recognized as the abiding reservoir of
Jewish numbers and talent, could be kept alive on a sort of artificial respirator.[12]
Employing the metaphor of a wheel and its spokes, Ahad Ha'am imagined that
a developing elite living in the ancestral homeland would send out teachers and
leaders to the diaspora. They, in turn, would attract the most idealistic members
of the nation to participate in building the best surety of a Jewish future.

I have chosen to reproduce a few pages from "Flesh and Spirit," an essay
in which Ahad Ha'am demonstrates his original and utilitarian reading of
Jewish history. Written in 1904, shortly before he left Russia for England, and
on the 700th anniversary of Maimonides' death, "Flesh and Spirit" appeared
in the pages of Ahad Ha'am's journal *Ha-Shilo'ah*. Note how Ahad Ha'am
links the title's dichotomy to various movements in the Jewish past, how his
view of Jewish survival informs the piece, and how his own brand of Zionism is justified. Note also the innately conservative nature of his approach and
his conception of Jewry as a living organism, a view that later critics subjected to merciless criticism on the grounds that such an organic (positivist)
approach was inconsistent with Ahad Ha'am's constant reiteration of Jewish
ethics as indivisible from Jewish nationality.

Ahad Ha'am moved to England in 1907, where he served as a purchaser
for the Wissotzky Tea Company (still in business). Ahad Ha'am enjoyed the
cosmopolitan atmosphere of London. He was on hand for the Balfour Declaration of 1917, a major step in Zionism's diplomatic progress. Negotiated
from the Zionist side by Chaim Weizmann, a pupil of Ahad Ha'am's, the latter's pessimism regarding Balfour led to considerable tension between the
two men. Ahad Ha'am spent the last five years of his life in Tel Aviv, but not
happily. Although honored and surrounded by friends and family, Ahad

Ha'am found himself unable to do serious work. In a letter to Shimon Dubnov, the principal proponent of diaspora autonomism, the Zionist Ahad Ha'am confessed, "I can study in peace and quiet: all in Palestine, of which I have dreamt for years. And in these ideal conditions I sit and I long for—London!"[13]

QUESTIONS FOR AHAD HA'AM, "FLESH AND SPIRIT," 146–58 (FROM LEON SIMON, *SELECTED ESSAYS OF AHAD HA'AM*)

Why is the metaphor of "Flesh and Spirit" an appropriate one for talking about the history of the Jewish people? What does each term in this metaphor stand for?

Do you see an implicit polemic against Christianity in this distinction between "Flesh" and "Spirit"?

Which are the two fundamental periods in Israel's history? What characterized each of them, in the broadest terms?

How does history operate in Ahad Ha'am's schema? Does Jewish history work any differently than other national histories? Can you tell from his treatment? What makes Jewish history different?

What interests Ahad Ha'am about Jewish history? How does his interest differ from that of the medieval rabbis? How does his interest differ from that of his friend, the great historian Shimon Dubnov?

If the Pharisees were the progenitors of rabbinic Judaism, and also the dominant force in the nation after the destruction of the Second Temple (70 CE), why does Ahad Ha'am *reject* traditional Judaism as the best path for the Jewish people at present?

Although there were several different ways of rejecting rabbinic Judaism at the end of the nineteenth century, Ahad Ha'am is convinced that only one of them is correct. Which contemporary parties does Ahad Ha'am oppose in this essay? Why must there be only one right answer for Ahad Ha'am, when Jewish diversity is so blatant?

In the last paragraph of this essay, Ahad Ha'am links the prophets and the Pharisees to a third party in the third stage (i.e., the contemporary stage) of Jewish life. Based on what Ahad Ha'am has said up to this point, what would be the nature of this third party? What extremes would it avoid? Other than moderation, why would this party be the rightful heir to the prophets and the Pharisees?

STUDIES BY AND ABOUT AHAD HA'AM

The essence of Ahad Ha'am's thought is readily available in three volumes translated by one of his many disciples, the British Zionist Leon Simon, who also wrote the first major English-language biography, *Ahad Ha'am* (Philadelphia: Jewish Publication Society, 1960). Leon Simon's *Ten Essays on Zionism and Judaism* (New York, Arno Press, 1973); *Selected Essays of Ahad Ha'am* (Cleveland: Meridien, 1962); and *Ahad Ha'am: Essays, Letters, Memoirs* contain all that is likely to interest the general reader. Ahad Ha'am is very accessible; the reader can start almost anywhere, beginning with the essays referred to here. "Moses," a semiautobiographical essay, is both revealing and scintillating. While there is much secondary scholarship, I especially recommend Jacques Kornberg, *At The Crossroads: Essays on Ahad Ha-am* (Albany: State University of New York Press, 1983); section six of Arthur Hertzberg's introductory essay in *The Zionist Idea: A Historical Analysis and Reader* (Philadelphia: Jewish Publication Society, 1997); and Steven J. Zipperstein's biography *Elusive Prophet: Ahad Ha'am and the Origins of Zionism* (Berkeley: University of California Press, 1993).

From "Flesh and Spirit"

Ahad Ha'am

In the period of the first Temple we find no trace of the idea that man is divisible into body and soul. Man, as a living and thinking creature, is one whole of many parts. The word *Nefesh* (translated "soul") includes everything, body and soul and all the life-processes that depend on them. The *Nefesh*, that is, the individual man, lives its life and dies its death. There is no question of survival. And yet primitive Judaism was not troubled by the question of life and death, and did not arrive at that stage of utter despair which produced among other nations the materialist idea of the supremacy of the flesh and the filling of life's void by the intoxication of the senses. Judaism did not turn heavenwards, and create in Heaven an eternal habitation of souls. It found "eternal life" on earth, by strengthening the social feeling in the individual, by making him regard himself not as an isolated being, with an existence bounded by birth and death, but as a part of a larger whole, as a limb of the social body. This conception shifts the centre of gravity of the Ego not from the flesh to the spirit, but from the individual to the community; and, concurrently with this shifting, the problem of life becomes a problem not of individual but of social life. I live for the sake of the perpetuation and the happiness of the community of which I am a member; I die to make room for new individuals, who would mould the community afresh and not allow it to stagnate and remain forever in one position. When the individual thus values the community as his own life, and strives after its happiness as though it were his individual well-being, he finds satisfaction, and no longer feels so keenly the bitterness of his individual existence, because he sees the end for which he lives and suffers. But this can only be so when the life of the community has an end of such importance as to outweigh, in the judgment of the individual, all possible hardships. For otherwise the old question remains, only that it is shifted from the individual to the community. I bear with life in order that the community may live: but why does the community live? What value has its existence, that I should bear my sufferings cheerfully for its sake? Thus Judaism, having shifted the centre of gravity from the individual to the community, was forced to find an answer to the problem of the communal life. It had to find for that life some aim of sufficient grandeur and importance to uplift the individual, and to give him satisfaction at a time when his own particular life was unpleasant. So it was that Israel as a community became, "a kingdom of priests and a holy nation," a nation consecrated from its birth to the service of setting the whole of mankind an example by its Law.

Thus Judaism solved the problem of life, and had no place for the two extreme views. Man is one and indivisible; all his limbs, his feelings, his emotions, his thoughts make up a single whole. And his life is not wasted, because he is an Israelite, a member of the nation which exists for a lofty end. Since, further, the community is only the sum of its individual members, it follows that every Israelite is entitled to regard himself as the cause of his people's existence, and to believe that he too is lifted above oblivion by his share in the nation's imperishable life. Hence in this early period of Jewish history we do not find any tendency to real asceticism, that is to say, to hatred and annihilation of the flesh. That tendency can only arise when life can find no aim in this world, and has to seek its aim in another. There were no doubt Nazarites in Israel in those days, who observed the outward habits of the ascetic; but all this, as I have said, was simply part and parcel of the practice of sacrifice. How far the Nazarites were removed from hatred of the flesh we may see from the fact that even Samson was regarded as a Nazarite.

This philosophy of life, which raises the individual above all feelings of self-love, and teaches him to find the aim of his life in the perpetuation and well-being of the community, has been condemned by many non-Jewish scholars as being too materialistic, and has been regarded as a proof of the inferiority of Judaism, which does not promise immortality to every individual, and a reward to the righteous after death, as other religions do. So great is the power of hatred to blind the eyes and pervert the judgment!

But a change came after the destruction of the first Temple, when the national disaster weakened the nation's belief in its future, and the national instinct could no longer supply a basis for life. Then, indeed, Judaism was forced to seek a solution for the problem of life in the dualism which distinguishes between body and soul. But the deep-rooted partiality to the body and material life was so strong that even the new theory could not transform it entirely. Hence, unlike other nations, the Jews of that period did not eliminate the body even from the future life, but left it a place beyond the grave by their belief in the "resurrection of the dead." The end of man's life was now, no doubt, the uplifting of the spirit, and the bringing it near to "the God of spirits"; but the body was regarded not as the enemy of the spirit, but as its helper and ally. The body was associated with the spirit in order to serve it, and enable it to achieve perfection by good actions. And therefore, even in this period, Judaism did not arrive at the idea of the annihilation of the flesh. It regarded such annihilation not as righteousness, but as a sin. The two elements in man, the physical and the spiritual, can and must live in perfect accord, not as enemies; and this accord is not a truce between two opposing forces, based on a compromise and mutual accommodation, but a real inner union. The spiritual element is to penetrate into the very heart of the material life, to purify it and cleanse it, to make all its complex fulness a part of the spiritual life. Such union does not degrade the spirit, but uplifts the flesh, which is irradiated by the spirit's sanctity; and their joint life, each linked with and completing the other, brings man to his true goal.

Talmudic literature is full of utterances which confirm the view here put forward. It is sufficient to mention, by way of example, Hillel's saying about the importance of the body,[14] and the repeated condemnations of those who mortify the flesh, especially the familiar saying: "Every man will have to give an account of himself for every good thing which he would have liked to eat, but did not."[15]

Even the two non-conformist sects, the Sadducees and the Essenes, which might seem at first sight to have stood for the two extreme views, really based themselves on Jewish teaching, and developed no extravagant theories about the life of the individual. The Sadducees did not incline towards the sovereignty of the flesh, nor the Essenes towards its annihilation. The truth is that the Sadducees, who endeavored in all things to revive the older Judaism, held to the Scriptural view in this matter as in others, that is, that the individual has only his life on earth, and eternal life belongs solely to the nation as a whole, to which the individual must subordinate his existence. The Essenes, on the other side, starting from the eternity of the individual spirit as the most fundamental of all principles, endeavored to hold aloof from everything that distracts attention from the spiritual life. But they never despised or hated the flesh; and Philo says of them that "they avoided luxuries, because they saw in them injury to health of *body and soul*."

In the Middle Ages, no doubt, Judaism did not escape the infection of alien theories based on hatred of the flesh; but the best Jewish thinkers, such as Maimonides, tried to stem the tide of foreign influence. They remained true to the traditional Jewish standpoint, and taught the people to honor the body, to set store by its life and satisfy its legitimate demands, not to set body and spirit at odds. It was only after the expulsion from Spain, when the Jews were persecuted in most countries of the Diaspora, that the Cabbalists, especially those of Palestine, succeeded in obscuring the light, and won many converts to asceticism in its grimmest form. But their dominance was not of long duration; it was overthrown by a movement from within, first by the sect of Sabbatai Zebi and later by Hasidism. The ground was cut from under their asceticism, and material life was restored to its former esteem and importance.

And yet we do find even in Jewish history traces of these two extreme views—the sovereignty of the flesh and its annihilation. But that characteristic tendency, which we have already noticed, to transfer the centre of gravity from the individual to the national life, is evident here also; and so the Jews applied to the national life those ideas which other nations applied to the life of the individual.

In the very earliest times there was in Israel a considerable party which adopted the materialistic view of the national life. The whole aim of this party was to make the body politic dominant above all other interests, to win for the Jewish State a position of honor among its neighbors, and to secure it against external aggression. They neither sought nor desired any other end for the national life. This party was that of the aristocrats, the *entourage* of the king, the military leaders, and most of the priests: in a word, all those whose private lives were far removed from human misery, which demands consolation. The spiritual aspect of the national life had no meaning for them. They were almost always ready to desert the spiritual heritage of the nation, "to serve other gods," if only they thought that there was some political advantage to be gained. Against this political materialism the Prophets stood forward in all their spiritual grandeur, and fought it incessantly; until at last it vanished automatically with the overthrow of the State. But certain modern historians are quite wrong when they assert that the Prophets hated the State as such, and desired its destruction, because they regarded its very existence as essentially inconsistent with that spiritual life which was their aim. This political asceticism, this desire for the annihilation of the flesh of the national organism as a means to the strengthening of its spirit, was in reality quite repugnant to the view of the Prophets. We have only to read those passages in which the Prophets rejoice in the victories of the State—in the time of Sennacherib, for instance—or bewail its defeats, to see at once how they valued the State, and how essential political freedom was, in their view, to the advancement of the very ideals for which they preached and fought. But at the same time they did not forget that only the spirit can exalt life, whether individual or national, and give it a meaning and an aim. Hence they demanded emphatically that the aim should not be subordinated to the means, that the flesh should not be made sovereign over the spirit. The Prophets, then, simply applied to the national life that principle which Judaism had established for the life of the individual: the unity of flesh and spirit, in the sense which I have explained.

The real ascetic view was applied to the national life only in the time of the second Temple, and then not by the Pharisees,[16] but by the Essenes. So far as the individual was concerned, the Essenes, as I have said, had no leaning towards hatred of the flesh. But they did adopt that attitude as regards the body politic. These spiritually-minded men saw corruption eating at the very heart of the Jewish State; they saw its rulers, as in the time of the first Temple, exalting the flesh and disregarding all but physical force; they saw the best minds of the nation spending their strength in a vain effort to uplift the body politic from its internal decay, and once more to breathe the spirit of true Judaism into this corrupt flesh, now abandoned as a prey to the dogs. Seeing all this, they gave way to despair, turned their backs on political life altogether, and fled to the wilderness, there to live out their individual lives in holiness and purity, far from this incurable corruption. And in this lonely existence, removed from society and its turmoil, their hatred of the State grew stronger and stronger, until even in its last moments, when it was hovering betwixt life and death, some of them actually did not conceal their joy at its impending destruction.

But these political ascetics had no great influence over the popular mind. It was not they, but another sect, called Pharisees, although they had no vestige of real asceticism,[17] who were the teachers and guides of the people, and who upheld the Jewish view which was handed down from the Prophets: that is, the combination of flesh and spirit. They did not run away from life, and did not wish to demolish the State. On the contrary, they stood at their post in the very thick of life's battle, and tried with all their might to save the State from moral decay, and to mould it according to the spirit of Judaism. They knew full well that spirit without flesh is but an unsubstantial shade, and that the spirit of Judaism could not develop and attain its end without a political body, in which it could find concrete expression. For this reason the Pharisees were always fighting a twofold battle: on the one hand, they opposed the political materialists within, for whom the State was only a body without an essential spirit, and, on the other side, they fought together with these opponents against the enemy without, in order to save the State from destruction. Only at the very last, when the imminent death of the body politic was beyond all doubt, did the root difference between the two kinds of patriots, who stood shoulder to shoulder, necessarily reveal itself; and then the separation was complete. The political materialists, for whom the existence of the State was everything, had nothing to live for after the political catastrophe; and so they fought desperately, and did not budge until they fell dead among the ruins that they loved. But the Pharisees remembered, even in that awful moment, that the political body had a claim on their affections only because of the national spirit which found expression in it, and needed its help. Hence they never entertained the strange idea that the destruction of the State involved the death of the people, and that life was no longer worth living. On the contrary: now, now they felt it absolutely necessary to find some temporary means of preserving the nation and its spirit even without a State, until such time as God should have mercy on His people and restore it to its land and freedom. So the bond was broken: the political Zealots remained sword in hand on the walls of Jerusalem, while the Pharisees took the scroll of the Law and went to Jabneh.[18]

And the work of the Pharisees bore fruit. They succeeded in creating a national body which hung in mid-air, without any foundation on the solid earth, and in this body the Hebrew national spirit has had its abode and lived its life for two thousand years. The organization of the Ghetto, the foundations of which were laid in the generations that followed the destruction of Jerusalem, is a thing marvellous and quite unique. It was based on the idea that the aim of life is the perfection of the spirit, but that the spirit needs a body to serve as its instrument. The Pharisees thought at that time that, until the nation could again find an abode for its spirit in a single complete and free political body, the gap must be filled artificially by the concentration of that spirit in a number of small and scattered social bodies, all formed in its image, all living one form of life, and all united, despite their local separateness, by a common recognition of their original unity and their striving after a single aim and perfect union in the future.

But this artificial building stood too long. It was erected only to serve for a short time, in the days when men firmly believed that to-day or tomorrow Messiah would come; but at last its foundations decayed, and its walls cracked and gaped ever more and more.

Then there came again spiritually-minded men, who revived the political asceticism of the Essenes. They saw at its very worst the scattered and enslaved condition of the dispossessed nation; they saw no hope of a return to the land; they saw, too, the organization of the Ghetto, in which there was at least some shadow of a concrete national life, breaking up before their eyes. Despair took hold of them, and made them absolutely deny bodily life to their nation, made them regard its existence as purely spiritual. Israel, they said, is a spirit without a body; the spirit is not only the aim of Jewish life, it is the whole life; the flesh is not merely something subsidiary, it is actually a dangerous enemy, a hindrance to the development of the spirit and its conquest of the world.

We need not be surprised that this extreme view produced its opposite, as extreme views always do, and that we have seen a recrudescence of that political materialism which confines the life of Israel to the body, to the Jewish State.

This phenomenon is still recent, and has not yet reached its full development. But past experience justifies the belief that both these extreme views, having no root and basis in the heart of the nation, will disappear, and give place to the only view that really has its source in Judaism, the view of the Prophets in the days of the first State, and that of the Pharisees in the days of the second. If, as we hope, the future holds for Israel yet a third national existence, we may believe that the fundamental principle of individual as of national life will be neither the sovereignty of the flesh over the spirit, nor the annihilation of the flesh for the spirit's sake, but the uplifting of the flesh by the spirit.

NOTES

1. According to Steve Zipperstein, author of *Elusive Prophet: Ahad Ha'am and the Origins of Zionism* (Berkeley: University of California Press, 1993), Israeli schoolchildren still are force-fed Ahad Ha'am's essays as examples of classic, modern Hebrew prose.

2. In this first essay, Ginzberg adopted the pen name Ahad Ha'am ("One of the People") that he has been known by ever since.

3. Ahad Ha'am, "Truth From the Land of Israel" in *Kol Kitve Ahad Ha'Am* (Tel Aviv: Dvir, 1956), 23–24. On Ahad Ha'am and Palestinian Arabs, see Shlomo Avineri, *The Making of Modern Zionism* (New York: Basic Books, 1981), 121–22.

4. Ahad Ha'am, "Slavery in Freedom," in *Selected Essays of Ahad Ha'Am*, ed. Leon Simon (Cleveland: Meridien, 1962), 171–94.

5. Initiated by Catherine the Great after the partitions of Poland, the Pale of Settlement was the area within the Russian Empire in which Jews were permitted to dwell.

6. Arthur Hertzberg's essay on Ahad Ha'am in *The Zionist Idea: A Historical Analysis and Reader* (Philadelphia: Jewish Publication Society, 1997), 51–72, stresses his class loyalties as an important influence.

7. B'nei Moshe served as Ahad Ha'am's sounding board. Its accomplishments were few and most of its members eagerly joined the mainstream Zionist movement after the advent of Herzl in 1897.

8. The frontispiece of *Altneuland* proclaimed: "If you will it, it is no fairy-tale [*Märchen*]."

9. I am indebted here to Jacques Kornberg's formulation in *At the Crossroads: Essays on Ahad Ha-Am* (Albany: State University of New York Press, 1983), xvi.

10. See Hertzberg, *The Zionist Idea*, 51–72.

11. Robert Seltzer, "Ahad Ha-Am and Dubnov: Friends and Adversaries," in Kornberg, *At the Crossroads*.

12. Ahad Ha'am had contempt for those who envisioned a "liquidation of the diaspora." He sarcastically asked how 10,000,000 Jews could be fed, housed, and employed in an agriculturally poor region.

13. Leon Simon, *Ahad Ha-Am* (Philadelphia: Jewish Publication Society of America, 1960), 268.

14. Vayikra Rabba, [Ahad Ha'am is citing the Midrash], 34.

15. Jerusalem Talmud, end of Kiddushin.

16. The word "Pharisee" is derived from the root *parosh*, which means "to separate," and is therefore usually regarded as meaning a man "separated" from the concerns of everyday life, i.e., a sort of hermit or ascetic. The author seems to accept this explanation. Others, however, regard the Pharisees as having stood for *national* separateness; others, again, derive the name from a secondary sense of the same root, "to explain, expound," and make the Pharisees the "expounders of the Law."—Ed.

17. See the previous footnote.—Ed.

18. Rabbi Johanan ben Zakkai obtained permission from the victorious Romans to retire with his disciples to Jabneh, where he kept alight the lamp of Jewish study, and thus secured the continuance of Judaism despite the overthrow of the Jewish State.—Ed.

Chapter Nine

Mordecai Kaplan

A Secularist (Re)Constructs Religion

KAPLAN'S LIFE AND TIMES (1881–1983)

> The first real encounter with a live philosophical issue I owe to Dr. Kaplan. He
> was, as I have earlier noted, not a warm personality, nor did he care much that
> he was plunging many of his students into a turmoil of belief. He had no sym-
> pathy at all for our discomfort, bludgeoning his way through our apologetic de-
> fenses. . . . Truth to tell, I disliked Dr. Kaplan as a teacher, yet I owe him a large
> intellectual and educational debt. Only later did I come to appreciate his blunt
> honesty and exemplary courage in defying orthodox beliefs and forging new
> paths in Jewish religious thought. And only later still did I come to regard him
> with genuine affection.[1]

These words, from the memoirs of Israel Scheffler, a distinguished professor
of education at Harvard, point to the characteristics that made Kaplan so formidable a figure: courage of conviction, extreme intellectual honesty, and insistence on making his ideas count in the wider world. A full century of activism gave Kaplan the opportunity to influence American Jewish life
profoundly as a teacher, writer, and rabbi. He founded and continues to serve
as the ideological touchstone of the Reconstructionist movement.

Kaplan began life in Lithuania, the son of a learned rabbi who brought his
family to New York when Mordecai was just a boy. Mel Scult reports that Israel Kaplan, Mordecai's father, initially worked for Rabbi Jacob Joseph, the
ill-fated chief rabbi of New York. Brought from Lithuania in 1882, Jacob
Joseph had plans to run New York like an old-world Jewish community (*kehillah*) and to impose uniform kashrut standards. Since many Jews from Eastern Europe were eager to overthrow the compulsory authorities of the *kehillah*

(not to mention starvation, pogrom, and conscription), and since New York's Jewish population dwarfed even the largest Eastern European communities, Jacob Joseph's plans came a cropper. Did young Mordecai get some of his American pragmatism from hearing about Jacob Joseph's travails or from observing the police riot that took place during Rabbi Joseph's funeral procession? Perhaps, although Kaplan continued to yearn for a modernized *kehillah* that would offer a broader basis of communal Jewish life than the synagogue could. More likely, Kaplan's profound Americanization derives from the education he received at City College of New York, where he graduated in 1900. His studies in sociology and pragmatism would be a decisive influence on his Jewish thinking. Combined with his excellent Judaic training, obtained first from his father, and then from the fledgling Jewish Theological Seminary (JTS), Kaplan was one of the few in his generation to be fully grounded in both traditional Judaic learning and cutting-edge American ideas.

Kaplan had a long career as a pulpit rabbi, first at Kehillat Jeshurun and then at the Society for the Advancement of Judaism. But Kaplan's influence probably owes even more to his role as principal of the Teachers' Institute at JTS, a position he was appointed to by no less a figure than Solomon Schechter, the JTS president and pioneering researcher of the Cairo Geniza.[2] Kaplan would remain at JTS until 1968, despite some periods of extreme controversy, and despite the tempting offer from Rabbi Stephen Wise, the spiritual leader of American Reform Judaism in the first half of the twentieth century, to assume control of the Jewish Institute of Religion.

By the 1910s and 1920s, in a series of essays, Kaplan emerged as the American Jewish community's most acute critic of American Jewish life. Despite a burgeoning population that would make America home to the world's largest Jewish community, and the incipient signs of an economic advance that would propel Jews from Hester Street tenements to Scarsdale estates, Kaplan looked with alarm at the community's religious development. Kaplan considered it obvious that if one-half of American Jews did not bother to belong to or attend synagogues, something was wrong organizationally. Kaplan also thought that the doctrines of all three branches of Judaism (e.g., Orthodox, Conservative, and Reform) were unresponsive to discoveries in the world of science, philosophy, sociology, and so forth. While he did not coin the well-known equation Orthodox = crazy, Reform = lazy, Conservative = hazy, Kaplan certainly thought that none of the branches of American Judaism grasped what being Jewish in America in the twentieth century was *really* about.

In a very fine book on Reconstructionist thinking, Rebecca Alpert and Jacob Staub have contrasted "belonging" with "believing" as a crux in Kaplan's ideology.[3] What this means is simply that Jews feel more organically bound to other Jews than they do to any particular set of beliefs or practices. Recognizing that ethnicity and shared immigrant experiences imparted most of the vibrancy to American Jewry, Kaplan urged a frank acceptance of this "social viewpoint." In this way, urged Kaplan, "We will then realize that our problem is not how to maintain beliefs or uphold laws, but how to enable the Jewish people to function as a highly developed social organism and to fulfill the spiritual powers that are latent in it."[4]

In social-scientific language drawn from American philosophers such as Dewey, Peirce, and James, and from secular Jewish thinkers in Eastern Europe such as Shimon Dubnov and Ahad Ha'am, Kaplan emphasized the "peoplehood" of Jewish existence. Every Jewish institution ought to reflect the fact that Jews saw themselves as part of a civilization, not just a religion. Synagogues, for instance, ought to be synagogue-centers that offered a setting for a variety of social activities. Congregations should be more than places of prayer, they should be loci of community (the contemporary *havurot* movement owes much to Kaplan). Zacharias Fraenkel, the grandfather of Conservative Judaism, had reminded Reform leaders in the 1840s that "Judaism is the religion of the Jews"; in other words, it is not just an abstract set of ethical principles. Kaplan now took this a good step further and declared, "Judaism . . . is the sum of everything about the Jewish people." In his first book, *Judaism as a Civilization*, Kaplan sums up this approach nicely:

> Judaism as otherness is thus something far more comprehensive than Jewish religion. It includes that nexus of a history, literature, language, social organization, folk sanctions, standards of conduct, social and spiritual ideals, esthetic values, which in their totality form a civilization.[5]

Kaplan undoubtedly described the nature of Jewish life in America accurately, especially in its second generation on American soil.[6] So it might be asked, Why did Reconstructionism fail to capture the loyalties of most American Jews in Kaplan's lifetime? Why does it remain, even today, at just over one hundred congregations and havurot, the smallest of the four denominations? Kaplan's opposition to Reconstructionism as an independent movement—the Reconstructionist Rabbinical College was founded in 1968—provides part of the answer. Kaplan preferred to influence the denominations from without, to exert a new sensibility without a formalized framework. Conservative and Reform Judaism in particular eventually "domesticated" many things initially advocated by Kaplan. Kaplan, who after all began his career as a modern Orthodox rabbi at Kehillat Jeshurun, also influenced Orthodoxy.

In a probing essay, sociologist Charles Liebman pointed to another reason for the limits on Reconstructionism's success: it was exactly Kaplan's frank and honest approach in focusing on the ethnic folk-religion of American Jews that was unappealing. Liebman writes,

> Most American Jews are not quite willing to admit to this virtue publicly. The entire basis of Jewish accommodation to America, the legitimacy of Jewish separateness, has been that Judaism is a religion, like Catholicism and Protestantism, and that Jews are not merely an ethnic group like the Irish or the Italians.[7]

To put it another way, Jews recognized that the depth of their infra-group loyalty could only be justified, even if inaccurately, in more traditional religious terms than Kaplan was wont to employ.

As a description of Jewish consciousness in the 1950s and 1960s, Liebman's analysis has much to commend it. But even a casual observer can see that the Jewish politics of "What will the gentiles say?" has given way to a more aggressive Jewish stance. In the multicultural America of today, another explanation must be sought for Reconstructionism's rather modest success. This phenomenon, in my opinion, stems mainly from a rejection of Kaplan's religious naturalism or transnaturalism (as opposed to supernaturalism). I have avoided, up to now, explaining why Kaplan stirred up so much controversy, and why his 1945 Sabbath Prayerbook was publicly burnt in a New York hotel room.

Despite the influence of the atheist Ahad Ha'am and despite his own lifelong support of Zionism, at that time an essentially secular enterprise, Kaplan asserted that Judaism is a *religious* civilization. What Kaplan meant by this is that every civilization has its own particular tendencies, its own genius. In the case of Jewish civilization, that genius was religion (for the Greeks, let us say, art; for the Romans, law; for the Irish, literature). Thus, any authentic Jewish civilization ought to be expressed largely (though not exclusively) in religious terms. Since religion is also a universal human need, nothing could be more natural than for a Jew to celebrate her/his blessings, mourn her/his sorrows, mark her/his life-cycle events in the midst of the community of Israel, through the sacred symbols (*sacra*) of traditional Judaism. In a large sense, the practice of any civilization is its own justification.

Kaplan recognized that many Jews, influenced by science's seeming ability to explain the physical universe, no longer believed in a personal God who stands outside that universe and commands it according to his will, or hears the individual prayers of his petitioners. Kaplan knew that many Jews, well-versed in the findings of biblical criticism, no longer believed in the Mosaic (and therefore divinely revealed) origins of the Bible. It should be recalled that Kaplan's intellectual coming of age coincided with the lowest ebb of prestige accorded religion by intellectuals since the French Enlightenment.

(The Scopes Monkey Trial, for instance, commenced in 1925.) One of Kaplan's own childhood teachers, the eccentric Arnold Bogumil Ehrlich, firmly believed that only an understanding of the multiplicity of biblical authors and the lateness of many biblical documents made the text comprehensible.[8] Without a belief in a personal God and without a belief in the direct revelation of the Bible (*torah min ha-shamayim*), what would become of the *sacra* of Jewish practice?

Kaplan's answer was striking and revolutionary. We must consciously revalue the key terms of tradition (God, Commandment, Prayer, Chosenness) in ways that are intellectually acceptable to highly educated, highly modernized Jews. God, for Kaplan, cannot be a person or being in the anthropomorphic sense, but is nevertheless very real *functionally*, that is to say, in the world. God becomes "the power that makes for salvation," the force that guides our self-improvement and our improvement of the world. God, for Kaplan, was more than just an idea. The *mitzvot* are not literally commandments, which would imply a commander, but a means of binding us closer together as a living Jewish community, closer to a sense of identification with a Jewish past, and a means of sanctifying the physical world that we inhabit. Prayer cannot be an individual supplication to a personally involved deity, but becomes "a power in nature that responds to human need, if properly approached." Community prayer, in particular, enables the individual to focus on public, as opposed to private, concerns. This method, which could be called "functional reinterpretation," saves a maximum of Jewish practice for meaningful fulfillment by a Jewish world that shares only a minimum of the traditional premises, or beliefs. Kaplan himself remained highly observant, as do many of his disciples.

Not every Jewish doctrine from the past can be functionally reinterpreted. Chosenness, for Kaplan, proved to be untranslatable in a palatable manner; it was too bound up with an ethnocentric perspective that Kaplan found incompatible with American and democratic values. The opening of the following reading selection from Kaplan cuts through any pretensions to Jewish superiority or "mission" in the following words:

> The Jewish quality of the religion of the Jews will not depend on claims to supernatural origin or claims to be more rational or more ethical than other religions. Its uniqueness will consist chiefly in the fact that it will be lived by Jews, and will be expressed by them through such cultural media as Jewish civilization will produce.[9]

In practice, Kaplan dispensed with expressions of Chosenness in his congregation's services and in all of the liturgical publications under his auspices.

It must have been jarring for congregants to have the traditional Torah blessing "who has chosen us from all the peoples" replaced by "who has drawn us
to his service." Kaplan's logical consistency and the sense of some midcentury Orthodox leaders that Kaplan was a wolf in sheep's clothing, led to the
burning of the 1945 Prayerbook. Kaplan's views invite critique from a traditionalist perspective. Eliezer Schweid, a contemporary Israeli philosopher
writes: "His [Kaplan's] theology preserves the longing for faith and tries with
excessive optimism to describe modern man's longing for transcendent faith
as if it were faith itself." But Kaplan would insist that Schweid misunder-
stands him. "The fact is," Kaplan once told the philosopher Arthur Cohen,
"that there is a third alternative to 'idea' and 'persona'; namely, that God is,
objectively speaking, 'process.' The process is that which in human nature is
experienced as transcendence."[10]

There is another dimension of Schweid's critique, aimed at all "secular" re-
constructions of Jewish values without traditional beliefs, but particularly
those in a highly acculturated setting, that touches Kaplan. Kaplan extolled
the idea of "living in two civilizations." For Kaplan, American Jews should
try to make themselves the heirs to the best of what Jewish and American civilizations had to teach. To Kaplan, this was more than an apologetic statement. While the Jewish and the American could sometimes create a synthesis, sometimes the role of one civilization was to correct the other. Judaism
could offer spiritual correction to the empty quest after material goods; America could reign in Jewish tendencies toward parochialism. For children of immigrants, whose Jewish belonging was unquestioned and whose background
gave them an intimate acquaintance with Jewish folkways, both civilizations
were acquired naturally. But fourth- or fifth-generation American Jews, or
converts to Judaism, clearly do not enjoy that advantage. Schweid contends
that the Jewish ingredients in this recipe will necessarily become lost in the
sauce. Clearly, many contemporary Jews need to acquire their sense of belonging. Whether that can be successfully accomplished remains an ongoing
challenge to American Jewry at large, but a sharper challenge to Reconstructionism with its view of Judaism as a civilization.

Democratic, American, Zionistic, forward-thinking, nonsexist,[11] deeply
committed to the future of Judaism, yet frank about what a modern Jew could
no longer believe with good conscience: these were Kaplan's values. They
seem to be values to which many American Jews subscribe. Thus the question tugs at our sleeves once more: Why aren't most American Jews Recon-
structionists? Perhaps the issue goes beyond the hypocrisy at the heart of
Liebman's analysis, described above. Perhaps, deep down, Jews want to believe in a God that transcends the world, want prayers to be personally addressed, and above all, want to know that belonging to the Jewish people—

whether by descent or by choice—is more than an accident of birth or an act of conversion. Whatever Chosenness means, American Jews are unwilling to dispense with it, just as they are unwilling to dispense with a view of God Kaplan would call supernatural. All in all, in my opinion, most Jews prefer their own spiritual agnosticism to Kaplan's transnatural certainties.

I have chosen a selection from Kaplan's first full-length classic, *Judaism as a Civilization*. Published in 1934 when he was fifty-three, the signs of Kaplan's maturity as a thinker are manifest on every page of the book. Whatever your answers to the following questions and whatever your feelings about Kaplan, I feel obligated to make a closing comment: Mordecai Kaplan was, without doubt, American Jewry's first important creative religious thinker.

QUESTIONS FOR KAPLAN,
"FUNCTIONAL METHOD OF INTERPRETATION"
(FROM *JUDAISM AS A CIVILIZATION*, 385–405)

The very title of Kaplan's work (*Judaism as a Civilization*) points to an original dimension in his thought. Why would anyone disagree with a presentation of Judaism as a "civilization"?

John Dewey's pragmatism was a major influence on Kaplan. Can you see how Kaplan applies Dewey to religion in general, and Judaism in particular?

Kaplan describes a "Historical School." What does Kaplan mean by this, and what are the two shortcomings of the Historical School, in his opinion?

Of the three denominations that existed in American Judaism in 1934 (Orthodox, Conservative, and Reform), where does this Historical School most naturally fit?

Has every age developed Judaism as decisively as Kaplan contends? Or, have modern Jews experienced a sea-change from all previous Judaisms?

Kaplan writes, "Revaluation of spiritual values is the conservation of spiritual energy." What does Kaplan mean by the term *revaluation*? Would it make any difference if the term were *reevaluation*? (A colleague of mine, a moderate Kaplanian, insists that *reevaluation* better captures Kaplan's ideas; I disagree.)

What is the difference between the revaluation that Kaplan counsels as appropriate for contemporary Jewry, and *transvaluation*, the term Kaplan would later employ to describe the preferred mechanism of change in Jewish ages past?

Kaplan contends that even if the transition from biblical to rabbinic Judaism was as radical as the transition from premodern to modern Judaism, objectively speaking, our contemporary, subjective, conscious awareness of religious change necessitates a new method (i.e., revaluation) from prior ages. Do you agree? Do you think the subjective factor is really so important?

When Kaplan discusses the permeation of Jewish civilization with the God-idea, what does he mean by permeation? And most of all, by the God-idea? Is the God-idea different from God? How?

Kaplan calls for the disengaging of the "psychological aspect" from "traditional lore and custom." What difficulties are inherent in that attempt?

Why does Jewish civilization need the God-idea for its very survival? How does this serve as a conservative force in Reconstructionism?

What is "the functional method of interpretation"?

Both utter rationalists and strident fundamentalists find Kaplan's "functional method of interpretation" objectionable. How and why would each group reject Kaplan? How would he respond?

STUDIES BY AND ABOUT KAPLAN

Kaplan was a prolific diarist, the first volume of his ten-thousand-page journal has been edited and published by Mel Scult, *Communings of the Spirit: The Journals of Mordecai M. Kaplan 1913–1934* (Detroit, Mich.: Wayne State University Press, 2001). Scult's biography, *Judaism Faces the Twentieth Century: A Biography of Mordecai Kaplan* (Detroit, Mich.: Wayne State University Press, 1993), promises to be the standard work for a long time. Kaplan fans can only hope that Scult will bring the diary and biography past 1934. Kaplan's essay "The Way I Have Come" is as close as he gets to autobiography. *The American Judaism of Mordecai Kaplan,* ed. E. Goldstein, M. Scult, and R. Seltzer (New York: New York University Press, 1990) contains some stellar analytical essays and offers many insights into Kaplan's personality. J. J. Schacter and Jeffrey Gurock have edited some wonderful essays on Kaplan's impact on American Orthodoxy, *A Modern Heretic and a Traditional Community* (New York: Columbia University Press, 1997). Rebecca Alpert and Jacob J. Staub ably present Reconstructionism today in *Exploring Judaism: A Reconstructionist Approach,* 2nd ed. (Elkins Park, Pa.: Reconstructionist Press, 2000).

From *Judaism as a Civilization*

Mordecai Kaplan

Chapter XXVI

The Functional Method of Interpretation

Reinterpretation—A means of eliciting latent values—The achievements and shortcomings of the historical school—The functional method of interpretation as a means of maintaining the continuity of the Jewish religion—The God-idea in the problem of reinterpretation—The variable God-idea in Jewish history— The emotional and conative aspects of the God-idea—Moral progress as reflected in the God-idea—What is implied in the revaluation of God-idea—The functional interpretation of the divine attributes—The functional interpretation of other-worldliness—Resistance to reinterpretation to be expected.

The Jewish quality of the religion of the Jews will not depend on claims to supernatural origin or claims to being more rational or more ethical than other religions. Its uniqueness will consist chiefly in the fact that it will be lived by Jews, and will be expressed by them through such cultural media as Jewish civilization will produce. But even before these media are cultivated on a scale commensurate with present spiritual needs, the religion lived by Jews can be given character and individuality by utilizing the vast storehouse of spiritual values that are implicit in its traditions. If the recorded experiences of Jewish prophet and sage, poet and saint will occupy a predominant place in the Jewish consciousness as it strives to adjust itself to life, the resulting adjustment will constitute Jewish religious behavior. The individuality of the Jewish religion cannot be described in advance. Only after a Jewish life or civilization is attained will there emerge a type of religion as unique as that which emerged from the Jewish civilization of the past.

Individuality is at first spontaneous and unshaped, says John Dewey. It is a potentiality, a capacity of development. . . . Since individuality is a distinctive way of feeling the impacts of the world and of showing a preferential bias in response to these impacts, it develops into shape and form only through interaction with actual conditions. . . . The imposition of individuality as something made in advance always gives evidence of a mannerism, not of a manner. For the latter is something original and creative; something formed in the very process of creation.

If the traditional Jewish religion is inherently capable of engendering the most significant human attributes—faith, hope, courage—if it can lead to social control and improvement and to the development of personality in the individual, it should be capable of revaluation in terms of present-day thought. Whereas in the past the theurgic element of the traditional values often eclipsed the ethical and spiritual consequences, now it will be necessary to stress the ethical and spiritual consequences to such an extent as to make evident their independence of the theurgic element. It may be asked: but why start out with traditional concepts, and then subject yourself to the arduous task of revaluation? Why not begin with utterly new standards and values? The answer is that the tendency to reinterpret derives from the basic human need of feeling that there is some objective truth to the course which human history has taken. If all that man achieved of culture and religion should turn out to be illusory, what meaning can human life have, as a whole? On the other hand, if we can discover some element of continuity between that which we find to be helpful to human life and development and that which was cherished by the ancients, we are fortified in our hopes and aspirations. *The advantage of utilizing traditional concepts is that they carry with them the accumulated momentum and emotional drive of man's previous efforts to attain greater spiritual power.*

To derive that advantage, it is necessary to develop a method of discovering in traditional Jewish religion adumbrations of what we consider an adequate spiritual adjustment to life. We must evolve a method of interpretation which, though it regard the traditional religious teachings and institutions as a product of social life, reflecting the limitations of the various periods of their origin, will yet discover to what extent those teachings and institutions made for faith, salvation and loyalty. By this means the pragmatic implications of the traditional teachings will be revealed and developed. Thus the forgotten mood of a people's civilization can be recaptured and given "a spiritual contemporaneousness."

That method is now being evolved. The principle underlying the work of the Historical School is that Judaism is not a static congeries of beliefs and practices definitely fixed for all time and handed down intact from generation to generation. The Historical School assumes that Judaism represents the changing cultural and spiritual life of a people subject to the vicissitudes of time and place. It expected to put new life into Judaism by interpreting it as a series of social phenomena subject to the natural laws of change that operate in the universe. The Historical School has not treated Judaism, especially since the biblical period, as a supramundane revelation somehow vouchsafed to a single people chosen for that purpose, but as a continual development of a living people adjusting itself to its environment and adjusting the environment to itself. Viewing Judaism as a dynamic process prepares the way for the synthesis of the Jewish social heritage with the best in the civilizations of our day, a synthesis so essential to the spiritual normality of the Jew.

However, the historical method of interpretation, as developed and applied up to now, has fallen short in two respects. In the first place, it has been too limited in its scope. The Historical School has subjected to its method of interpretation the material of the rabbinic period in Judaism, but has contributed little to the study of the Scriptures in the light of scientific research. With the characteristic inconsistency of the Historical School, Henry Malter wrote: "Our religion restrains us from any criticism of the Bible because *torah min ha-shamayim* is one of the main principles of the doctrine of Judaism. No such prohibition exists against criticism of the Talmud. The Bible is the word of God; the Talmud is the work of men, no matter how great or glorious." We can, of course, understand why it has refrained from submitting the Bible to its method of investigation. The Bible has been the Jews' "Holy of Holies." To subject it to scientific analysis before the greater part of Jewry sensed the actuality of the living spirit of the Jewish people would have been to deprive the Jew of his spiritual mainstay. Rabbinic Judaism, the traditional religion of the Jewish people, is popularly regarded as derived from, and dependent for its validity upon, the written word of the Torah. So long as this idea prevails, any attempt to study the Bible from the historical point of view will be considered a blow at the very vitals of Jewish religion. But that reason is no longer valid. The negative implications of biblical criticism have percolated to the general mind, and unless they are countered by a positive intellectual readjustment, they are bound to render the Jewish religion even more inoperative than it is already.

Secondly, the Historical School has fallen short in having failed to reckon with the fact that *the significance of an idea or an institution is to be sought not only in its overt expression but also in its implications.* These implications need not necessarily have been recognized by those who first voiced the idea or evolved the institution. It is only in retrospect as we review the consequences in thought and action of any tradition that we begin to sense its full significance. To identify those consequences which are essential to a comprehension of the larger significance of a traditional belief or custom, it is necessary to approach that belief or custom from the psychological point of view. Had the Historical School utilized that approach in its study of traditional Judaism, it would have inaugurated the spiritual readjustment so essential to Jewish life. It would not merely have piled up archeological data, but would have revealed the elements in Judaism which are of permanent value. It would have brought back to the Jew the spirit that groped after self-expression in the traditional teaching and the aspiration that animated the ritual observance. "It must be admitted," writes I. Elbogen, in his survey of the achievements of the *Jüdische Wissenschaft*, which is the creation of the Historical School, "that the *Jüdische Wissenschaft* made but little effort, when it was in the heyday of its career, to formulate a new world-outlook for Judaism."

The Jewish religion must be so reinterpreted that it will be able to further the values which have become the conscious objects of all higher human striving. These values are the product not only of any single religious philosophy, or ethical tendency, but of the various social and intellectual forces that have entered into the shaping of modern civilization. In reinterpreting the traditional values of any spiritual heritage or civilization, we are conserving accumulated energy that would otherwise go to waste. *Revaluation of spiritual values is the conservation of spiritual energy.* It helps to conserve and foster all tendencies, individual and social, which make for the complete development of the individual and the progressive unification of mankind.

The ideas expressed in the ancient Jewish literature, and the institutions that have become identified with Jewish life, should be regarded as attempts to express in terms of beliefs and practices the needs and desiderata of a fuller life than man had been able to attain. What these needs and desiderata were, can be discerned in some of the consequences in thought and action which resulted from those ideas and institutions. The task of reinterpretation consists first in selecting from among the ideational and practical consequences of the traditional values those which are spiritually significant for our day, and then in turning those consequences into motives of thought and conduct. Functional interpretation, therefore, implies a knowledge of the background of the teaching or institution interpreted, of the various contexts in which that teaching or institution occurs, and most of all a knowledge of human nature as it functions in society and in the individual. Reinterpretation is the process of finding equivalents in the civilization to which we belong for values of a past stage of that or another civilization. While there is a qualitative difference between such values, yet in their relation to their respective civilizations or, considered morphologically, they possess equivalence.

Assuming that there has taken place no qualitative change in human nature during the last two or three millennia, we may take for granted that whatever objectives we now accept as worthy and desirable have been anticipated by some of the avowed objectives of the past. For modern ideals to be without ancestry would imply that human nature has altered radically in the past hundred years or so. If we search diligently, we shall find that traditional aspirations are pregnant with implications that are highly significant for our day.

It must be remembered that we are not dealing with questions of fact. To interpret the past functionally does not mean to follow in the footsteps of the traditional harmonizers who tried to prove that the Scriptures had anticipated every recently discovered scientific fact. Functional reinterpretation is concerned with man's yearning to find himself in a universe that is friendly to his highest purpose, to fulfill the most valued potentialities of his nature and to achieve a social order that is founded on justice and peace. These yearnings are as constant as human nature. If it is our purpose to continue any particular spiritual heritage, we can do so by reconstructing mentally the aspirations implied in its teachings and institutions. Every tradition is rich in these aspirations, for it could not have become a tradition without them. By rendering these implications explicit, we supply momentum to all social and spiritual endeavors which have as their aim the unhampered and complete self-fulfillment of the individual and the increasing measure of cooperation among individuals and groups.

This type of interpretation consists chiefly in disengaging from the mass of traditional lore and custom the psychological aspect which testifies to the presence of ethical and spiritual strivings. The effect of discovering the psychological element in a tradition is that the tradition ceases to be regarded as something to be accepted or rejected. A third alternative presents itself, that of employing it as a symbol for a spiritual desideratum in the present. Which desideratum it shall be can best be determined by choosing from among the implications and consequences of the tradition the one relevant for our day.

How necessary it is to apply this type of interpretation to the contents of the Jewish past can best be appreciated, perhaps, when we realize that the values which have been incorporated into other civilizations have been only those of the first two stages of the Jewish civilization. The prophetic ideals evolved during the period of the First Commonwealth, and the messianic ideals crystallized during the period of the Second Commonwealth, have become the common possession of mankind. But the same cannot be said of Talmudism, or of medieval Jewish philosophy and poetry. So far the only one who has hinted at a value of universal significance to be derived from the last twenty centuries of Jewish suffering and striving has been Shimon Dubnov. He regards the ideal of steadfastness to a cause and the capacity for martyrdom as the universal value which emerges from the third stage of Judaism's history. But even that value is scarcely apparent to the average person of today to whom the greater part of the literary content produced by Judaism during its third stage seems, in its uninterpreted form, completely irrelevant to his own spiritual needs. It is only by means of the functional method of interpretation that all the life and thought that have gone into Judaism since the destruction of the Second Temple can be so rendered that the particularistic and national mode in which they are cast will become transparent enough to permit the universalistic and human to shine through. This has to some extent been attempted by Moritz Lazarus in his *Jewish Ethics* and Hermann Cohen in his *Die Religion der Vernunft*. But while they both succeed in idealizing many of the leading religious and ethical ideas in Judaism, their deductions suffer largely from the absence of historical perspective. They read much more into, than out of, the statements they interpret.

Nothing about the Jewish civilization of the past is so conspicuous as its permeation with the God-idea. Physical phenomena, historical events and moral duties acquire their significance from their relationship to God. As handed down, the conception of God which is the *leitmotif* of the Jewish civilization is theurgic in character; that is, it implies divine interference with the continuity of nature for the sake of man. To some people the elimination of the theurgic element from the God-idea is equivalent to the abandonment of the belief in God, and an act which must lead to the disintegration of the Jewish social heritage. If we approach the Jewish civilization with the purpose of understanding its psychological—not its logical—reality, its conception of God should interest us not for what it seeks to tell concerning the metaphysical nature of the Deity, but for the difference it made in the behavior of the Jew. We should analyze the Jewish conception of God in order to learn how it functioned in the life of the Jewish people. If it in any way made for that justice which spells the fullest possible opportunity for the individual to give play to his highest intellectual and spiritual powers, and for that love which spells the growing capacity to make our common humanity the basis of co-operation, it should be capable of revaluation in terms of present-day thought.

To understand how it is possible for a God-idea to undergo change without producing a break in the continuity of the civilization to which it belongs, we must realize that it does not function by itself, but through that pattern of emotional, volitional and ideational reactions which may be described as religious behavior. Before considering, however, the God-idea in the process of operation with the other elements of religious behavior, it is necessary to note that the human mind has evolved two different types of God-ideas: one consists of both percepts and concepts; the other, much rarer type, consists of concepts only. In the religion of primitive peoples, the God-idea is of the first type for, despite the conceptual ramifications it may later acquire, its fundamental content is always some real or imaginary entity, some object or identifiable being. The primitive man was able to conceive everything, animate or inanimate, as informed with divine qualities. The focal object of his religious behavior might be any being or thing in the heavens above, the earth beneath, or the waters beneath the earth. Only at a comparatively late stage of civilization does the worship of other than the human form come to be abhorred. When this happens, the God-idea already consists to a marked degree of concepts.

Even in the most primitive religions, the God-idea is never altogether free from conceptual thinking, since the object or being regarded as divine is *ipso facto* conceived as endowed with the qualities of power and purposiveness. If purposiveness be the essential characteristic of personality, then we may say that together with the percept which entered into the God-idea—with the focal object of that idea—more or less vague conceptions of power and personality were always present.

Thus far the God-idea as a synthesis of perceptual image and conceptual abstraction. When philosophy invaded the field of religion, all mental representations of God were considered inconsistent with ideal religious behavior. No form, whether that of object or of human being, was deemed compatible with the God-idea. For the more speculatively minded, the perceptual element had to be banished altogether from the God-idea. The God-idea was now an abstraction distilled out of the conceptions of power and personality which had always accompanied the perceptual elements in the God-idea. *The qualities of perfection and infinity which the philosophers ascribed to God were not additional qualities superimposed upon the traditional concepts of power and personality, but were simply the extension, in thought, of those qualities.*

The main contribution of philosophy to religion has thus consisted of a change not merely in the focal object of religious behavior, but in the *type* of focal object. In unphilosophic religion the focal object of religious behavior was always an identifiable being either real or imaginary. In philosophic religion the focal object was treated as far too different from reality as conceived by the human mind to be accounted an entity or identifiable being in the same sense as any known or imagined entity. This gave rise to the tendency in premodern philosophy to define the nature of God negatively rather than affirmatively. When it was said, for example, that there was only one God, the philosophers added, "But there is no unity like unto his unity." Likewise every one of the other attributes ascribed to God was interpreted in terms of what God was not. The tendency of philosophic religion in modern times is to be even more emphatic than it was in the Middle Ages in deprecating any identifiable being as the focal object of religious behavior. Nevertheless, modern philosophic religion is more inclined than medieval to define the focal object of religion in affirmative fashion by identifying God with some aspect of reality, or with reality as a whole, viewed from some particular standpoint. It does not hesitate for example, to identify God as the *life* of the universe, or as the *meaning* of reality.

When we trace the history of the religious behavior of the Jewish people, we find that the God-idea which was the source of that behavior varied with the different stages of its civilization. We know that after the Israelites established themselves in Canaan they worshipped YHWH in the image of a bull. What psychological factors contributed to the attitude of derision and abhorrence which developed against that image in Israel it is difficult to discover. It is possible that what contributed most to the elimination of bull worship was the sacred ark which the Israelites had brought with them from the wilderness. But whatever percept the earlier Israelites had of YHWH, there can be no doubt that for the Prophets, YHWH was essentially an anthropomorphic being. Some prophets, like Ezekiel, may have had a distinct mental image of YHWH, while others, like Isaiah, pictured his form in vague outline.

When the Jewish religion came into contact with philosophic thought as it did in the case of the Alexandrian school, and later in the Middle Ages beginning with the period of the Geonim, it had completely emancipated itself from the need of any perceptual image of God. In fact, the Jewish philosophers not only treated the perceptual image of God as dispensable, but they very emphatically condemned it as on a par with idolatry. Despite the insistence of the philosophers, however, upon a purely conceptual representation of God, and the expression of that insistence in the formal creed of Maimonides, the vast majority of the Jewish people have not been seriously troubled about the philosophic objections to conceiving God as a magnified being. In fact, the uncompromising tendency of Maimonides and his successors to declare any but a purely conceptual idea of God heretical called forth opposition on the part of the unphilosophic Talmudists.

To this day, there is no intellectually formulated conception which has required authoritative recognition in Judaism as the only true idea of God. The inevitable conclusion to which we are led by the consideration of the evolution of the God-idea in the history of the Jewish people, and of the part played by it in civilization in general, is that *the Jewish civilization cannot survive without the God-idea as an integral part of it, but it is in no need of having any specific formulation of that idea authoritative for all Jews.*

The foregoing refers to God only as the focal object, or object of reference, in the pattern of reactions, which in their totality constitute the religious behavior of the Jew. To get the full significance of that behavior, and to appreciate the nature of its functioning, we have to consider also its emotional and conative aspects.

The emotional phase of religious behavior is compounded of the emotions of awe and trust which are the principal ingredients of the sense of holiness. There is, however, a marked difference between the cognitive and the emotional aspects of religious behavior in the degree to which they are affected by cultural development. The cognitive element, as we have seen, may vary from the crudest percept with a minimum of concept, to the most abstract concept with a complete negation of percept; the emotional phase, however, is the same in the most diverse forms of religious behavior. Whether the negative element of fear or the positive element of confidence predominate in the compound, emotion is not a matter of progressive development, but rather the result of individual temperament, or of the outward circumstances which are at times depressing and at times exhilarating. A savage will manifest the same intense religious emotions as the most highly cultivated person. It is evident, then, that the emotional phase in Jewish religious behavior would in no respect be different from the manifestation of that phase in the religious behavior of any other people.

It is chiefly the conative aspect of a people's religion that reveals its distinctive element. This aspect of a religion finds expression in the activities and restraints which are exercised with reference to objects or situations of vital interest to the adherents of that religion. What is of vital interest depends upon the state of cultural development. Under primitive conditions, only those objects and situations which appeal directly to the elementary needs of human nature excite interest. Food, mating and the maintenance of life and well-being are the only interests of savage society. Objects and situations which are directly connected with these ends and which excite interest simultaneously in a number of people evoke communal activities and restraints. In turn these activities and restraints focus further attention upon the objects and situations and bring them to the fore of consciousness. These latter thus become the main sources of the percepts and concepts that are projected into the focal object, or object of reference, in religious behavior; that is, into the object or being which is identified as a god.

As soon as man emerges from the savage state, he tends to develop derivative interests. As William James puts it, "Things not interesting in their own right borrow an interest which becomes as real and as strong as that of any natively interesting thing." The only things interesting in their own right are those which have to do with the satisfaction of the elementary needs. But the activities and restraints connected with objects and situations which are interesting in their own right acquire a derived interest that may attain an intensity not only equal to, but sometimes even greater than some of the elementary interests. *The cultivation of derivative interests is the chief function of a civilization.* If they retain their connection with the basic wants of human nature, they can with advantage serve as the norm of human living. Such a norm constitutes part of the higher life and makes for greater abundance of well-being. When man's elementary needs are stifled or even neglected through overemphasis upon derivative or spiritual interests, religion revenges itself by becoming either ascetic and dehumanized, or romantic and voluptuary.

The pragmatic significance of religious behavior turns upon the nature of the activities and the restraints through which it expresses itself. The pragmatic consequences of any religious idea—the conception of God, the conception of the messiah, or any similar idea—need not be the object of conscious recognition or reflection. If those activities and restraints refer merely to elementary needs, we have a very low type of religious behavior. That is the type of religion whose deities were the concrete and externalized expression of man's elementary needs—they were the gods of rain, of fertility, of war. As soon as these activities and restraints refer to interests which even for a time eclipse the elementary ones with which they are connected, there result two important consequences: first, the activities and restraints are modified to conform with the more developed social and ethical needs that arise; second, the God-idea is made to reflect the modified or more ethical nature of the activities and restraints.

Evidences of this development are discernible in the religions of Babylon, Egypt, Greece and Rome. The social and ethical standards that gave rise to their changing legal codes could not but modify their conception of the deity that was the focal object of the religious behavior. *But in the case of no people did the activities and restraints which constituted religious behavior undergo such a revolutionary change, and bring about so radical a transformation in the conception of the focal object of religious behavior, as in that of Israel.*

This radical transformation of religious behavior was attempted by the Prophets. As a result of their activity, the ethical element in the priestly *torot* was stressed, and God came to be conceived as creator of the universe, and sovereign of all mankind. The unity attributed to God in the Jewish religion has altogether different implications from the unity attributed to God by the Greek philosophers. The *conation* accompanying the concept of the unity of God in Jewish religious behavior consists in treating mankind as one, whereas no such pragmatic consequence is implied in the philosophic conception of divine unity. Though the reconstruction of the religion of Israel, which took place after the return from Babylon, did not altogether reap the fruits of the prophetic revaluation, enough of the prophetic impulse remained to affect Jewish religious behavior ever after. The prophetic inspiration suffused with a sense of high worth or holiness those activities and restraints which made for the holiness of life, for the fostering of human personality, and for the unification of society.

The revaluation of the traditional Jewish religion will be possible, therefore, only if we recognize that its significance does not derive from the cognitive element of its God-idea, but from the *conduct* in which that idea has found expression. Jewish religious behavior requires *an* idea of God, but were it contingent upon a particular idea of God, the continuity of the religious heritage would be broken. Since, however, the Jewish civilization succeeded in retaining its own continuity and that of its religion, despite the changes in the God-idea, it has proved itself exempt from the necessity of commitment to one authoritative conception of God. But though the Jewish civilization is not tied down to the God-idea of the *Tannaim*, the *Amoraim*, or of the Jewish philosophers of the Middle Ages, it cannot afford to become secular and omit the God-idea altogether. The only alternative is to reinterpret the God-idea in such a way as to allow for the differences in intellectual outlook. For some people only perceptual or demonstrable things are real, and of supreme importance. The focal object of their religious behavior might then be some anthropomorphic being. *There is nothing in Judaism viewed as a civilization to preclude an anthropomorphic or any other God-idea, provided its emotional and conative expression in religious behavior make for what are now recognized as the highest ends of human aspiration.* But most rational people today cannot bring an anthropomorphic God-idea to the necessary emotional and conative expression. They prefer to identify God with that aspect of reality which elicits the most serviceable human traits, the traits that enhance individual human worth and further social unity. Since those traits constitute what we value most in human personality, it may be said that the modern thinker tends to base his conception of God upon the cosmic implications of human personality.

It is interesting to note how the foregoing analysis of religious behavior throws light upon the three types of spiritual leaders that the human race has produced—the prophet, the philosopher and the mystic. Whereas the function of the priest has been to maintain the *status quo* of spiritual attainment, the prophet, the philosopher and the mystic have contributed, each in his own way, to the development of moral and spiritual values. The prophets have always concentrated their efforts upon the conative expression; the philosophers upon the cognitive aspect, and the mystics upon the emotional. Whenever an upheaval in social and cultural life makes the traditional religion inoperative, it is necessary for the prophetic type of activity to assert itself in the conative expression of the spiritual life in order to bring about a readjustment in the moral and social standards. The philosopher and the mystic then follow with their activity, and consolidate in intellectual and emotional terms the result of the change that is effected in individual conduct and social institutions.

Only pedantic literalists would insist that the God-idea can have meaning only in religion based on the acceptance of supernaturalism and other-worldliness. They forget that we are so constituted that we have to keep on using old words and operate with traditional ideas, though with each generation experience is enriched, and the language in which that experience is expressed necessarily acquires new meaning. This is especially true in the case of terms which designate the distillation of social experience. Take, for example, words like justice, liberty, education. At one time, gruesome punishment meted out in a spirit of revenge was the prevalent idea of justice, and the ideal of liberty was so conceived as to be compatible with the institution of slavery. What was once considered education would now pass for learned ignorance. Would it ever occur to us to adopt some other method of designating one's ego than by the use of the personal pronoun, "I," because our conception of the entity denoted by it has been completely revolutionized?

Words, like institutions, like life itself, are subject to the law of identity in change. It is entirely appropriate, therefore, to retain the greater part of the ancient religious vocabulary, particularly the term "God." As long as we are struggling to express the same fundamental fact about the cosmos that our ancestors designated by the term "God," the fact of its momentousness or holiness, and are endeavoring to achieve the ideals of human life which derive from that momentousness or holiness, we have a right to retain their mode of expression.

> In attempting to deal with living emotions, says John Cowper Powys, with those nameless subjective feelings which underlie such historic words, it seems wiser to direct the introspective mind toward each particular feeling rather by means of the older symbols than by means of the newer ones, just because these traditional names—'will,' 'soul,' 'universe,' 'nature,' 'ego,' and so forth—have by long use on the high roads of human intercourse acquired such a rich thick emotional connotation that, however mythological they may be, they are more suggestive of what lies behind all words than the newer, more logical terms, coined by clever modern thinkers, so puzzlingly obscure except to the initiated, and of necessity so abstract and thin.

One wonders what inhibited the author from adding just one more term, "God."

The reinterpretation of the traditional religious values and concepts is resisted by the enemies of religion as vigorously as by the reactionaries and fundamentalists. This resistance of the so-called rationalists is motivated by an animus hardly compatible with rationalism. It is difficult to understand why religion should not be accorded the same right of revising and correcting itself as science and philosophy. We need only recall the crude guesses that went by the names of science and philosophy in olden times to realize that it is not the results attained that constitute the identity of an intellectual or spiritual discipline, but the impulse behind them. Religion conceived in terms of supernatural origin is the astrology and alchemy stage of religion. The religion which is about to emerge is the astronomy and chemistry stage of religion. Instead of resorting to belief in miracles, theophanies and external authority as the sanction for its teachings, religion will, henceforth, resort to the study of the needs of human nature which have found their satisfaction in the complex of beliefs, practices and emotions that center about the idea of God. Those needs form the common denominator between the religion of the past and the religion of the future.

Once we have learned to reinterpret the God-idea in terms of function, there is no difficulty in applying the same method of reinterpretation to the *attributes* that traditional religion has associated with God. Our chief interest is in the attributes which form part of the religious, and not necessarily of the philosophic consciousness. The attributes of God which were formulated by the Jewish philosophers of the Middle Ages are reinterpretations of the religious conceptions of God in terms of specific systems of thought. Thus the attributes of absoluteness, infinity and incorporeality do not represent original elements in the God-idea of Judaism. They served the purpose of establishing a certain functional identity between the God-idea of Scriptures and that of the philosophies current in the past. Our task is with the qualities ascribed to God in the sacred writings and prayers of the Jewish people, where God is conceived as creator, helper, king, lawgiver.

Much of the wisdom and aspiration of our ancestors is lost upon us because we no longer speak their language, though we may speak to the same purpose. The effort to recover the permanent values inherent in traditional religion is handicapped by the lack of imagination. An inflexible mentality takes every word in texts of ancient origin literally and ignores the *nisus* which created the word. If we disengage from the language of adoration the spiritual desiderata implied therein, we discover that the attributes ascribed to God represented the social and spiritual values formerly regarded as all-important. Those attributes are by no means limited in their meaning and application to the theurgic conception of God.

Just as the God-idea progressed from a perceptual image to a conception like the one which identifies God as the sum of all those factors and relationships in the universe that make for unity, creativity and worthwhileness in human life, so can the attributes of God, which once were externalized and concrete, be translated into modern terms and made relevant to modern thinking and living. Men attributed to God their own highest desires and aspirations. They called him creator, protector, helper, sovereign and redeemer. These terms can now be identified with the highest and most significant aims of human existence, and achieve a new force and vitality through this conscious process of identification. We can no longer believe that God is a mighty sovereign, or that the universe is the work of his hands. In the light of the present development of the God-idea, however, we can see that God is manifest in all creativity and in all forms of sovereignty that make for the enhancement of human life.

Let us take, for example, the attribute of God as creator. Were we to approach it from the standpoint of medieval metaphysics, we would at once involve ourselves in the complicated problem of *creatio ex nihilo*, and land in a philosophic *cul de sac*. If we proceed by the functional method of interpretation, we can discern in the belief that God created the world as an expression of the tendency to identify the creative principle in the world with the manifestation of God. This approach to the problem of creation is in keeping with the trend of modern religious metaphysics. In a sense, it is the very antithesis of the approach of traditional theology, yet, emotionally and volitionally, we can deduce the same practical and socially valuable results from the one approach as from the other—from the conception of *God as the creative principle* of the universe as was derived in the past from the conception of *God as the creator* of the universe. For the creative principle is compatible in human life only with intelligence, courage and good-will, and is hindered in its operation by arrogance, greed and uncontrolled sexual desire.

God as helper and protector may be identified with the powers of nature which maintain life, and with the intelligence that transforms the environment by subjugating and controlling the natural forces for the common good of humanity. In any act of social cooperation and good-will, in the striving for finer human relations, in man's courage and moral resilience, in his conquest of fear and death, we can discern the operation of the divine principle—God made manifest. Likewise, whenever we experience a sense of stability and permanence in the midst of the universal flux, we experience the reality of God as helper.

The attributes of God as redeemer and sovereign can also be translated into terms of contemporary needs. According to tradition, when God revealed himself to Israel at Sinai, he made himself known not as the creator of heaven and earth, nor as the sovereign of mankind, but as the redeemer of Israel. In terms of the present world-outlook, man's desire for freedom, his struggles to attain it, reveal the striving of the divine in man. The cosmic life urge is displayed in restiveness under restraint. When the life urge becomes self-aware in man's efforts to shake off intolerable restraint, God as redeemer is manifest.

The sovereignty of God denotes the primacy of spiritual values in human life. That God is sovereign means that those aims, standards and interests which center about the belief in God are ends to which all other aims, standards and interests are subordinate as means. Thus for the individual so to strive after wealth that it becomes to him the standard of all values, is a denial of the sovereignty of God. So are the attainment of power for its own sake and the subservience to power, regardless of the manner in which it was acquired or the purpose to which it is applied. In domestic life, the primacy of the spiritual values means placing love and the spirit of sacrifice above any selfish purpose. In economic life, the primacy of the spiritual means realizing that men count more than things, that production is not an end in itself. In national life, from the standpoint of internal relations, the primacy of the spiritual values implies aiming toward creation of opportunities for the many rather than maintaining privileges for the few; from the standpoint of external relations, it implies that international dealings be motivated by a desire for peace and cooperation rather than for war and domination.

The difficulty in effecting the transition between the last stage of traditional religion and the religion of the future lies in the changed emphasis from other-worldly to this-worldly life. In traditional religion, the sense of at-homeness in the world, the fulfillment of personality and group loyalty were bound up with the belief that the present world was destined to give way to a new heaven and a new earth. Only by believing that this world would be super-seded by another did man reconcile himself to life on earth; only the ultimate liberation of the soul from earthly needs rendered this life worthwhile; only that group which helped secure one a share in the world to come was gen-uinely significant. If we acquire the habit of viewing the traditional belief in the world to come, not from the standpoint of objective truth, but from that of its functional aspect, we can easily discern in it a meaning for our day. Inter-preted functionally, the traditional conception of the world to come expresses man's discontent with the things as they are and his yearning for the things as they ought to be. From this viewpoint, the important element in this belief is not the fantastic picture of the ideal world, but the inner urge of which it was an expression; namely, the compulsion to look forward to a condition of hu-man existence which would be free from the physical, spiritual and social ills that detract from life's worthwhileness. In former times, man was not famil-iar enough with the processes of nature to realize that he himself could effect the desired transformation. Not having observed nature with sufficient care to note its uniformities and plasticities, he was unable to conceive how the ideal world could rise out of the actual world. *The human mind will have to un-dergo considerable development before it will learn to treat its own initiative in bringing about a better world as part of the process whereby God is actu-alizing the world to come.*

With all their wisdom and insight the ancients did not arrive at the truth which has been distilled out of the sufferings of the human race, the truth that the kingdom of God is a paradox, an inner contradiction that must somehow be resolved. For ages men have put their faith in conformity and obedience to authority. In the eighteenth century, a reaction set in and men began to look upon the absolute freedom of the individual as the chief end. Ever since then, the pendulum of human life has been swinging between extremes of despotism and anarchism. But so far no serious attempt has been made to discover a method whereby men might act both interdependently and independently, and achieve the world to come through a harmonious interplay of individualism and collectivism.

The world to come is none other than this world redeemed from slavery and war, from want and suffering, from disease and crime. Bitter experience has made humankind realize that only by reckoning with the polarity of human nature will it be possible to achieve the better world-order, the world to come. Every human being is both an *ego* and an *alter*, a self and an other. The *ego* or the self hungers for the satisfactions that yield individuality and selfhood. The *alter*, or other, yearns for absorption in a larger self, in an enveloping permanence and order and meaning. This polarity is an inescapable part of the nature of things. Human life is most complete when it reckons with its double aspect. Then it approximates a mode of life which is in accord with the law of God as writ in the nature of man. In an ideally ordered world these two tendencies of human nature would find fulfillment.

All forms of the spiritual life are an organization and synthesis of conflicting tendencies and impulses in human nature, and the spiritually ordered world must provide for the realization of such a synthesis. For synthesis it must be. We cannot fulfill the two impulses alternately; we cannot first cooperate and then be free, and imagine that we have achieved the desideratum. In that case, freedom and unity would in the end destroy each other as they have always done. We must so order the world that the two impulses of human may find complete expression in one and the same effort, in one and the same practical manifestation of our desire to establish the kingdom of God. The adjustment between individuals, classes and nations should be guided by this consideration. Good government depends upon the recognition of this functional principle. For only in a social order based on peace can the two impulses be expressed and synthesized.

Some will always assume a deprecatory attitude toward the attempt to reinterpret the Jewish values from a modern, functional standpoint on the ground that Jewish religion would attain a form that its Jewish forebears would not recognize. They argue that, since our aim is to maintain the continuity of Judaism, we are defeating that aim when we impose modern categories of thought upon literature and institutions of Judaism. A basic error in approach is at the root of this contention. It proceeds from the assumption that those who are to determine whether or not the continuity of a culture is maintained are its founders or initiators, and not its spokesmen in the generations following. Those who make that assumption, therefore, believe that since the founders are no longer alive when the problem of continuity arises, we must be possessed by their spirit and act as their proxies in deciding whether the adaptation of the culture to the exigencies of the times preserves the identity of the culture or not. This is essentially the point of view of all the orthodoxies that have acted as a dead-weight upon human progress. The only ones to decide whether the continuity of a culture is maintained are those who are actually confronted with the problem. *The past or its proxies can no more pass judgment upon the present than the child can sit in judgment upon the man.*

Suppose we were to apply the orthodox criterion to the spiritual life of the Jewish people during the last three thousand years. Can we, for instance, assert that a Samuel or a David would have recognized in the Judaism of a Raba or an Abbaye, *Amoraim* of the fourth century, their own beliefs and practices? It is true that the *Amoraim* regarded the heroes of the Bible as living the life of Talmudic Jews. But we know that this was a gross anachronism. Fortunately, the sense of psychological continuity need not be based upon such an illusion.

Spirituality, or the aspiration toward the good life, is the common denominator of all civilization worthy of the name. They differ, however, in the particular form this aspiration assumes and in the emphasis it receives. The Judaism of the past was no doubt a spiritual civilization, but it was circumscribed in its spirituality by a limited knowledge of God and the world. The enlarged knowledge of God and the world will enable the Judaism of the future to function more completely and more effectively as a spiritual civilization.

Even those who believe in the finality of traditional truths will probably concede that today we can avail ourselves of a larger knowledge of the world than the Jews of the past could. The proposition, however, that correlative with enlarged knowledge of the world is an enlarged knowledge of God, seems absurd to them. To the traditionalists it is self-evident that the ancients knew more about God than we can ever hope to know, for did he not reveal and explain himself to them? Yet the proposition must stand, and it is basic to any attempt to construct the Judaism of the future as a spiritual civilization. Our knowledge of God is determined by our knowledge of reality. As our knowledge of reality is enlarged, our knowledge of God is deepened. Today we find it possible for a civilization to express itself spiritually and to feel the sense of destiny without claiming to have experienced theophany, without resorting to a conception of direct cause-and-effect relationship between obedience to God and the fortunes of the individual, and without having to assume that the only way a new world will ever emerge out of the present chaos will be through some supernatural cataclysm. The spirituality of the Jewish civilization in its fourth stage can dispense with all these assumptions. It will consist mainly in the effort to foster knowingly and deliberately the historical tendency of the Jewish religion to progress in the direction of universal truth and social idealism.

NOTES

1. Jeffrey Schein, "Mordecai Kaplan and the Contemporary Agenda of Jewish Education," *Reconstructionist* 60, no. 2 (Fall 1995): 24–25.

2. The Cairo Geniza, found by accident, offers a fairly complete view of Jewish Mediterranean society in the Middle Ages. Jewish law prohibits the burning of all books with God's name. In the case of the Cairo community, they also buried plenty of other documents, too.

3. Rebecca Alpert and Jacob Staub, *Exploring Judaism: A Reconstructionist Approach*, 2nd ed. (Elkins Park, Pa.: Reconstructionist Press, 2000).

4. Mordecai Kaplan, "The Reconstruction of Judaism," 1920, in *The Jew in the Modern World*, ed. Paul Mendes-Flohr and Jehuda Reinharz (New York: Oxford University Press, 1980), 397.

5. Mordecai Kaplan, *Judaism as a Civilization* (Philadelphia: Jewish Publication Society of America, 1981), 178.

6. The "ethnic" Jewishness of my own upbringing, beyond stories about the immigrant experience, would be this: on Sunday mornings I would line up with my father to buy bagels and the *New York Times* with dozens of other Jews in a predominantly Jewish neighborhood, all of whom thought John F. Kennedy was the greatest thing since Franklin Delano Roosevelt and most of whom appeared in synagogue mainly on Rosh Hashanah/Yom Kippur and at life-cycle events.

7. Charles Liebman, "Reconstructionism in American Life," *American Jewish Yearbook* 71 (1970): 96.

8. One of the little ironies of modern Jewish thought is that Kaplan received Bible instruction from Arnold Bogumil Ehrlich, an accomplished but often heretical and quirky scholar who temporarily converted to Christianity.

9. Kaplan, *Judaism as a Civilization*, 385.

10. Mordecai M. Kaplan and Arthur A. Cohen, *If Not Now, When?* (New York: Schocken, 1973), 38.

11. Nonsexist, that is, by the standards of the day. Kaplan followed his father's example by providing his daughter Judith (also the first proper bat mitzvah in Jewish history) with a high-quality education in Hebrew, French, music, and so forth. He also championed the mixed seating of men and women. On the other hand, Kaplan had a very traditional marriage and could describe "women of both sexes" who shied away from his reforms. See Carole S. Kessner, "Kaplan and the Role of Women in Judaism," in *The American Judaism of Mordecai Kaplan*, ed. Robert Seltzer and Mel Scult (New York: New York University Press, 1990).

Part Three

RECOVERING *KEDUSHAH* (THE SACRED) IN A PROFANE AGE

INTRODUCTION

The German sociologist Max Weber coined a word that I particularly like to describe the secularization process: *Entzauberung*, which means "demysti-fication," or "demagicification." To me, this word captures the loss of a world where God was assumed to be intimately present and where every de-cision was charged with religious and moral significance. Few traditional societies better exemplified this world than that of Eastern European Jewry before the Holocaust, as fixed in the popular imagination by the milkman Tevye. Tevye, Yiddish writer Sholom Aleichem's central character, could chat with God as naturally and unselfconsciously as with a neighbor. No as-pect of Tevye's and Golde's (Tevye's wife) life was devoid of Jewishness (*Yiddishkeit*). We modern Jews, on the other hand, are accustomed to a more divided existence. We live in a world where rational calculation of eco-nomic benefit, geographic mobility, urban life, the business cycle, and our job schedules predominate. Except for segments of the Orthodox world, our daily and weekly cycle does not revolve around the performance of *mitzvot*, and even in Orthodox circles one could argue that a more theological and less instinctual concept of *mitzvot* prevails. As God's immanence recedes, our sense of the sacred or holy (*kedushah*) is dulled.

A searching article by the historian Haym Soloveitchik makes clear what *Entzauberung* means in a contemporary context:

In 1959, I came to Israel before the High Holidays. Having grown up in Boston and never having had an opportunity to pray in a *haredi* yeshiva,[1] I spent the entire High Holiday period—from Rosh Hashanah to Yom Kippur—at a fa-mous yeshiva in B'nei Brak. The prayer there was long, intense, and uplifting, certainly far more powerful than anything I had previously experienced. And yet, there was something missing, something I had experienced before, something perhaps I had taken for granted. Upon reflection, I realized that there was introspection self-ascent, even moments of self-transcendence, but there was no fear in the thronged student body, most of whom were Israeli born. . . . What was absent among the thronged students in B'nei Brak and in other contemporary services—and, lest I be thought to be exempting myself from this assessment, absent in my own religious life too—was that primal fear of Divine judgment, simple and direct.[2]

Moses Maimonides (1135–1204) noted that service to God based on love is superior to service to God based on fear. Yet it would be foolish to deny that both fear and love traditionally played a great role in the piety of the average Jew. According to Soloveitchik, that fear has fallen victim to modernity, and if that is true in the yeshiva of B'nei Brak, it is obviously true in Shaker Heights, Skokie, and Scarsdale. This alienation, this distancing of God and people, may be said to be the problem that the four thinkers in this section deal with repeatedly. All four grew up in traditional Jewish communities and confronted modern ones. Three of the four (Salanter, Heschel, and Soloveitchik) came from an Eastern European background yet spent many years in the West. The fourth (Kook) encountered the most radically secularist Jewish society of all, the pioneer (*chalutz*) communities of early Zionism.

By way of introducing Israel Salanter, Abraham Isaac Kook, Joseph Soloveitchik, and Abraham Joshua Heschel, a few words on the divisions within Eastern European Jewry seem essential. Beginning with Israel Baal Shem Tov (1700–1760), who was awarded the acronym "Besht," Hasidism emerged as a pietist movement that challenged the rabbinic status quo. The intellectual roots of Hasidism lay mainly in the medieval mystical tradition (i.e., *kabbalah*). Hasidism held that the holy or righteous man (i.e., the *tzaddik*, or *rebbe*) had the power to intercede with the heavens. This emphasis on dynastic and charismatic leadership departed from the relatively meritocratic and intellectual standards of traditional rabbinic promotion. These features sound elitist, yet Hasidism possessed enormous appeal for the Jewish masses. The hasidic focus on joyful and ecstatic prayer, the importance placed on the subjective religious experiences of the worshipper, the cultivation of a sense of inner redemption under increasingly oppressive external circumstances, all contributed to *hasidim*'s popularity. Spread initially by Yiddish-speaking preachers, within a couple of generations Hasidism won the loyalties of roughly half of Eastern European Jewry. Before the Holocaust, Hasidism dominated Poland, the Ukraine, and White Russia.

Hasidism's emerging critique of traditional rabbinic leadership and education did not go unchallenged. In Lithuania, Rabbi Elijah ben Solomon Zalman (also known as the Vilna Gaon) championed a more responsive and practical yeshiva education, a recommitment to the basic sources of rabbinic Judaism, and a greater openness to Western learning as a tool for the clarification of Judaism.[3] His reforms, carried on by talented disciples, led to a flourishing of Eastern European *yeshivot* in the nineteenth century. The confrontation of Hasidism and its opponents (literally, *mitnaggdim*) was quite nasty, involving bans of excommunication, denunciations to the czarist government, and physical violence. In many communities throughout Eastern Europe, the Jewish population was split between *hasidim* and *mitnaggdim* who refused to pray together, buy meat from each other's butchers, or marry each other's children.

In time, the hostilities lessened, in large measure because of the emergence, by the 1820s and 1830s, of a third force in Jewish life: the Haskalah, or Jewish Enlightenment. Leaders of both movements realized that the Haskalah, with its commitment to modernization, secularization, and cultural integration, constituted a far greater threat to traditional Jewish life. By the second half of the nineteenth century, it was clear that traditional Jewish life was beginning to undergo some of the same transformations Western European Jewry had experienced several decades earlier. To be sure, the path of secularization differed in the czarist regime. The size and concentration of the Jewish population in Russia, Poland, and the Baltic states dwarfed that of the West. With the brief exception of Alexander II, the czars did not permit the integration of Jews into the national fabric as had occurred west of the Elbe River. Although the socioeconomic apex of Eastern Jewry might have been prepared to "Russify" or "Polonize," for the vast majority secularization took place without structural assimilation. Only in the Pale of Settlement did modern Jewish political parties (the Bund, Zionism, the Agudah) come into existence. These tensions challenged Tevye's world, and the figures discussed below must be seen as respondents to these tensions.

Many stories are told about Israel Salanter, founder of the *musar* movement. One, attributed to a Lubavitch Hasid, captures the respect paid Salanter by both *mitnaggdim* and *hasidim*: "After many generations God had pity on the unfortunate *mitnaggdim* and sent them the soul of a *rebbe*— Rabbi Israel Salanter." In Vilna, Salanter had been an innovative educator, establishing adult study groups to help propagate Jewish learning among businessmen, women, and the uneducated. In Kovno, Salanter and his disciples had introduced the study of ethics (*musar*) into the curriculum of the yeshiva world. Nearing age fifty, Salanter left for Koenigsberg, Germany. There he formulated a number of projects to bring Judaism back into the lives of German Jews. Unifying these activities was Salanter's desire to make moral behavior central to being a good Jew. Jews needed to train themselves through study, repentance, and *mitzvot* to be as careful in business dealings as in keeping kosher, and to be as aware of God at the marketplace as in the synagogue. "Fear of God," holds one of the Proverbs, is the beginning of wisdom. Salanter believed this firmly and wished to reinstill this sense in the modern Jew. As you read Salanter's letter, you might find him, compared to Heschel and Soloveitchik, antiquated and uncongenial. But he belongs with them as a figure who realized how difficult it would be to maintain *kedushah* in a secular age.

Abraham Isaac Kook, the greatest figure in twentieth-century Jewish mysticism, experienced an intimate relationship with God that he felt was essentially beyond the power of words to describe. Whereas Salanter tried to convey a feeling of fear of God (*yirah*), and Heschel a sense of joy in the fulfillment of the Commandments (*simchah l'mitzvah*), Kook's outpourings evidence a man whose senses were flooded with the unity and glory of God's creation. In his own person, Kook bridged the worlds of the Eastern European yeshiva and the emerging Zionist enterprise in present-day Israel. Not surprisingly, this synthesis proved unacceptable to most of his contemporaries. The traditional Jews who lived in Israel mainly for pietistic reasons regarded the secular settlers as heretics; the settlers looked upon the ultra-Orthodox as irrelevant throwbacks to a diaspora whose time had come—and gone. Kook saw both parties as necessary components of the Redemption.

Abraham Joshua Heschel, the descendant of hasidic rabbis, emerged as the most renowned Jewish theologian in the second half of the twentieth century. While Martin Buber had done much to prepare the groundwork for a wider reception of Hasidism by translating and commenting on its tales, Heschel may be credited with bringing a hasidic sensibility to all of Jewish life—and beyond. In several theological gems, Heschel tried to explain the necessity of spiritual quest in a modern world. Although trained in philosophy at the University of Berlin and in traditional Judaism in Eastern European *yeshivot*, Heschel was born and lived as a Hasid. The initial imprint was a deep one— Heschel's writings often seem more like "spiritual" than "philosophical" classics. Arnold Eisen comments:

> Heschel frustrated those who believed him potentially the greatest Jewish theologian of the century by spending much of his work seeking to evoke the awe and wonder at things and at oneself which he believed led human reason to jump beyond itself to God. If he could not conjure up that experience, then talk of revelation and *mitzvot* would fall on deaf ears.[4]

To me, Heschel's most moving works are those such as *The Sabbath* and *The Earth is the Lord's* that capture the splendid holiness of Jewish life in Eastern Europe. These evocations do not, however, contain the core of Heschel's "theology of pathos" or "depth theology," which Heschel expounded most fully in

Man Is Not Alone and *God in Search of Man.* Since I am good friends with two people far better qualified than I to expound Heschel's theology, I have asked one of them, Rabbi Roger Klein, to write the introduction to this chapter.

Joseph Baer Soloveitchik, the scion of Lithuanian yeshiva giants, has a lineage no less impressive than Heschel's. His works illustrate the ways in which a totally committed halachic life may nurture a first-rate philosophical personality. Scholars of medieval thought debate whether Moses Maimonides represents an integrated or a schizophrenic religious personality. Does the author of the Aristotelian-philosophical *Guide of the Perplexed* really see eye-to-eye with the author of the classic legal text *Mishneh Torah*, or do the two works represent a thinker at war with himself? I suspect that Soloveitchik, heavily influenced by Maimonides, will generate a similar debate. He is at one and the same time *The Lonely Man of Faith*, an existentialist hero seeking God in a universe that doubts the legitimacy of such a quest, and the supremely confident *Halachic Man*, armed with a worldview that confronts all phenomena from a sure perspective.

As the above-cited quote from Joseph Soloveitchik's son, Haym, indicates, making *kedushah* real in a profane world continues to challenge even the most committed Jews. Salanter, Kook, Heschel, Soloveitchik: saint, mystic, Hasid, philosopher—differing yet recognizable types in Jewish tradition. Yet all four were engaged in the act of translation. Namely, translating the essence of a world that faced deterioration and then destruction. Reading the works of these spiritual giants offers a good first step in understanding the nature of the quest for *kedushah* under different circumstances and without any certain models.

NOTES

1. A yeshiva is an institute of higher Jewish learning. *Haredi* is a Hebrew word from a root meaning "to tremble, to shake." *Haredi* is usually translated into English as "ultra-Orthodox." An easy if shallow way of distinguishing *haredi* from centrist or modern Orthodox is dress—*haredi* men wear a black hat over their Kippot and only white and black clothing; *haredi* women always have their heads covered by a scarf or wig. The classic portrait of the *shtetl*, *Life Is Like People*, has been criticized as static and overly sentimental. (To be sure, most Jews would choose Long Island over Anatevka.)

2. Haym Soloveitchik, "Rupture and Reconstruction: The Transformation of Contemporary Orthodoxy," *Tradition* 28, no. 4 (1994): 98–99.

3. Emanuel Etkes, *Israel Salanter and the Musar Movement* (Philadelphia: Jewish Publication Society, 1993).

4. Arnold Eisen, *The Chosen People in America* (Bloomington: Indiana University Press, 1983), 180.

Chapter Ten

Israel Salanter

Restoring "Fear of Heaven" to Human Behavior

SALANTER'S LIFE AND TIMES (1810–1883)

Rabbi Israel [Salanter's] compassion for humankind seemed limitless. He wanted every Jew to have a great share in the world to come and to escape the pangs of hell, worse even than the suffering of this world. To this end, he strove always to be among the people, to live in different cities and countries, though by nature he preferred seclusion. Wherever he went, he summoned people to repentance and good deeds.[1]

We have encountered several "types" in this book: the heretic (Spinoza), the apologist-educator (Mendelssohn), the ideologues (Hirsch and Geiger). But, until now, we have not yet encountered the saint. The stories attesting to Israel Salanter's sainthood are legion and striking: On one Yom Kippur, while a cholera epidemic was raging, Salanter encouraged those suffering greatly to eat and keep their strength as a matter of *pikuach nefesh* (the saving of a human life). On another Yom Kippur Eve, Salanter spent the evening babysitting. He had come upon a six-year-old child who had fallen asleep while looking after her infant sister. Salanter considered it more important to see to the girls than to attend Kol Nidre services. Another tale relates that on the day of his death, Salanter comforted the watchman who had been assigned by the Koenigsberg community to notify them when the great man passed away. According to Louis Ginzberg, who studied with Salanter's disciples, the latter's remaining possessions were a single suit of clothes, a prayer shawl (*tallith*), and phylacteries (*tefillin*).[2]

The best testimony to Salanter's sainthood, however, is that his initiatives, actions, and personal example of how to improve or perfect human behavior

165

spawned a movement whose legacy remains. Ironic as it may seem, no other figure in Eastern European life—not even the founder of Hasidism, Baal Shem Tov—can claim that distinction. The *musar* movement, with its influence on *"musar"* *yeshivot*, its influence on adult education in the Orthodox world (the *kollel*), and its highlighting the importance of moral qualities (*middot*) as a specific area of study and concern, all these may be traced back to this remarkable and enigmatic figure. Before relating what little we know about Salanter's personal life, some definition of the term *musar*—the term with which Salanter is most closely identified—is called for.

My Hebrew-English dictionary defines *musar* as "morals" or "ethics." But the word also means to "chastise, correct, reprove, instruct." Hebrew is a concrete language, and the three-letter root itself is also related to the words "binding" and "fettering." Concern with morals and ethics, of course, typifies all religious traditions. Within Judaism, the Bible and the rabbinic literature never travel very far without contending with these issues. But there also exists a discrete tradition of *musar* literature whose interests are more exclusively and explicitly concerned with improving human character. The best-known and best-loved portion of the Mishnah, "Chapters of the Fathers" (*Pirkey Avot*), is an example of *musar* literature from the formative rabbinic period. Bahya Ibn Pakuda's "Duties of the Heart" is another *musar* classic, written against the background of the declining fortunes of Spanish Jewry in the medieval world. Rabbi Moshe Haym Luzzato's "Path of the Upright" was a Renaissance example of *musar* literature written by a young mystic. But Israel Salanter's "Epistle of Musar" (reproduced at the end of this introduction) is the modern *musar* classic par excellence.

We can say much more about Israel Salanter's overall background than about the particulars of his early life. Israel (Lipkin) of Salanter grew up in a traditional rabbinical family in Lithuania, and spent the formative years of his life in this northeast corner of Europe, so rich in Jewish intellectual accomplishment. Salanter's father, Ze'ev Lipkin, was a rabbi and teacher. More unusual, Salanter's mother, Leah, published works on the Bible and Talmud. When Yehuda Leib Gordon satirized the repressed role of Jewish women in Eastern European life, Moshe Leib Lillienblum supposedly took Leah Lipkin as his stellar counterexample. Regrettably, we know little more about Salanter's mother than this isolated fact, and even less about Salanter's wife. Her family was the main financial support of the Salanters during the early years of their marriage, and she clearly bore the brunt of raising their children, for Salanter spent many solitary years headquartered in the West. Salanter's relationships with his children were mixed. While his eldest son followed in his footsteps, another son (Yom Tov Lipman Lipkin) broke from traditional Jewish life and became a renowned mathematician.

Salanter learned from his father and mother first. He learned the Talmud from Rabbi Hirsch Braude, a capable scholar of the old school. But the more profound influence was that of Rabbi Joseph Zundel, who uttered the apparently galvanizing injunction to his protégé: "If you want to lead a pious life, study *musar.*"

Ultimately, Salanter migrated westward, spending the last years of his life bolstering Orthodox Judaism in several German cities and eventually Paris. Nevertheless, he represents the first of many Eastern European figures we will encounter in this book whose development took place in a purely Jewish setting and whose intellectual sources were overwhelmingly Judaic. Although he was an exact contemporary of Geiger and Hirsch, one looks in vain for any counterpart to the sort of intellectual influence that non-Jews such as Baur or Hegel exercised on these German intellects. Despite Yizhak Ahren's claims that Salanter studied Kant and was influenced by his ideas on the unconscious, one can thumb through his letters (unfortunately untranslated) and find continual references to all strata of the Judaic tradition but, so far as I can tell, none whatsoever to gentile thinkers.

In his lifetime, Salanter was claimed by every important religious stream within Eastern European Judaism. Lithuanian yeshiva leaders objected that their students did not need to practice the self-abasing techniques of *musar*, but they recognized Salanter's moral perfection. The pietist *hasidim* conceded that the yeshiva world had finally produced a righteous leader (*tzaddik*). The secularist, modern-minded Enlighteners (*maskilim*) tried to claim Salanter as a supporter of secular learning on the basis of his many friends among the secularly educated German-Orthodox leadership and his innovative teaching techniques. Possibly not since Moses Mendelssohn (1729–1786) did any Jewish figure enjoy such a unanimously untarnished prestige. In the memoirs of Yudel Mark and in Ginzberg's thumbnail sketch, the desire to portray Salanter as synthesizer of these three streams is evident.

But in reality Salanter was principally the product of the world of the solidly anti-hasidic Lithuanian yeshiva. The Israeli scholar Immanuel Etkes has demonstrated that Salanter continued tendencies in educational and yeshiva reform that began with the famous Vilna Gaon, and which were continued by the Gaon's leading student, Chaim of Volozhin (Volozhin became the greatest of the nineteenth-century *yeshivot*). Like the Vilna Gaon, Salanter considered secular subjects legitimate only when put to the service of traditional Torah values (unlike the *maskilim*). Practical *halachah*, the study of the law that would lead to more informed and considered practice, was a hallmark of the Vilna school and of Salanter's *musar* movement.

The doctrine of *yirah*, fear of God, held a prominent place for the Vilna Gaon, for Chaim of Volozhin, and for Salanter. Certainly, Salanter did not embrace the joyful, ecstatic mode favored by the hasidic movement, nor did he present himself (or his disciples) as *tzaddikim*, righteous men who could somehow intercede with the higher powers. Salanter was uninterested in kabbalah and the mystical tradition, which were pivotal to Hasidism.[3] Yet the Lubavitch Hasid who said, "After many generations God had pity on the unfortunate *mitnaggdim* [opponents of Hasidism] and sent them the soul of a rebbe—Rabbi Israel Salanter. But those bunglers deadened his spirit too," was not altogether wrong.[4]

Salanter's lifelong love of Israel (*ahavat Yisrael*) and his populistic educational activities during his Vilna years (1840–1848), stood in contrast to the other disciples of the Vilna Gaon, a dyed-in-the-wool elitist. His focus on the personal, emotional, and psychological also recalls Hasidism more than the Lithuanian *yeshivot*. The extremely vocal and emotional self-criticism practiced in *musar yeshivot* approximated in tone if not substance the hasidic worship style that their opponents considered so offensive.

Saintliness is a characteristic, but not a profession. What did Salanter actually do? Although he wrote essays, letters, and sermons, he was most active as an organizer, rabbi, and teacher. All major scholars of Salanter agree that his ideas and methods developed as he moved from Salant to Vilna to Kovno to Germany. His public mission really began in Vilna in the 1840s when Salanter decided that *ba'alei batim*, or "husbands and fathers" (the literal translation of *ba'alei batim* would be "homeowners"—but I doubt that many Vilna Jews owned their own homes), needed to continue their Jewish education as adults. Salanter extended his popularizing elements to women and untutored men, an unusual step in the Eastern European context. In Vilna, Salanter established the *kollel* system, whereby a few hours a week would be set aside for the study of legal and moral material chosen for their applicability to the "real" world as opposed to the yeshiva. In the next generation, Salanter's disciples extended this system and it remains an influence today, even where the Jewish community no longer shares the relatively high level of observance that Salanter could expect in Vilna. Salanter's pedagogic innovations also brought him to the attention of the Russian government. Pressured to join the government-sponsored Rabbinical Seminary, with which the czarist regime hoped to foster a break from traditionalism and ultimately a conversion to Christianity, Salanter fled Vilna for Kovno, Lithuanian Jewry's second city.

During the eight years he spent in Kovno, Salanter continued to reach out to the Jewish *ba'alei batim* that he had taught in Vilna. Indeed, despite being a strong center of the Jewish Enlightenment (Haskalah), Kovno also became a capital city of the *musar* movement. In addition to this audience, Salanter also turned in a more elitist direction. He established conventicles (*musar kloizn*) dedicated to the study of the *musar* literature that he had done much to have disseminated while he was still in Vilna. He began to see a need to train rabbis and scholars who would integrate Torah study with the study of *musar* classics. The mainstream Orthodox leadership looked askance at this attempt to alter the traditional curriculum, but the opposition never reached the same heights of vituperation that characterized the counterassault against Hasidism in the days of the Vilna Gaon. From 1851 to 1857, when Salanter traveled to Germany for medical reasons, he taught at the Nevyozer *kloiz*. Nevyozer became the most important cell of the *musar* movement, and Salanter created a new type of yeshiva leadership, which placed a hitherto unheard-of emphasis on the moral and spiritual (as opposed to the purely intellectual) growth of the yeshiva students.

Salanter spent the last years of his life in Germany and France, strengthening Orthodoxy in two countries where the vast majority of the Jews had long since abandoned traditional Judaism for forms deemed more compatible with modern citizenship. While Salanter's move probably surprised his disciples, he had a ready explanation:

> When horses panic and start galloping downhill, anyone who tries to stop them midway risks his life. The horses will trample him. But after the horses have rushed down the hill it is possible to halt and bridle them. So too, with the Jewish communities. In the large Russian cities, they are still in headlong flight and nothing can be done for them. But the communities abroad have long ago leveled off and now something can be done for them.[5]

Despite this hopeful assessment, many of Salanter's initiatives in the West met with failure. His plans for a modern Yiddish-language Talmud translation and commentary came to naught, as did his plan for an Aramaic-Hebrew dictionary to make the Talmud more accessible to those Jews who had never benefited from yeshiva training. (The larger, more difficult part of the Talmud, that is, the *gemara*, is in Aramaic, not Hebrew.) Salanter's desire that the Talmud be taught to educated gentiles in German universities bespeaks incredible naïveté, as the Talmud was a text generally despised among the German Protestants who dominated the theological faculties. Even a *musar* journal, *Tevunah* (*Understanding*), appeared for only two years.

Thus, Salanter's primary legacy remains the accomplishments of the 1840s and 1850s. We have said something about the institutional dimension of this accomplishment; we now turn to the key ideas articulated in these decades. What was the idea behind Salanter's doctrine of human nature and the means of perfecting it? The best way to answer this question is to examine the most famous of all Salanter's writings, the "Epistle of Musar," composed during the Kovno years and published for the first time in 1858 in Koenigsberg. By then, Salanter and his disciples had developed the institutions that would preserve the *musar* idea. Although the questions that follow should help you work your way through the "Epistle of Musar," which I have been permitted to reprint in its entirety, I will concede that my students often find the letter uncongenial. Salanter takes sin and punishment much more seriously than most contemporaries do and one can hear more than a bit of the preacher in the teacher. Still, Salanter's doctrine of reward and punishment, quaint as it seems, may after all be the best way to instill the pursuit of moral excellence, his ultimate goal.

QUESTIONS FOR SALANTER, "EPISTLE OF MUSAR"

Salanter begins this essay with the assertion "Man is free in his imagination but bound by his reason." Is this true? Is this a bad thing? Is this different from Rousseau's assertion that "Man is born free but everywhere is in chains"?

What is the image of human psychology that Salanter puts forth? Is there any difference between Salanter's view and that of the earlier sages, who also acknowledged that man possesses both a good and an evil inclination?

What is spiritual accounting (*heshbon ha-nefesh*)? What precludes people from making this spiritual accounting?

Neither knowing the right thing (Plato) nor reveling in the right thing (Hasidism) suffices to keep men (and presumably women) walking the straight and narrow. Why is this?

Do you think Salanter's pessimism is justified? Do you think Salanter's pessimism is Jewish?

How does Salanter correlate public versus private sin with the eras of the First and Second Temples? Which kind of sin is more serious? Which is more difficult to extirpate? Which is more relevant for our modern condition? (It is worthwhile comparing Salanter's "historiography" to Ahad Ha'am's discussion of these two periods in "Flesh and Spirit.")

Salanter talks about two categories of sin: lust/desire and bad habits. What does Salanter find puzzling about the second category of sins, which includes gossip and jealousy, for instance, and which do not yield any tangible benefit to the sinner?

What does Salanter prescribe as an antidote for each kind of sin?

How does one make sin habitually revolting to the sinner?

How does fear of God (*yirah*) serve in the battle against sin?

Why is it appropriate to reproach a fellow Jew when one sees him or her transgressing?

What is Salanter's view of the righteous man (the *tzaddik*)? What is your view?

What does *sin* mean to you? How do you deal with it?

STUDIES BY AND ABOUT SALANTER

With the exception of the "Epistle of Musar," I am not aware of material in English by Salanter. Jacob Mark and M. Gerz's brief recollections of Salanter and other *musar* figures in Lucy Dawidowicz's superb collection *The Golden Tradition* (New York: Schocken, 1967) are well worth consulting. Chaim Grade's two-volume novel *The Yeshiva* wonderfully (if critically) evokes the spirit of the *musar* yeshiva. Louis Ginzberg, *Students, Scholars and Saints* (New York: Meridien, 1958), offers a dated but still vivid thumbnail sketch of Salanter from a figure who heard stories of the master from Salanter's direct disciples. More academic and challenging, but worth the effort, is Immanuel Etkes, *Rabbi Israel Salanter and the Mussar Movement*, trans. Jonathan Chipman (Philadelphia: Jewish Publication Society, 1993). Kaminetsky and Friedman, *Building Jewish Character* (Fryer Foundation: 1975), contains essays on the application of *musar* traditions to modern Orthodox education. Hillel Goldberg has written extensively on Salanter, most accessibly in *From Berlin to Slobodka: Jewish Transition Figures from Eastern Europe* (Hoboken, N.J.: Ktav, 1989).

From "Epistle of Musar"[6]

Israel Salanter

Man is free in his imagination but bound by his reason. His imagination leads him wildly in the direction of his heart's desire, not fearing the inevitable future, when God will punish him for all his deeds, and he will be chastised by severe punishments, he alone, no other will be substituted for him; he himself will reap the fruit of his iniquities. It will be the very person who commits the sin who will be punished.

It is bitter. Man cannot say: "This is (*my*) sickness, and I must bear it." The sufferings of this world are small matters, indeed, [comparing them] with the penalties for the sins. Man's soul abhors it [to such a degree] that a day will be considered like a year. Woe to [our] imagination—this evil foe. It is in our hands and in our power to put it far away from us by lending a listening ear to [our] reason, to seek wisely the attainment of truth, by taking into account the gain obtained through a transgression in comparison with the loss [incurred through committing it.] And what is to be done? Imagination is an overflowing stream wherein reason can drown, unless we place it aboard a ship, i.e., the emotion of the soul and the storm of the spirit.

(Epistle of Musar)

In all things and matters there is to be found a general and particular principle (or specific, generic and individual). If there is no general principle there can be no particular, for the particular principle has in it no more than is found in the general principle. However there may be a general principle from which no particular can be deduced. Hence the general principle is of primary importance, and [as secondary principles] the particulars are derived from it.

Now, then, let us observe our religious duties which we owe to our Creator, may He be praised—indeed it is an important matter—and see what is the general idea from which we draw the specific principles.

[Even] without knowledge and understanding we do recognize the belief that permeates us that God is the Judge, to mete out to man his due, in accordance with his deeds. (If his way of life be wicked and grievous he will be severely punished either in this world or in the world to come, the everlasting world. Man does not realize to how great an extent [the punishment] will be meted out both as regards quality and quantity. However, if his deeds are pure and upright,—he will be called blessed—[and he will be recompensed with] celestial pleasures in this [world] and even more so in the next [world], in a wonderful [Garden of] Eden, [of a nature] that is far beyond human intellect and senses to comprehend.) This is our first step in the worship of God, may His Name be praised.

Thus we find statements of our sages, of blessed memory: (in Makkoth 24a) "Habakkuk summed up [all the precepts] in one, 'But the righteous shall live by his faith.'" And in Baba Bathra (78b): "'Wherefore do the *Moshelim* say, come ye to *Heshbon*' which means: Those that exercise control over their inclinations (*Yezer ha-Ra'*) say, come and let us take stock (*Heshbon*), let us balance the loss entailed by the performance of a *Mizvah* against its gain and the gain obtained by a transgression against the loss it entails."

However it is bitterness of spirit and sadness of heart: this general principle lies dormant in us, hidden in the secret recesses of the heart, not seen from the outside, unless we apply ourselves to cultivating our hearts in the furtherance of *Musar* thoughts. And, therefore, even this general principle may not possess the controlling influence of binding our bodily limbs with the bonds of *Fear*. And hence no particular principle can be derived from this general principle, to preserve us from the iniquities to which we are exposed. We are at all times being ensnared in the pitfalls of cardinal sins, which are sky high, such as sins committed by our tongue (slander), and dishonest business transactions, and above all else neglect of the study of Torah. Generally speaking, upon close reflection we find that there is hardly one sound limb in the whole body, because every man is valued in relation to his worth: "The greater the man the greater his evil inclination." (Sukkah 52a) Thus one is apt to stumble over immense cardinal sins [the magnitude of which, as a consequence of the blindness of our hearts we are really incapable of perceiving, (as in the case of common sins) unless we look through a telescope. (That enables us to see such objects that though large like the stars in heaven, which are larger then the globe of the world, we see them as small objects because of the limitations of our sight, and by this telescope we can see them much larger, though still they are infinitesimally smaller than they are in reality. Even so it is in our case.) This is *Pure Reason* based upon established faith. We find our sins in substance very grave indeed.]

This we can support by the statement of our sages, of blessed memory (Yoma 9b). Why was the First Temple destroyed? Because of three things that prevailed there: idolatry, incest and bloodshed; but why was the Second Temple destroyed, since the people did occupy themselves with the study of the Torah and observed its precepts and practiced charity? — Because unwarranted hatred prevailed there. *Both Rabbi Johanan and Rabbi Eliezer say*: As for the former generations their sins were made public and thus the end of their captivity was revealed, as for the latter their sins were not made public and their fate was not revealed. The underlying idea of this Talmudic statement is: "The iniquity of the former were revealed," i.e. the gravity and profundity of their sins were so apparent, even without applying them to intelligent scrutiny, while "the sins of the latter ones," [which could only be perceived after sharp scrutiny proved to be much more grave and cardinal, because immense and countless transgressions branch out from them, may God save us]. And the Amoraim further inquired (*ibid.*) "Who were better, the former generations or the latter ones?" To which the answer was given: "Look well at the Temple, it was restored to the former generation but was not restored to the latter one." This, indeed, brings us back to our previous quotation that "the greater the person" [as during the period of the second Temple when one engaged in the study of the Torah. Yoma, *ibid.*] "the greater his evil inclination." Which leads him to be caught in the snares of immense sins, as the power of which to lead one to evil is well known to the seeker after the truth.

Now, however man may view it: what can one do, seeing that the day of death is hidden from all, and its advent is sudden and God will call man to account for all his deeds which he performed [during] the days of his life, none of them shall be missing. More bitter than death will be the end from which there is no escape, and no place of refuge to go to.

This, then, is the meaning of the sentence "For to him that is joined to all the living there is hope; for a living dog is better than a dead lion," (Ecc. 9:6) as the sages of blessed memory have interpreted (Yalkut) "As long as a man is alive he has hopes to repent but when he dies all hope is lost, etc."

Therefore as long as the breath of life is within us let us hasten to mend our ways. Surely, because of the stumbling blocks, the road is precipitant for us; we do not tremble at the day of death although we remember it, as our sages, of blessed memory, expressed it in Shabbath (31b), "Perhaps you might say it is due to forgetfulness etc.; even though we behold with our own eyes the demise of mortals like ourselves, it does not give us strength of soul to return to our Creator, may He be praised, with all our heart, before Whom we shall ultimately come for judgement," Who will question us concerning all our evil doings. This is indeed contrary to the verse of the Scriptures (Eccl. 7:2) "It is better to go to the house of mourning, / Than to go to the house of feasting; / For that is the end of all men / And the living will lay it to his heart."

We must therefore say that it is the multiplicity of our sins which dulled our hearts and changed them into stone, as it is expressed in the statement of our Rabbis, of blessed memory in Yoma (39a), *interpreting* the verse of Leviticus 11:63: "Neither shall ye make yourselves unclean *with them that you should be defiled thereby." Read not V'nitmelhem, (that you should become defiled), but V'nitamatem (that you become dull-hearted,)* etc. and for this very reason even our sins are concealed from *us, and* we are not so quickly aware of them. Just as our Rabbis have expressed in Kiddushin (60a) "When a man commits a sin and repeats it, it becomes to him as though permitted." And these (sins) surround us upon the Day of Judgement, as our Rabbis, of blessed memory, said (Avodath Kochavim 18a "those sins that (usually) man tramples upon (in this world) surround him," etc. Now, is, God forbid, our hope lost? Is there, far be it, no remedy for us?

IT IS ONE THING, WE HAVE FOUND IT, IT IS AN ART NOT A LABOR, LET US CONVERSE A LITTLE AND RELIEVE OURSELVES.

Let us examine closely the case of iniquities. We find that there are two distinct species: One species springs from unrestrained lust, to desire that which is pleasant for the present moment, without our heeding the consequences, that in the end they may be disastrous. An example of this we find in mundane affairs. The foolish man or he whose mind is weak loves to indulge in the delicacies which are sweet to his palate, forgetting that they may cause him grave diseases. For this reason our Rabbis said in Avoth (2:15): "Who is wise? He who foresees the result of an act." This saying is identical [*in thought*] with the one our Rabbis expressed in Sotah (3a): "No one commits a sin unless a spirit of madness entered into him." This then is the entire task of man, dedicated to the service of God, may He be praised, to meditate and reflect on the awesomeness of God, the fear of His retribution, through the study of the books of *Musar, Aggadoth* and sermons of our Rabbis, of blessed memory. These will make him hear with his own ears and visualize almost with his own eyes, the intensity of the punishment, both in quantity and quality, which will stand before his very eyes, as our Rabbis said in Sanhedrin (7b): "Forever should [a judge, being apt, *because of his position* to go astray, yet the same caution should be taken by every man] a man think of himself as *if a sword was suspended over his body* and hell was gaping beneath him." If man will do so, his heart will have understanding, and he will repent and be healed.

Truly, the wickedness of man is great upon the earth; no one seeks after righteousness, nor is there any one who has understanding of the Fear of God, ready to set aside fixed periods for the exercise of reverence of God, to draw understanding out of belief, concealed within the secret recesses of the heart, in order to extend it and to uphold it, to give it strength and fortitude, and to vest in it the proper authority—to rule over the organs of the body that they do not overstep the bounds of *the Torah* and act in accord with the Torah. *This is the second category.* We do not find in the affairs of this world an example of this nature. There is no one who is beset by troubles who does not take time in thinking how to escape them. Now then, lust is not the cause (*of this category of sins*)—and this is really something to wonder at, and it is amazing—of one's neglect to meditate upon the fear of God and the correction by His punishment. *Such transgressions can not be classified under the first category, since lust (per se) is insufficient to be the cause.* They are rather an outcome of the spirit of uncleanliness which clings to man in order to cause him to sin, especially in those matters which pertain to speech. What advantage, indeed, does the man of (*evil*) tongue derive?—As our Rabbis, of blessed memory, said (vide: 'Arachin 15b).

Herein do we find an explanation of the two systems (*of thought*) regarding the *Yezer Tov* and *Yezer Ra'*. One system (*of philosophy*) well known, is that which holds that the Evil Inclination is due to the Force of Uncleanliness in man which entices him to sin, and that the Good Inclination is due to the Force of Sanctity in man which leads him to all that is good. This is the system expounded by a great many philosophers. The second system (*of thought*) holds that the Evil Inclination is due to the force of man's lust which seeks out that which is of a momentary pleasure, and cleaves unto it passionately, whereas the Good Inclination is the result of common sense which looks into the future. It is the awesome fear of God and His grave judgements (*that make man*) choose that which is useful, suppressing desire so as ultimately to attain the highest pleasure, that wondrous beatitude which is indescribable.

As we see, people vary in the degree of their sinfulness: some cling to one sin, others to another. Some will rather sin in their neglect of the study of the Torah than fall short in conducting business honestly or give alms, and there are others who do the opposite. And the same is true with other transgressions: One man cannot be compared with another. If the Evil Inclination were due to the Force of Iniquity which entices man, why then does it not seduce all men equally, (*to commit the same sins*) [unless we do not observe their roots]. But if we assert that the Evil Inclination is due to the Power of lust, then this case is quite understandable: One's lust depends largely upon one's temperament [one's birth, nature, age and interests.] Since people's temperaments differ, their transgressions differ also.

However, this explanation, too, is not completely adequate: *We ourselves witness men committing heinous sins not caused by lust.* At times lust even stands in their way, as for example, in the case of the man who desires greatly and pursues illusory honors, while despising the honors (*he would derive*) from fulfilling a *Mizvah*, et al. This may be attributed only to the spirit of uncleanliness which confounds him, causing him to do evil even against his vain desire.

Yet it is perfectly clear that the above two systems (*of thoughts*) are right: The Evil Inclination is due to both, force of lust and spirit of uncleanliness. Similarly the Good Inclination: it is both the right thinking (not yet corrupted by transgressions and passions) that sees the future result (*of an act*) and the spirit of holiness in man.

Now, man is composed (*of a dual nature*): physical and spiritual, just as when he was fashioned by his Creator. The physical (*part*) is visible to all, while the spiritual can only be perceived through the actions and behavior of the body. All of man's devices and plans to hold his soul in the body center only about the body alone, so as to strengthen it by wholesome food and to guard it against all injuries and mishaps—thus does man watch over the soul which abides in his body. However there is no natural way (*of doing so*) [through spirituality; as a matter of course, the chief concern of safekeeping the soul in the body depends largely on the soul itself, in accordance with its worshipping its Creator, blessed be He,] in seeking devices as to how the soul should be kept in the body—because no one sees or feels it by itself. What, then, is to be done about it?

Thus it is with the worship of God, may His Name be praised. The essence of it is to strengthen the two Good Inclinations—due to the Force of Sanctity and the Right Thinking [which have not been corrupted], and to thrust aside the two Evil Inclinations, due to the force of uncleanliness and lust. This depends upon a physical aspect, (*namely*) to feed it (the *Yezer ha-Ra'*) with wholesome nutriment, which are meditation, fear, and *Musar* which springs from the True Torah. This is expressed by our Rabbis, of blessed memory, in Baba Bathra (16a): Job sought etc. and what did they (Job's friends) reply to him? "Yea, thou doest away with fear etc." "The Holy One Blessed be He created the Evil Inclination, he also created for him the Torah as a palliative." They had taught us that the palliative of the Torah is the fear which emanates from its teachings, as expressed in the Scriptural verse: "Thou doest away with fear." This is a physical characteristic, clearly perceived by the human eye, as a means of curing infirmities of the soul. Would that man dedicate his heart and soul to the fear (*of God as expressed*) by the Torah. Would in general, that man knew and understood from the Torah that for every transgression there is (*in sotre*) a heavy penalty, and that (*for the observance of*) every precept there is (*in sotre*) a great and wonderful reward; would that in particular, and this is most important, one studied *the law* of every transgression separately, for haughtiness—the portion relating to haughtiness, for honest business dealings the portion (of the Torah) concerned with that and thus for each transgression the precepts in the (*portion of the*) Torah thereto appertaining.

The most important and chief (*method*) in the application of these curative powers of the Torah for the maladies of the evil inclination is to study with vigor and with profound meditation all the laws pertaining to that very transgression, the Halakah about it with all its ramifications. For we see with our own eyes that there are many transgressions which man naturally (or *by his nature*) would restrain himself from committing and would not commit if conditions somehow rendered them difficult. Then again there are none more flagrant sins than these, yet man would very easily commit them. For instance: a large part of our people, almost everyone of them, would not partake of food without washing their hands, God forbid, even though the delay by this (rite) increased their hunger and discomfort. However, (*the sin of*) slander, a much graver offence, they will very easily commit, even without great passion for it. Now, then, we see that the main point in guarding ourselves from committing a sin is to make it habitual and natural not to commit it. For, if man should try hard *to walk* in the paths of *Musar*, exerting himself to guard (*against*) slandering, with all his energy and mind (as is proper) yet, as long as his habits and nature remain unchanged, so as not to have a natural propensity to speak slanderously, it would still be easier (*for that person*) to commit the sin of speaking slander than to eat, God forbid, without washing the hands. The same is (*true*) of all (*other*) types of sins, depending upon the man, the period and the country. Even countries differ, they vary in their types (*of sins*); the communities of each individual country abstain easily from certain sins considered by them naturally repellent. And this much is well known that one's nature can be changed only through incessant study and behavior. And therefore, the chief basis and strong pillar (*of this theory*) is: one should prepare himself to be on his guard against transgressing and (*ready*) to observe the precepts through the perusal of that Halakah which is related to that transgression or to that precept. Particularly, the study must be profound, for only by this (*method*) will the soul acquire a natural aversion to that sin. Similarly, in our country the prohibition against non-Kosher meats and the like, are so rooted in the Jewish soul that one does not have to force oneself or curb one's desire to keep away from them: they are loathsome to one. It is unthinkable that a dealer in Kosher meats, upon discovering some inner parts (*of an animal or fowl*) which arouse his suspicion as to their Kashruth, would not seek the advice of a Rabbi, although the latter's decision might cause him financial loss [(although no one else but the dealer is aware of it)]. Fear of Heaven is upon him by natural habit, far be it from him to be malicious and to be the cause of a Jew perpetuating (*the sin of eating Terephah*).

But, on account of our many sins, in business it is quite the contrary. Men will not, of their own accord, order an investigation of a robbery or theft before a charge is brought against them; and even then, after being accused they will vehemently deny the charges with all manners of evasions. However in the Torah all (*sins*) have the same status. One negative command is on a par with another. According to law: "Ye shall not eat any flesh that is torn of beasts of the field," "Ye shall not eat of anything that dieth by itself," or (*the negative law of*) "Thou shalt not oppress thy neighbor nor rob him," and others like them. And just as it is ingrained in the Jewish soul that there is no distinction between any form of *Terephah* and whatever the Rabbi rules not fit must be thrown away, and the law fulfilled. Likewise, a similar concept is found in money matters: to take away money that belongs to one's fellow man is considered robbery by the Torah and the negative commandment of "thou shalt not rob" is thus violated. Yet we see, (*to our chagrin*) that even learned and God fearing people are not always observant in respect to this negative law—a transgression for which neither the Day of Atonement, nor the Day of Death gives atonement.

However, if one should devote himself with all his heart and soul to a profound study of those *Halakoth* pertaining to money matters, in *gemarah* and Codes according to the best of his ability—with the chief object of becoming familiar with what is prohibited and what is permitted [at the beginning he would find it difficult to comply with those laws, because the passion in such matters is very strong, and it is also not in keeping with customs (of business)]. How much more difficult a matter it is to imbue man even gradually, with the idea that such laws are on an equal basis with the (*dietary*) laws. Thus when one finds oneself addicted to unusual sins, as fornication or the like, of which our *(sages)* of blessed memory said "a few people indulge in fornication, and that only because passion had the upper hand over them, making it appear as a permissible act"—[besides meditating in *Musar* and devotionals as found in *Aggadah*, in midrash and *Musar*-book pertaining to these matters] should be: studying those *Halakoth* dealing with such matters with thoroughness, with the purpose of putting them into practice. At first one should try mending one's ways in matters where the Evil Inclination is not strong; as we find in Hullin 4b about a known heretic in whose house leaven was kept over the Passover, thereby violating the negative commandment of "It shall not be seen nor found." We take it that he must have changed it (for bread of a non-Jew, in order to lessen the violation). We base our assertion on the supposition that the apostate (heretic) complied with this regulation. Should we not be ashamed, should not our hearts be faint seeing the meanness of our souls in comparison with people of a former generation, when a *mumar* who kept leaven bread in his home over the Passover, possessed a natural inclination to lessen this sin, which was committed without lust. But in our generation, unfortunately we fall into the category of those who "commit a sin with defiance;" even in regard to sins to which we are addicted we do not commit them so as to lessen one prohibition. Our evil deed is as great [as is the deed of a defiant apostate]. And the chief cure for this malady is [besides the meditation upon Fear, as one cannot describe the greatness of the punishment of one who commits a transgression defiantly in comparison with one who does so just because of lust; and we drag down upon our own souls (ourselves) severe punishments when there is no desire] to study those *Halakoth* profoundly, everyone in accordance with his ability. [It is of great importance to know them, they are not mentioned in the books of the latter Rabbis, and one must spend much time in research in original sources.] Thus *this* system will gradually show results in helping one gain enough spiritual strength to save one from purgatory, at least to prevent one from committing a transgression defiantly. Then, by constantly interesting oneself in those laws that pertain to usual sins, it will give strength *(to a person)* to acquire a different disposition towards committing sins, and he will not think of transgressing the laws even if it should prove to be a difficult task. Now in the cure the Torah offers for the *Yezer ha-Ra'* there is yet another spiritual aspect [of which man's intellect and senses are unable to grasp the cause]. This is what our Rabbis declare in Sotah (21a), "While one is engaged in the study of the Torah it saves him, etc." It makes no difference in what section of the Torah one is engaged, it delivers him from sin. Whether one studies the law of "an ox that gores a cow" or the like, one will be saved from engaging in slander, although there is absolutely no connection whatsoever between these two matters. The spirituality of the Torah, in itself, protects one.

And upon careful analysis it may be observed that all our efforts in the direction of ridding ourselves of the Evil Inclination are all physical, that is meditating on the Fear (*of God*) and studying of the laws, as said above. For the second cure—the spiritual—comes of itself, and it is called accidental remedy, since the commandment to study the Torah is a positive precept by itself, belonging to the category of *Halakoth* dealing with the study of the Torah. A man is commanded to pursue the study of the Torah in order to know how to regulate his life with regard to the precepts and with regard to worldly affairs, without taking into account the distinction, whether his Inclination overpowered him much or little. Man must constantly engage in study to fulfill the precept of study even if his Inclination does not overpower him. But he does not have to study more than is obligatory, and fulfilling the precept of studying the Torah, brings a spiritual cure upon his Evil Predilection, in one manner or another.

Indeed the physical aspect (*of the matter*) is: meditation in (*the subject of*) Fear of God, and study of the Laws which is a self-cure and is called a cure. And man must of necessity know how to treat of this malady. Just as in physical ills the malady is commensurable with the cure, both in quantity and quality, similarly with spiritual ills, the cure should be based upon the condition of the malady. In the degree that his Evil Inclination gets hold of him, in the same degree should he increase his reflection upon Fear of God and the study of the *Halakoth*, as explained above. And should one fail to use the physical remedy (*as prescribed*) then the spiritual remedy—that is the study of the Torah—will not avail one to any great degree (*in overpowering*) the Evil Inclination. It is the same as in other human characteristics: spiritual activity, that is the action of the soul, depends upon activity of the body. And, lo! the enemy who lies in wait for man is the Evil Inclination, which is active in every way and means, seeking to turn his heart into stone, so as not to feel his multitudinous sins and not to see his own failings. It will also make man incapable of reflecting on the Fear of God, and of seeking a healing medicine, a physical cure.

A man should, therefore, devote himself (*to the duty*) of uplifting others, of arousing them to meditation on devotion and *Musar*. Since man's eyes are open to see (*faults*) of others and he is aware of their imperfections, and realizes that they need ethical instruction considerably, he should therefore apply himself zealously to *Musar* study, so that others may follow him, and Fear of God will increase, (*in the world*), and he will be responsible for the merit of others. And in consequence, gradually the study of *Musar* will lead one in the path of righteousness and *correctness*, that (*study of Musar*) being both the spiritual and physical cure. For "as for him who causes many to do good deeds no sin is perpetrated by him" declared our Rabbis of blessed memory in Yoma, 87.

How great, then, should this precept be in the eyes of man to set his heart and soul so as to guide people in the study of *Musar*, in order to save their souls from purgatory. "And he who has compassion upon human beings is rewarded in that Heaven has compassion upon him" (Shabbath 151b). And there is no greater compassion than to remind and arouse people to study Fear. For then they will see with their eyes, hear with their ears, and understand with their heart the immensity of the danger before them and they will bemoan their end, to return to God, praised be He, to depart from evil and do good, in a lesser or greater degree. The man who arouses people to this (*task*) will have a share in all that will result from it, and enjoy the eternal Eden the like of which no eye has yet seen. Human intellect in all its power is unable to grasp and to recognize well the quantity and quality of the public good which will ensue to men from such seemingly trivial act. The labor is but little and the reward is inestimable, and immeasurable. Therefore a man should devote his intellectual abilities to the great worthy cause, if he be indeed a man possessing a soul.

NOTES

1. Jacob Mark, "Truth and Legend about Israel Salanter," in *The Golden Tradition*, ed. Lucy Dawidowicz (New York: Schocken, 1967), 171–78.

2. Louis Ginzberg, *Students, Scholars and Saints* (New York: Meridien, 1958), 191.

3. On Salanter's indebtedness to kabbalah there is a dispute between Immanuel Etkes and Hillel Goldberg. Etkes contends that even if Salanter read kabbalistic literature, he exhibits little kabbalistic influence; I believe that Etkes is in the right.

4. Mark, "Truth and Legend."

5. Mark, "Truth and Legend."

6. I have deleted the commentary for the "Epistle of Musar" in Menachem Glenn, *Israel Salanter: Religious-Ethical Thinker, the Story of a Religious-Ethical Current in Nineteenth Century Judaism* (New York: Bloch, 1953) and comments to *Iggeret ha-Musar* for the simple reason that they presume a knowledge of Hebrew and familiarity with the rabbinic style of writing (*melitzhah*) that cites or alludes to a panoply of other sources in almost every line.

Chapter Eleven

Abraham Isaac Kook

Mysticism and Nationalism

KOOK'S LIFE AND TIMES (1865–1935)

> Modern Zionist thought is the creation of a whole galaxy of passionate and
> extraordinary men, but even among them a few stand out as original. Abra-
> ham Isaac Kook is one of this handful.

> —Arthur Hertzberg

By the time of his death in 1935, Rabbi Abraham Isaac Ha-Cohen Kook was
recognized as the greatest mystic in modern Judaism. The basic facts of his
life are known, yet Rav Kook was an enigma in his own day and remains one
until the present. Even when scholars speak of the "inspiration" Kook drew
from Rabbi Loew of Prague and the "influence" of the kabbalah, their assig-
nation of his intellectual lineage is strikingly vague. Kook's thought world
proceeded mainly from within—though he was wholly grounded in every aspect of Jewish learning.

The mysteries surrounding Kook can be multiplied. Although Kook married the daughter of the illustrious rabbi of Ponivesh (or Ponivetz), little has
been written about their relationship. Rabbi Kook's son, student, and recognized disciple, Rabbi Zvi Yehuda Kook (1891–1981), took his father's
thought in directions that, from an outsider's perspective, look parochially
Jewish, militaristic, and at odds with the spirit of his father's writings. Even
Kook's unique relationship with the secular pioneers and their intellectual
leadership remains largely untold. Yosef Hayyim Brenner rejected Kook's
views, yet walked (literally) in his footsteps on one occasion when the latter
was going to synagogue, and he regarded him as a kindred spirit. Kook wrote
a warm letter of welcome to the national poet, Chaim Nachman Bialik, when

he migrated to Israel, yet he wrote scathingly to Eliezer ben Yehuda, the father of modern Hebrew and another giant in the Zionist pantheon.

The campaign of vilification that Kook suffered at the hands of the ultra-Orthodox extremists of Jerusalem and the years he spent abroad, in London and in St. Gallen, Switzerland, are known only in general outline. All this only adds to the mystery that surrounds Rav Kook. This mystery can be partly dispelled by acquaintance with his thoughts, which, in contrast to his life, have received their due proportion of scholarly attention. Nevertheless, many of Kook's outpourings lie in manuscript and have not been published, much less translated into English. Every interpreter of Kook is quick to point out that his legacy still awaits proper assessment.

Shlomo Zalman, Kook's father, the local rabbi of Grieve, came from a hasidic background. Kook's mother, Peninah (Pearl), came from the world of the Lithuanian yeshiva. Like Israel Salanter and to a lesser extent Joseph Soloveitchik, Kook combined in his person the best of both these worlds. His thought evidences halachic expertise, yet he was essentially a mystic. In a 1908 letter, Kook cites admiringly the words of Rabbi Israel Baal Shem Tov, the founder of Hasidism, and the Vilna Gaon, his fierce opponent.[1]

By age nine, Kook had learned all that his local elementary school (*heder*) instructor could teach him. Known locally as the "cross-eyed genius," by fifteen Kook began his peregrinations through the Pale of Settlement, pursuing the Torah at every step of the voyage. Kook attended the famous Volozhin yeshiva, then headed by the famed Rabbi Naphtali Zvi Yehuda Berlin (the Netziv). Volozhin spawned some of the greatest students of the Torah and also some of Israel's greatest heretics. But despite his insistence in using spoken Hebrew (the "Holy Tongue" was not usually employed when discussing profane matters), Kook remained fervid in prayer and in observance. One childhood friend remembered the profuse tears that Kook would shed before Tisha B'Av, the day commemorating the destruction of the two Jerusalem Temples. His friend pointed out that he too longed for the Holy Land. But Kook replied, "Neither you nor your father are priests. But I am a Cohen [Priest]."[2] Many of the Volozhin students seemed to regard Kook as odd. But the Netziv and the Hofetz Hayim, two of the greatest figures in turn-of-the-century Eastern Orthodoxy, recognized Kook's unique qualities and befriended him.

A few years after his marriage, Kook served as a rabbi in Zoimel and Boisk, two towns in the Pale of Settlement. But Kook had his eyes fixed on Zion and was paying attention to the emerging Zionist movement. To the surprise of his friends and supporters, Kook accepted a call to serve as rabbi in Jaffa in 1904. This was hardly an obvious career move: The spade had been sent to Tel Aviv, now a city of a million, only two years earlier. Jaffa, unlike Jerusalem, Hebron, Tiberias, or Sefat, was not even one of the four

holy cities of Judaism. The Jaffa rabbinate would need to deal with secularist Jewish settlers, mainly Russian youngsters who had deliberately revolted
from the Jewish life of their parents, which Kook very visibly represented.
(Whether at the inauguration of the Hebrew University of Jerusalem in 1925
or at other secular events, Kook is always easy to pick out of the photo with
his full beard, black attire, and large *streimel*,[5] his high level of observance
was unmistakable.)

Kook's decision to come to *Eretz Yisrael*[6] inaugurated a very fruitful ten-
year period in his life. Mystical experiences, which Kook struggled to convey in poetry and prose, alternated with a variety of practical affairs. Despite
his love of Israel (and indeed all of humanity and the animal kingdom as
well), Kook found himself embroiled in controversy. Probably the most famous dispute concerned the *shemittah*. *Shemittah*, a biblical injunction to
Jews to allow their lands to lie fallow every seventh year as a shabbat to the
Lord, presented a severe challenge to the early colonists. Given the exigencies of early Zionist settlements, full observance of the *shemittah* would
have been an economic disaster. Kook found a way to commute it: fictive
land sales to non-Jews combined with special harvesting methods would allow agriculture to take place within halachic parameters. Traditionalists in
Jerusalem were outraged, but Kook stood his ground. Baron Edmond de
Rothschild, who in the 1889 *shemittah* controversy first devised the fictive
land sales, attempted to force more religiously observant colonists into farm-
ing. Contrary to his own lenient ruling, Kook declared that any colonist was
free to observe the *shemittah* in its strictest sense. (Kook interpreted the *halachah* stringently in issues ranging from women's rights and milking cows
on Shabbat to conducting autopsies).

To say that Kook stood above all parties is a gross understatement. He
would participate in folk dances with Jewish atheists while wearing full rabbinic regalia. He aggressively promoted Palestinian-grown citrons (*etrogim*)[7]
as superior to those grown in Corfu, and encouraged viticulture—the fact that
we now enjoy the superb wines of the Golan and Central Plains is due partly
to Kook. (He had a head for business and was persuaded to serve as communal rabbi by his father-in-law.) Yet Kook also authored tracts on the importance of proper *tefillin* placement on the forehead and on the mystical significance of Hebrew letters, vowel signs, and cantillation notes. Criticizing a
negativistic and superspecialized rabbinate, Kook the mystic sought the living God at the core of the religious experience:

> Matters have come to a point where the true meaning of Torah, the higher level
> of the Torah, has been made void, where the deepest aspect of the soul has been
> crushed, where the capacity to think has been weakened, where our spiritual

state and that of the world that is dependent upon us has been brought to a state of fearful decline. . . . Are you advocating *Kabbalah, musar,* philosophy, literature, poetry? All these are bankrupt. . . . Such arguments are enough to choke the voice of God calling within us in the depths of our souls and penetrating to all worlds: *Seek me and Live.*[8]

On a trip to Germany in 1914 to attend a conference of non-Zionist Orthodox rabbis of the recently founded *Agudat Yisrael,* Kook found himself stranded when the First World War broke out. Lodged by Rabbi Isaac Dov Bamberger, a member of a distinguished rabbinic family, in the charming town of St. Gallen, Switzerland, Kook used the next two years to study and write. Legend has it that at St. Gallen he lay with a stone under his pillow in remembrance of Jacob (Gen. 28:11) and out of solidarity with the suffering of the Jews of Palestine. Fortunately for the Zionist movement, Kook accepted a rabbinical position in London, which he held until 1919. Fortunate, because Kook was on hand for the negotiations that surrounded the issuing of the Balfour Declaration of 1917—opposed by several highly placed British Jews. Kook impressed British leaders such as Arthur Balfour and Lloyd George who were Bible enthusiasts and thus captivated by Kook's messianic vision of Jewish restoration to the land of Israel.

The British Mandate over Palestine began in 1920, issuing in a new period for the Zionist movement. One result was to transfer high levels of self-governance to the respective religious communities in Palestine. Kook returned to *Eretz Yisrael* serving as chief Ashkenazic rabbi. (He served until his death in 1935.) Within a couple of years, Kook had established a yeshiva that now sits in the heart of the Jewish Quarter of Jerusalem and bears its founder's name (*Merkaz ha-Rav*). He also founded a movement of Orthodox Jews (Banner of Jerusalem) composed of followers ideologically unable to join the religious Zionist movement, Mizrachi, but also dedicated to the rebuilding of Palestine. The 1920s and 1930s were a critical decade in building a Zionist nucleus for a full-fledged state, and Kook set an important example by fully participating in these events.

This period of Kook's life was even more marked by controversy than his first sojourn in *Eretz Yisrael.* While the extremist Orthodox made him miserable most often, the Labor Zionists took their turn, especially when Kook defended Avraham Stavsky, falsely convicted of the murder of Chaim Alosoroff. Alosoroff, a popular labor leader, was murdered while strolling with his wife on a Tel Aviv beach, an incident that horrified the Jewish inhabitants to a degree that can only be compared to the reaction that followed the murder of Yitzhak Rabin. Three suspects, all right-wing revisionist activists, were tried for the murder. Public sentiment against the killers ran high, but the trial was full of irregularities. Kook, after interviewing Stavsky in prison, declared that he would swear during the holiest part of the Yom Kippur service when it fell on a Shabbat that Stavsky was innocent!

Admittedly, the expanse of Rav Kook's thought is so overwhelming that any summary is bound to do it an injustice. Taking a page from Shlomo Avineri's useful thumbnail sketches of Zionist thinkers, I will address only three aspects of Kook's thought: (1) his conception of the mystical qualities inherent in *Eretz Yisrael*, (2) his dialectical evaluation of the relationship between secular Zionism and Judaism, and (3) the universal, messianic significance of the Jewish renaissance.[9]

The notion that geography affects character is neither new nor implausible. Yehuda Halevy, the eleventh-century philosopher and poet, contended that prophecy could only take place in the ancestral homeland. During the Enlightenment, Montesquieu argued that climate affected the form of a particular nation's government. Put an Englishman in Italy for a few years and we are not surprised when his disposition gets sunnier as his complexion gets darker. In the nineteenth century, nationalists emphasized the integral relationship between a nation's character and its geography: Germans were forest people, Semites desert people, and so on. Kook's vision blends Halevy with nineteenth-century nationalism and expresses itself in unmistakably kabbalistic images:

> In the Holy Land man's imagination is lucid and clear, clean and pure, capable of receiving the revelations of Divine Truth and of expressing in life the sublime meaning of the ideal of the sovereignty of holiness; there the mind is prepared to understand the light of prophecy and to be illuminated by the radiance of the Holy Spirit. In gentile lands the imagination is dim clouded by darkness and overshadowed with unholiness, and it cannot serve as the vessel for the outpouring of the Divine Light.[10]

For Kook, Jewish attachment to *Eretz Yisrael* is a metaphysical, not merely an emotional, reality. "Deep in the heart of every Jew, in its purest and holiest recesses, there blazes the fire of Israel."[11] Implicitly (and elsewhere explicitly), Kook condemned the life created in the lands of the diaspora as unredeemed; the very return to the land, the very air and soil of *Eretz Yisrael* would bring a healing to the alienated Jewish soul. On this point, the Zionist thinker who most invites comparison with Kook is Aharon David Gordon. Gordon, a Tolstoy-influenced, secular Russian, traveled to Palestine in his fifties to work the land as a farmer and to preach the "religion of labor." An apocryphal story has it that Gordon once remarked to Kook that "the great heretics and the great believers understand one another." True or not, the story points to their common belief that *Eretz Yisrael* itself possesses the ability to rejuvenate Jewish character.

The second facet of Kook's thinking that so shocked contemporaries was his insistence that secular colonists performed a divine task when they developed the land, even if they were unaware of it, indeed, even if they denied any religious component to their activities. How else could one explain "secularists" being drawn to an arid, backward, often unwelcoming land? In the diaspora, the spirit had been cultivated by students of the Torah, but the body of Israel had atrophied. When the body was healed, the spirit of Israel would assert itself. This is one of the many metaphors that Kook used to express the divine dialect of what was happening before his very eyes. (The Jewish population of Israel grew from 90,000 to 400,000 during Kook's chief rabbinate, and the physical development of the land was equally striking.)

In a vein entirely foreign to the older pietists, who considered the Zionist settlers outright sinners and heretics, Kook could admiringly describe the "healthy flesh and blood, strong and well-formed bodies, and a fiery spirit encased in powerful muscles" that the return to *Eretz Yisrael* would engender.[12] Curiously, this focus on physical well-being is often associated with Max Nordau's call for a "Judaism of muscle." Nordau, Herzl's deputy and a European philosopher of renown, represented an entirely secularist position within Zionism. Kook reacted harshly to Nordau's proclamation that "Zionism has nothing to do with theology." Israeli philosopher Aviezer Ravitsky has demonstrated that it took Kook a longer time than is usually assumed to accept that the secularist still belonged to the community of Israel. In the end, Kook's messianic optimism won out. He confidently declared that a secular Zionism "has sufficient potency to be a theme of propaganda and, to some extent, win adherents for a limited span of time, but secularity cannot offer us a permanent directive for life."[13] Whatever the early Zionist settlers thought, they were unwittingly and unconsciously doing the work of the Lord.[14]

Messianism has always threatened stability, rational decision making, and good political judgment. The early sages advised that if you were planting a sapling and someone told you that the Messiah was coming, it would be better to finish planting and then go out and greet him. The disastrous Sabbatian explosion of 1665–1666, the last major messianic uprising, had wreaked havoc upon the order of the Jewish communities. A key prohibition, "it is forbidden to hasten the end," was used by traditionalists in justifying their opposition to Zionism. Other religious Zionists, who organized the Mizrachi Party, were careful to distinguish the patient building up of the land from the messianic process itself; the sacred from the profane. That is why, at the Sixth Zionist Congress, Mizrachi representatives supported Herzl's investigation into a temporary East African refuge for the Jews of czarist Russia.[15] Kook, however, had no doubt the messianic era was at hand. He likened Herzl to Messiah ben Yosef, the "pre-Messiah" whose physical labors and ultimate demise would precede the arrival of Messiah ben David—the real item.

Two features of Kook's messianism deserve emphasis. One, rather than pack his bags and his lunchbox and wait passively for the messianic redemption (which is exactly what many ordinary Jews did during the Sabbatian movement in the seventeenth century), Kook busily prepared for the great day by building up the land. Two, rather than fantasize about the terrible punishments that would befall the nations (typical of medieval messianic imaginings), Kook considered the Jewish renaissance the greatest possible boon for humanity. Jacob (Israel), Esau (Christianity), and Ishmael (Islam) would be restored to their essential brotherhood, bathed in the light of compassion. Judaism's goal, he said, "is not to absorb or destroy the other faiths . . . but to perfect them toward a higher development, so that they may free themselves of their dross, and they will automatically attach themselves to the root of Israel. . . . This applies even to pagan faiths and certainly so to those faiths that are partly based on the light of Israel's Torah."[16]

This harmonizing, universalistic, peaceful vision is not what most Israelis associate with "Kookism." Rather, Kookism today is associated with the settler movement and an ultranationalism that expresses itself aggressively toward Palestinian Arabs. The story of Kookism after Kook goes well beyond the parameters of this chapter; still, the problems inherent in his utterances deserve mention. When Kook died in 1935, the Nazis had only begun their reghettoization of German Jews (many of whom emigrated to Israel from 1932 to 1939). The Nazis had not yet destroyed the world that gave birth to Kook. Inevitably, Kook's optimism regarding the nations was hard to maintain in light of the Holocaust and the growing animosity of Palestinian Arabs. In addition, epochal events such as Israeli independence and the reunification of Jerusalem demanded practical and theological application of Kookism to new realities. This alone would have reshaped Kook's legacy. But Kook also suffered from a weakness common to many visionaries, namely, a tendency to depreciate problems likely to be encountered on the way toward realizing the dream. As Ravitsky notes, Kook refused to recognize that secularism was not a mere transitional phenomenon, but was here to stay. Equally significant, Kook did not pay heed to the nasty realities of politics. That an Israeli state might act much like other states was beyond his ken. I conclude this discussion with Kook's bird's-eye view of Israel's political fortunes from the destruction of the Second Temple (70 CE) until his own day. It demonstrates both the weaknesses inherent in his mystic perspective, and its abiding beauty.

Forces from without compelled us to forsake the political arena of the world, but our withdrawal was also motivated by an inward assent, as if to say that we were awaiting the advent of a happier time, when government could be conducted without ruthlessness and barbarism. That is the day for which we hope. . . . It is not meet for Jacob to engage in political life at a time when statehood requires bloody ruthlessness and a talent for evil.[17]

QUESTIONS FOR KOOK, *LIGHTS FOR REBIRTH* (FROM HERTZBERG, *THE ZIONIST IDEA*, 419–30)

What is Kook's critique of the Jewish diaspora? Can you see why this might put him at odds with other Orthodox figures from Eastern Europe?

What is Kook's view of the possibility of a truly secular Zionism? Can you see why that might put him at odds with the Zionist mainstream?

What does Kook mean when he refers to the holiness of the land of Israel (*Eretz Yisrael*)? Can a piece of land really be holy, in your opinion? What would make it holy? What are the possible religious and political implications of accepting the holiness of a piece of land?

Arthur Hertzberg describes Kook as a "mystic" and a "messianist." What is a mystic? What is a messianist? What factors in these essays incline you to agree (or disagree) with Hertzberg's verdict?

What aspects of the young Zionist settlers attracted Kook? What role did they play in his overall vision of transformation of the Jews? Of the land of Israel?

In what ways was Kook's ideal educational program different from the education that he himself received in Lithuania?

Why was Kook so sure that the Jewish return to the ancestral homeland would have such a revolutionary effect on Judaism the religion? Has this return had a revolutionary effect on Judaism, or on Jewish life? The effect that Kook anticipated?

What were the implications for the nations of the world of a return of the Jews to their homeland, in Kook's opinion? Who would accept this view? Who would reject it?

Is it possible today to remain as optimistic as Kook in the coming of redemption and in Israel's role in helping to bring redemption about?

STUDIES BY AND ABOUT KOOK

The two best places to read more about Kook in English are Arthur Hertzberg, *The Zionist Idea* (New York: Atheneum, 1979), and Ben-Zion Bokser, *Abra-*

ham Isaac Kook (New York: Paulist Press, 1978). There are many Hebrew works on Kook's life and thought, but the material in English is also adequate for the general reader. Jacob Agus, *Banner of Jerusalem* (New York: Bloch, 1946), presents the basic facts of Kook's career. A brief summary of his thought is available in Shlomo Avineri, *The Making of Modern Zionism* (New York: Basic Books, 1981). The most probing analysis of Kook and his legacy for contemporary Israel (in English) is Aviezer Ravitsky, *Messianism, Zionism, and Jewish Religious Radicalism* (Chicago: University of Chicago Press, 1996). Ravitsky represents a consciously left-wing, Orthodox position, and his judgment regarding Kook's legacy is severe but well supported. Ezra Gellman, ed., *Essays on the Thought and Philosophy of Rabbi Kook* (New York: Cornwall, 1991), provides topically organized reflections. The Jewish organization Avi Chai sponsored and published presentations on the fiftieth anniversary of Kook's death (1985), which appeared as *The World of Rav Kook's Thought* (1991).

From *Lights for Rebirth*

Abraham Isaac Kook

Our national life, both intrinsically and in its relationship to all mankind, has had a long career. We have existed for a long time, and we have, therefore, expressed ourselves in many ways. We are a great people, and our mistakes are equally great; therefore, our woes and the consolations to follow them are both on the grand scale.

It is a fundamental error to turn our backs on the only source of our high estate and to discard the concept that we are a chosen people. We are not only different from all the nations, set apart by a historical experience that is unique and unparalleled, but we are also of a much higher and greater spiritual order. Really to know ourselves, we must be conscious of our greatness. Else we shall fall very low.

Our soul encompasses the entire universe, and represents it in its highest unity. It is, therefore, whole and complete, entirely free of all the disjointedness and the contradictions which prevail among all other peoples. We are one people, one as the oneness of the universe. This is the enormous spiritual potential of our innate character, and the various processes of our historical road, the road of light that passes between the mountains of darkness and perdition, are leading us to realize the hidden essence of our nature. All the mundane sine-quanons [*sic*] of national identity are transmuted by the all-inclusiveness of the spirit of Israel.

It is impossible to lop off any branch from the great, leafy tree of our life and to give it an existence of its own. Every fiber of our being would be roused to opposition and, in total self-awareness, we would react with all the inner strength at our command. The long road of our history has been determined by the hope for complete renascence of ourselves and of everything that is ours. Nothing can be ignored—not a single line in the image of our people dare be erased.

Yes, we are stronger than all the cultures of the ages and more enduring than all the permanencies of the world. Our longing is to reawaken to life in the amplitude of our ancestors—and to be even greater and more exalted than they were. We have made great moral contributions to the world, and we are now ready to become its teacher of joyous and vibrant living. Our spirit is unafraid of the passing ages; it gives birth to these ages and puts its stamp upon them. The power of our creativity is such that it impresses the most sublime spirituality on the practical stuff of life. As life evolves toward higher forms, this creative power increases, and the process of its fashioning the world into tangible expressions of the spirit becomes ever more marvelous to behold. All this will reach its highest fulfillment when our Jewish life is renascent in all its facets.

Society today is in a state of movement and tumult; but how poor and stultifying is this age, and how vast is the void that remains in the heart, after all the high-pitched emotions of wars and rumors of wars—for all of this is bereft of ultimate purpose and represents only the passing life of one or another group of men. Nor is there much greater value even to broad social revolutions, especially when these are attended by major upheavals which inflame the heart and confuse the mind. Without an ultimate spiritual ideal which can raise the whole of man's striving to the level of the highest forms that reason and sublime emotion can conceive, no movement can be of any value, or long endure.

But let us return to the Divine purpose, which is to realize the general good through the perfection of every person and group. It is not enough to exemplify this ideal at a moment of high emotion. To approach the estate of spiritual wholeness and to be assured of survival, a society must express the ideal clearly in every aspect of its soul. That which is beyond the reach of language will be said, in all its force, by the future all-encompassing and eternal divine order.

True, in the days of our decline the sparks of spiritual light are dim, and they are present, for the most part, in the memories embodied in our traditional way of life, in all the religious commandments and rules which stem from the past and look toward the future. But these conserve enormous vitality, and the dust that spiritual callousness has allowed to collect on them will be shaken off by a really serious movement of national renascence. The fiery sparks will become visible; they will join in becoming a great divine flame, warming the world and illuminating its uttermost reaches.

Our present is but a translated shadow of our great past; it is always turned toward the lofty future, a future that is so exalted that it lights up the present and gives it dimensions of active power unwarranted by its real estate, which is one of waiting and longing for the future. Everything depends on the value of the past and the future: Some pasts and futures can give light and warmth only to the most immediate present, and others are great enough to make of the present, which lives by their power, an age that is truly alive and creative. Our past is a great one, and our future is even greater, as is evidenced by our striving for the ideals of justice that are latent in our souls. This great force inspirits our present and gives it full life. From the deep range of our memories we draw many examples, a particular kind of wisdom and creativity, a unique outlook on the world, *mitzvot*, traditions, and customs—all suffused with spiritual content, love, and gentleness, and nurtured by the dew of life, heroism, and majesty—by our own gentleness, our own heroism, and our own majesty.

Apart from the nourishment it receives from the life-giving dew of the holiness of Eretz Israel, Jewry in the Diaspora has no real foundation and lives only by the power of a vision and by the memory of our glory, i.e., by the past and the future. But there is a limit to the power of such a vision to carry the burden of life and to give direction to the career of a people—and this limit seems already to have been reached. Diaspora Jewry is therefore disintegrating at an alarming rate, and there is no hope for it unless it replants itself by the wellspring of real life, of inherent sanctity, which can be found only in Eretz Israel. Even one spark of this real life can revive great areas of the kind of life that is but a shadow of a vision. The real and organic holiness of Jewry can become manifest only by the return of the people to its land, the only path that can lead to its renascence. Whatever is sublime in our spirit and our vision can live only to the degree that there will be a tangible life to reinvigorate the tiring dream.

As the world becomes spiritual and the spirit of man develops to higher levels, the demand becomes ever stronger in man that he live in accordance with his true nature. This call contains much truth and justice, and it is incumbent upon the moral leadership that they purify it and direct it into the right channel. Man increasingly discovers God within himself, in his correct impulses; even those inner drives which appear on the surface to stray from what is conventionally held to be the true road, man can raise to such a high level that they, too, contribute to the ultimate good.

On awakening to life, the community of Israel will rediscover its courage and dignity. The purity and holiness that it used to demonstrate in submission is ever more being displayed through the courage of the soul in deeds of national heroism. These two states will become one, and, in their uniting, heroism will become all the greater because it will have been made sweeter by holiness.

There is an eternal covenant which assures the whole House of Israel that it will not ever become completely unclean. Yes, it may be partially corroded, but it can never be totally cut off from the source of divine life. Many of the adherents of the present national revival maintain that they are secularists. If a Jewish secular nationalism were really imaginable, then we would, indeed, be in danger of falling so low as to be beyond redemption.

But Jewish secular nationalism is a form of self-delusion: the spirit of Israel is so closely linked to the spirit of God that a Jewish nationalist, no matter how secularist his intention may be, must, despite himself, affirm the divine. An individual can sever the tie that binds him to life eternal, but the House of Israel as a whole cannot. All of its most cherished national possessions—its land, language, history, and customs—are vessels of the spirit of the Lord.

How should men of faith respond to an age of ideological ferment which affirms all of these values in the name of nationalism and denies their source, the rootedness of the national spirit, in God? To oppose Jewish nationalism, even in speech, and to denigrate its values is not permissible, for the spirit of God and the spirit of Israel are identical. What they must do is to work all the harder at the task of uncovering the light and holiness implicit in our national spirit, the divine element which is its core. The secularists will thus be constrained to realize that they are immersed and rooted in the life of God and bathed in the radiant sanctity that comes from above.

Despite the grave faults of which we are aware in our life in general, and in Eretz Israel in particular, we must feel that we are being reborn and that we are being created once again as at the beginning of time. Our entire spiritual heritage is presently being absorbed within its source and is reappearing in a new guise, much reduced in material extent but qualitatively very rich and luxuriant and full of vital force. We are called to a new world suffused with the highest light, to an epoch the glory of which will surpass that of all the great ages which have preceded. All of our people believes that we are in the first stage of the Final Redemption. This deep faith is the very secret of its existence; it is the divine mystery implicit in its historical experience. This ancient tradition about the Redemption bears witness to the spiritual light by which the Jew understands himself and all the events of his history to the last generation, the one that is awaiting the Redemption that is near at hand.

The claim of our flesh is great. We require a healthy body. We have greatly occupied ourselves with the soul and have forsaken the holiness of the body.

We have neglected health and physical prowess, forgetting that our flesh is as sacred as our spirit. We have turned our backs on physical life, the development of our senses, and all that is involved in the tangible reality of the flesh, because we have fallen prey to lowly fears, and have lacked faith in the holiness of the Land. "Faith is exemplified by the tractate *Zeraim* (*Plants*)—man proves his faith in eternal life by planting."

Our return will succeed only if it will be marked, along with its spiritual glory, by a physical return which will create healthy flesh and blood, strong and well-formed bodies, and a fiery spirit encased in powerful muscles. Then the one weak soul will shine forth from strong and holy flesh, as a symbol of the physical resurrection of the dead.

NOTES

The epigraph for the chapter is taken from Arthur Hertzberg, *The Zionist Idea* (New York: Atheneum, 1979), 417.

1. Jacob Agus, *Banner of Jerusalem* (New York: Bloch, 1946).

2. Cited in Agus, *Banner of Jerusalem*, 10–11.

3. The *tallith* (prayer shawl) is the four-cornered fringed garment whose wear is mandated in the Bible.

4. The *tefillin* (phylactery) is the wooden box with leather straps ritually wrapped around arm and forehead in the morning and in the evening. Like the *tallith*, the *tefillin* is also mandated wear in the Bible.

5. A *streimel* is the large fur hat, often made of beaver, usually worn by married (male) adherents of Hasidism. Although some form of head covering dates back at least to the early rabbinic period, the *streimel* became fashionable wear in the late Middle Ages.

6. *Eretz Israel* is Hebrew for "The Land of Israel."

7. An *etrog* is a lemon-like fruit used during the Sukkot holiday.

8. Ben-Zion Bokser, *Abraham Isaac Kook* (New York: Paulist Press, 1978), 357.

9. Shlomo Avineri, *The Making of Modern Zionism* (New York: Basic Books, 1981), 189.

10. Arthur Hertzberg, *The Zionist Idea* (New York: Atheneum, 1979), 421.

11. Hertzberg, *The Zionist Idea*.

12. Hertzberg, *The Zionist Idea*, 431.

13. Bokser, *Abraham Isaac Kook*, 11.

14. This paragraph relies heavily on Aviezer Ravitsky, *Messianism, Zionism, and Jewish Religious Radicalism* (Chicago: University of Chicago Press, 1996), 79–144.

15. Ehud Luz, *Parallels Meet* (Philadelphia: Jewish Publication Society, 1988).

16. Bokser, *Abraham Isaac Kook*, 29.

17. Jacob, or Israel, is taken here to represent the Jewish people.

Chapter Twelve

Joseph Soloveitchik

Halachah *and Existentialism*

SOLOVEITCHIK'S LIFE AND TIMES (1903–1993)

I remember when I was very young I was a solitary boy, afraid of the
world. But I had one friend, and he was—do not laugh—the Rambam
[Rabbi Moshe Maimonides 1135–1204][1]

Paradox surrounds the life and works of Rabbi Joseph Soloveitchik, heir to a
dynasty of Lithuanian Torah giants. He was an intensely reserved man, whose
confessional outpouring, *The Lonely Man of Faith*, constitutes a classic of
Jewish existentialism. He was an essentially private man, who served American Orthodoxy indefatigably from 1941 to 1985, in both Boston and New
York. He was a reticent judge in halachic matters who, arguably, ordained
more rabbis (about two thousand) than anyone, ever. A writer thoroughly at
home in both European philosophic and traditional Jewish literatures, whose
every line deserves a careful unpacking, Soloveitchik remains accessible to
the untutored or nonobservant reader in a way totally surprising given his
background and worldview. We can do no more here than note these para-
doxes in passing, and try to impart some small taste of one of the most complex figures in modern Jewish thought.

We are all the products of our families and our background, but this is especially true for a figure like Soloveitchik. Viewed from the outside, Soloveitchik's earliest education might be characterized as a mile deep but only an inch
wide. Soloveitchik's intellectual and familial ancestry stretches straight back to
the Vilna Gaon, the premier modernizer of Torah study and guiding spirit behind the flowering of yeshiva life in the nineteenth century. The traditions of
the Lithuanian *yeshivot*, especially the intellectually rigorous Brisker school,
played the decisive role in Soloveitchik's intellectual formation—most of

which, by the way, he acquired from his father, Moshe, and from tutors. The substance of that education was talmudic: so much so, that Soloveitchik arrived in Berlin *mushlam*—with a complete mastery of the two-and-a-half-million-word Talmud. A story has it that once Moshe Soloveitchik and a visitor differed on the wording of a passage in Maimonides' law code, the *Mishneh Torah*.[2] Rather than go to the bookcase, Moshe asked his son to recite the entire passage by heart. Ordained as a rabbi (in his teens) by some of the greatest luminaries of the day, Soloveitchik's ordination contained the approbation that the *halachah* should always be decided according to his opinion!

Soloveitchik received no *formal* secular education. Growing up, he had virtually no contact with the non-Orthodox Jewish world, and none whatsoever with the gentile one. Nevertheless, this picture of insularity is easily overdrawn. Through his mother Pesha's encouragement, Soloveitchik acquainted himself with European literature. In his teens, his mother further urged him to acquire a secular education through private tutors. Even on purely Jewish grounds, the picture of a Brisker "clone" is misleading. Although the Brisker school opposed both Hasidism and Zionism vociferously,[3] Soloveitchik had an early and significant exposure to Habad (that is, Lubavitch) Hasidism through a household tutor. Moreover, Naphtali Zvi Judah Berlin (the Netziv) and Rabbi Meir Berlin, also related through marriage, were far more receptive to religious Zionism than the paternal side of the family.[4] In any event, Soloveitchik emerged from his Eastern European youth with perfect aplomb, entered Berlin University at twenty-two, and acquired a doctorate in philosophy. Soloveitchik wanted to write on Plato's influence on Maimonides, but nobody was sufficiently qualified to direct him. Instead, his doctoral dissertation dealt with the great Jewish arch-rationalist and champion of Immanuel Kant, Hermann Cohen. Soloveitchik received his doctorate in 1932, only a few months before the Nazis would ring down the curtains on that remarkably creative culture—general and Jewish—associated with the Weimar Republic.

With his wife Tanya (née Lewitt), who also held a doctoral degree, Soloveitchik moved to America, aided by the fact that his father was already serving as the intellectual head of New York's Orthodox Seminary (RIETS). Thus began the long, fruitful chapter of Soloveitchik's life in America, where he would remain until his death in 1993, visiting Israel only once in all those years. His service included the establishment of the Maimonides school in Boston, the first modern Orthodox day school in America; the Orthodox chief rabbinate in Boston; additional pastoral duties in New York; advanced lectures on Talmudic subjects and equally advanced lectures on general and Jewish philosophy at Yeshiva University;[5] service on U.S. government committees; and, not insignificantly, a life busy doing mitzvahs, using his great prestige wherever it could do some good. Even this accounting does not begin to give a sense of Soloveitchik's influence on two generations of American Orthodoxy. Reading the eulogies for Soloveitchik, who passed away at ninety after several years of suffering from Parkinson's disease, one understands why no better appellation could be found than the one that was used most commonly: "the Rav," the rabbi's rabbi.[6]

From what students of the Rav tell me, the full power of his eloquence was manifested especially in Yiddish. His annual talk on his father's *yahrzeit* lasted four to five hours, packed the auditorium of Yeshiva University, and was considered one of the intellectual highlights of the Jewish year. It should be recalled that Soloveitchik wrote principally in Yiddish and Hebrew and that he did not switch over to English as a lecturing language until the 1960s. It should also be recalled that while all the Soloveitchiks wrote a great deal, they published very reluctantly, dogged by the possibility that they could find a way to say things a little better, a little more precisely. Much of Soloveitchik's opus remains in manuscript or in Hebrew essays that are accessible only to the very learned. But the following three works can be read profitably, if only with some effort, by the interested layperson.

Any discussion of Soloveitchik's thought must begin with *Halachic Man* (*Ish ha-Halachah*), the first major work of Soloveitchik's that saw the light of day, and which alone would have been sufficient to establish his reputation as a Jewish thinker of the first rank. Employing the typological model, his favorite rhetorical posture, Soloveitchik distinguishes cognitive man from homo religiosus. On page 7 of *Halachic Man* he writes:

> Homo religiosus, like cognitive man, seeks the lawful and the ordered, the fixed and the necessary. But for the former, unlike the latter, the revelation of the law and comprehension of the order and interconnectedness of existence only intensifies and deepens the question and the problem. For while cognitive man discharges his obligation by establishing the reign of a causal structure of lawfulness in nature, homo religiosus is not satisfied with the perfection of the world under the dominion of the law. For to him the concept of lawfulness is in itself the deepest of mysteries.[7]

Given this description, we might expect to find halachic man, also a typological figure and the obvious "hero" of the book, closer in style to homo religiosus (translated loosely: a/the man of faith). Surprisingly, this is definitely not the case. "To whom may he [halachic man] be compared? To a mathematician who fashions an ideal world and then uses it for the purpose of establishing a relationship between it and the real world."[8] Certainly the mathematician comes closer to the model of cognitive man than of homo religiosus. But Soloveitchik means something more by this striking analogy. The cognitive style of halachic man is not that of the experimental scientist who gathers data and then, ex post facto, devises a theory to fit the phenomena. Rather, halachic man, like a mathematician, comes to the world armed with perfect formulas a priori and sees how reality matches up. Looking at the sun setting in the Western sky, halachic man recognizes (cognizes?) the various obligations that the sunset brings: recitation of the evening *Shema*, matzah, the counting of the omer, and so forth. Halachic man does not have either the time or the desire to contemplate his navel: he is far too busy applying God's Torah to the world.

Although the entirety of *Halachic Man* merits discussion, many of Soloveitchik's treatments of *teshuvah* (repentance) strike me as a noteworthy highpoint. *Teshuvah*, a cardinal Jewish doctrine, is usually translated as "repentance," but that is too internal and subjective a word to capture the sense of the Hebrew root, which means "to turn" or "to return." In Judaism, *teshuvah* signifies a concrete change of direction, an objective, discernible turning to modes of behavior that are pleasing to God and beneficial for other humans. "The gates of *teshuvah* are always open." Anyone, anytime, can turn and be reconciled with God without the means of an intercessor or sacrament. Soloveitchik's discussion of *teshuvah* begins typically, with a seeming contradiction in Maimonides over whether or not verbal confession is a necessary component of *teshuvah*. In fact, as Soloveitchik explains, there is no contradiction but rather two teachings, corresponding to two forms of *teshuvah*. *Teshuvah* can be merely reactive and retrospective, oriented toward divesting the person of the status of sinner and averting punishment. This level of *teshuvah* truly could be translated as repentance, and remains largely reliant on the grace of God. But the ideal *teshuvah*, from the halachic perspective, also contains proactive, forward-looking, and self-reliant elements. In fact, *teshuvah*, properly performed, reorients the entire person toward a better existence and constitutes a perfect example of what Soloveitchik terms halachic man's "creative capacity."

The Halachic Mind, originally written in 1944 under the title "Toward an Epistemology of the *Halachah*," was published when Soloveitchik was already ill and without his permission. Although an unfinished symphony, *The Halachic Mind* sets out a methodology of religious investigation that is decidedly modern yet triumphantly Orthodox. Although it goes without saying that Soloveitchik believes in the perfection of the Torah given by God at Mount Sinai,[9] this book's contribution to modern Jewish thought can be grasped by recalling Alexander Pope's statement that "the proper study of mankind is man." Soloveitchik would take Pope's dictum further and apply it as well to the world of religion. The phenomenology of the person at worship (including prayer, repentance, and performance of the *mitzvot*) yields the raw data that the student of religion assesses after the fact to draw up the correct doctrines of that religion. The origins of that religion are as irrelevant to its validity as knowing what Pythagoras put on his oatmeal the day he intuited his famous theorem. Soloveitchik has some critical words to say about Samson Raphael Hirsch's and Maimonides' overly bold constructions of God's motives. His harshest criticisms, however, are reserved for the liberal religious thinkers of the last two centuries who "plunge" into the realms of ethics, aesthetics, and politics and present their findings as "religious" teachings.[10]

The Lonely Man of Faith, the opening of which has been reproduced at the end of this chapter, stands as a classic of religious existentialism, a probing examination of the dilemma of a religious person in a secular age. Dedicated to the memory of Soloveitchik's then recently departed wife Tanya, *The Lonely Man of Faith* first appeared as an essay in *Tradition* (1965) and was later republished in book form to wide acclaim. The body of this essay contrasts two human types, Adam I and Adam II. Soloveitchik ingeniously takes the two accounts of God's creation of humans (Gen. 1:26–28 and Gen. 2:4ff) as the textual peg on which to hang this typology. Adam I represents the man of the world: dignified, majestic, capable, successful, calculating, self-sufficient, satisfied with the acclaim of society. Adam II represents the religious man, longing and lonely, who accepts the need to surrender something of himself (a rib, for instance) in order to be complete. Adam II seeks meaning and transcendence in the encounter with the Other and with God, and finds spiritual fulfillment only within a covenanted community.

As the intellectual leader of American Orthodoxy for many decades, Soloveitchik was forced to confront many of the burning issues of the day, though his personality led to extreme reticence. Not only did Soloveitchik write exquisitely on the role of women in Judaism in essays such as "The Covenantal Role of Sarah," he permitted, on at least one occasion, a woman's intoning the benediction for the dead (*kaddish*), traditionally a male prerogative. Soloveitchik took the position in "Confrontation" that interreligious dialogue was at the deepest level an impossibility, and therefore, should be avoided. Soloveitchik's deprecation of non-Orthodox Judaism, though not non-Orthodox Jews, was exemplified by his decision that it would be better not to hear the *shofar* blown than to hear it in a synagogue without a *mehitzah*, a barrier between men and women. On the whole, Soloveitchik did not seek the fray. His political quiescence in the 1960s and 1970s contrasted strongly with the engaged activism of A. J. Heschel, a fellow survivor of the Eastern European tragedy.

Having lodged these reservations about Soloveitchik's legacy, let me conclude by suggesting that no one in this century has presented halachic Judaism with more integrity—intellectually and emotionally—than the Rav. His student and son-in-law Aharon Lichtenstein wrote, "It is as the scholar and philosopher of Halakhah that he is significant."[11] Yet this evaluation underestimates Soloveitchik, for on every page he wrote, one is constantly aware that here is a great man, a great Jew, and a towering religious personality.

QUESTIONS FOR SOLOVEITCHIK,
THE LONELY MAN OF FAITH

(These questions relate only to the opening few pages—really the prologue to the main part of the essay. I am confident that if you understand the beginning, the rest of the essay will also be comprehensible.)

The opening of this essay can be called existentialist. What is existentialism and how can existentialism be found in an atheist (Camus), a devout Christian (Kierkegaard), and an observant Jew (Soloveitchik)? After finishing the opening, ask yourself: Is there anything specifically Jewish here? Specifically Orthodox?

What does (and does not) Soloveitchik mean when he speaks of his loneliness?

Why is the "man of faith" necessarily alienated from modern society? What are the various sources of that alienation? What impedes the man of faith from communicating with the contemporary world?

How does Soloveitchik make the quest for self-knowledge (arguably a Greek, not a Judaic, ideal) a "kosher" endeavor?

What does Soloveitchik mean by the term *interpretive gesture*? Why is he at such pains to stress that this interpretative gesture is wholly subjective?

"Moreover, I have not even been troubled by the theories of biblical criticism which contradict the very foundations upon which the sanctity and integrity of the Scriptures rest." This is an unexpected statement from an Orthodox Jew who also mastered the European culture of his day, including Bible criticism. *Why* isn't Soloveitchik troubled by these theories?

Soloveitchik acknowledges that the Bible contains two accounts of creation. What do modern biblical scholars conclude from this incongruity? What does Soloveitchik conclude?

Looking at the four points of incongruity with which this selection concludes, can you imagine some differences in the nature of Adam I and Adam II?

STUDIES BY AND ABOUT SOLOVEITCHIK

The Lonely Man of Faith remains Soloveitchik's most accessible work in English. Nothing Soloveitchik wrote is "easy," but I hope that this introduction will whet the reader's appetite for the rest of this essay. Rabbi Aharon Lichtenstein's biographical essay in Simon Noveck's *Great Jewish Thinkers* series provides some good material on the Rav's life, but the evaluation of his works does not do justice to the scope of the Rav's general interest to students of religion. *The Soloveitchik Heritage: A Daughter's Memoir* (Hoboken, N.J.: Ktav, 1995), a memoir by the Rav's sister, Shulamith Soloveitchik Meiselman, provides a picture of the background of an extraordinary family.

Pinchas Peli, an Israeli scholar, has edited a book of talks and lectures titled *Soloveitchik on Repentance* (New York: Paulist Press, 1984), which can be read piecemeal or in its entirety. Peli's article "Hermeneutics in Rav Soloveitchik: Medium or Message," *Tradition* 23, no. 3 (Spring 1988) is a good exposition of his use of *derasha*. *Tradition*, a centrist Orthodox journal, regularly deals with Soloveitchik's legacy. Eugene Borowitz's discussion of the Rav in *Choices in Modern Jewish Thought: A Partisan Guide*, 2nd ed. (West Orange, N.J.: Behrman House, 1995) offers a clear overview. Soloveitchik has generated considerable academic discussion: most of it, regrettably, will be too technical to interest the general reader.

From *The Lonely Man of Faith*

Joseph Soloveitchik

It is not the plan of this essay to discuss the millennium-old problem of faith and reason. Theory is not my concern at the moment. I want instead to focus attention on a human-life situation in which the man of faith as an individual concrete being, with his cares and hopes, concerns and needs, joys and sad moments, is entangled. Therefore, whatever I am going to say here has been derived not from philosophical dialectics, abstract speculation, or detached impersonal reflections, but from actual situations and experiences with which I have been confronted. Indeed, the term "lecture" also is, in this context, a misnomer. It is rather a tale of personal dilemma. Instead of talking theology, in the didactic sense, eloquently and in balanced sentences, I would like, hesitantly and haltingly, to confide in you, and to share with you some concerns which weigh heavily on my mind and which frequently assume the proportions of an awareness of crisis.

I have no problem-solving thoughts. I do not intend to suggest a new method of remedying the human situation which I am about to describe; neither do I believe that it can be remedied at all. The role of the man of faith, whose religious experience is fraught with inner conflicts and incongruities, who oscillates between ecstasy in God's companionship and despair when he feels abandoned by God, and who is torn asunder by the heightened contrast between self-appreciation and abnegation, has been a difficult one since the times of Abraham and Moses. It would be presumptuous of me to attempt to convert the passional, antinomic faith-experience into a eudaemonic, harmonious one, while the Biblical knights of faith lived heroically with this very tragic and paradoxical experience.

All I want is to follow the advice given by Elihu, the son of Berachel of old, who said, "I will speak that I may find relief"; for there is a redemptive quality for an agitated mind in the spoken word, and a tormented soul finds peace in confessing.

I

The nature of the dilemma can be stated in a three-word sentence. I am lonely. Let me emphasize, however, that by stating "I am lonely" I do not intend to convey to you the impression that I am alone. I, thank God, do enjoy the love and friendship of many. I meet people, talk, preach, argue, reason; I am surrounded by comrades and acquaintances. And yet, companionship and friendship do not alleviate the passional experience of loneliness which trails me constantly. I am lonely because at times I feel rejected and thrust away by everybody, not excluding my most intimate friends, and the words of the Psalmist, "My father and my mother have forsaken me," ring quite often in my ears like the plaintive cooing of the turtledove. It is a strange, alas, absurd experience engendering sharp, enervating pain as well as a stimulating, cathartic feeling. I despair because I am lonely and, hence, feel frustrated. On the other hand, I also feel invigorated because this very experience of loneliness presses everything in me into the service of God. In my "desolate, howling solitude" I experience a growing awareness that, to paraphrase Plotinus's apothegm about prayer, this service to which I, a lonely and solitary individual, am committed is wanted and gracefully accepted by God in His transcendental loneliness and numinous solitude.

I must address myself to the obvious question: why am I beset by this feeling of loneliness and being unwanted? Is it the Kierkegaardian anguish—an ontological fear nurtured by the awareness of nonbeing threatening one's existence—that assails me, or is this feeling of loneliness solely due to my own personal stresses, cares, and frustrations? Or is it perhaps the result of the pervasive state of mind of Western man who has become estranged from himself, a state with which all of us as Westerners are acquainted?

I believe that even though all three explanations might be true to some extent, the genuine and central cause of the feeling of loneliness from which I cannot free myself is to be found in a different dimension, namely, in the experience of faith itself. I am lonely because, in my humble, inadequate way, I am a man of faith for whom to be means to believe, and who substituted "credo" for "cognito" in the time-honored Cartesian maxim.* Apparently, in this role, as a man of faith, I must experience a sense of loneliness which is of a compound nature. It is a blend of that which is inseparably interwoven into the very texture of the faith gesture, characterizing the unfluctuating metaphysical destiny of the man of faith, and of that which is extraneous to the act of believing and stems from the ever-changing human-historical situation with all its whimsicality. On the one hand, the man of faith has been a solitary figure throughout the ages, indeed millennia, and no one has succeeded in escaping this unalterable destiny which is an "objective" awareness rather than a subjective feeling. On the other hand, it is undeniably true that this basic awareness expresses itself in a variety of ways, utilizing the whole gamut of one's affective emotional life which is extremely responsive to outward challenges and moves along with the tide of cultural and historical change. Therefore, it is my intent to analyze this experience at both levels: at the ontological, at which it is a root awareness, and at the historical, at which a highly sensitized and agitated heart, overwhelmed by the impact of social and cultural forces, filters this root awareness through the medium of painful, frustrating emotions.

As a matter of fact, the investigation at the second level is my prime concern since I am mainly interested in the contemporary man of faith who is, due to his peculiar position in our secular society, lonely in a special way. No matter how time-honored and time-hallowed the interpenetration of faith and loneliness is, and it certainly goes back to the dawn of the Judaic covenant, the contemporary man of faith lives through a particularly difficult and agonizing crisis.

Let me spell out this passional experience of the contemporary man of faith.

He looks upon himself as a stranger in modern society, which is technically minded, self-centered, and self-loving, almost in a sickly narcissistic fashion, scoring honor upon honor, piling up victory upon victory, reaching for the distant galaxies, and seeing in the here-and-now sensible world the only manifestation of being. What can a man of faith like myself, living by a doctrine which has no technical potential, by a law which cannot be tested in the laboratory, steadfast in his loyalty to an eschatological vision whose fulfillment cannot be predicted with any degree of probability, let alone certainty, even

---

* This is, of course, a rhetorical phrase, since all emotional and volitional activity was included in the Cartesian *cogitatio* as *modi cogitandi*. In fact, faith in the existence of an intelligent *causa prima* was for Descartes an integral part of his logical postulate system, by which he proves the existence of the external world.

by the most complex, advanced mathematical calculations—what can such a man say to a functional, utilitarian society which is *saeculum*-oriented and whose practical reasons of the mind have long ago supplanted the sensitive reasons of the heart?

It would be worthwhile to add the following in order to place the dilemma in the proper focus. I have never been seriously troubled by the problem of the Biblical doctrine of creation vis-à-vis the scientific story of evolution at both the cosmic and the organic levels, nor have I been perturbed by the confrontation of the mechanistic interpretation of the human mind with the Biblical spiritual concept of man. I have not been perplexed by the impossibility of fitting the mystery of revelation into the framework of historical empiricism. Moreover, I have not even been troubled by the theories of Biblical criticism which contradict the very foundations upon which the sanctity and integrity of the Scriptures rest. However, while theoretical oppositions and dichotomies have never tormented my thoughts, I could not shake off the disquieting feeling that the practical role of the man of faith within modern society is a very difficult, indeed, a paradoxical one.

The purpose of this essay, then, is to define the great dilemma confronting the contemporary man of faith. Of course, as I already remarked, by defining the dilemma we do not expect to find its solution, for the dilemma is insoluble. However, the defining itself is a worthwhile cognitive gesture which, I hope, will yield a better understanding of ourselves and our commitment. Knowledge in general and self-knowledge in particular are gained not only from discovering logical answers but also from formulating logical, even though unanswerable, questions. The human logos is as concerned with an honest inquiry into an insoluble antinomy which leads to intellectual despair and humility as it is with an unprejudiced true solution of a complex problem arousing joy and enhancing one's intellectual determination and boldness.

Before beginning the analysis, we must determine within which frame of reference, psychological and empirical or theological and Biblical, our dilemma should be described. I believe you will agree with me that we do not have much choice in the matter; for, to the man of faith, self-knowledge has one connotation only—to understand one's place and role within the scheme of events and things willed and approved by God, when He ordered finitude to emerge out of infinity and the Universe, including man, to unfold itself. This kind of self-knowledge may not always be pleasant or comforting. On the contrary, it might from time to time express itself in a painful appraisal of the difficulties which the man of faith, caught in his paradoxical destiny, has to encounter, for knowledge at both planes, the scientific and the personal, is not always a eudaemonic experience. However, this unpleasant prospect should not deter us from our undertaking.

Before I go any further, I want to make the following reservation. Whatever I am about to say is to be seen only as a modest attempt on the part of a man of faith to interpret his spiritual perceptions and emotions in modern theological and philosophical categories. My interpretive gesture is completely subjective and lays no claim to representing a definitive Halakhic philosophy. If my audience will feel that these interpretations are also relevant to their perceptions and emotions, I shall feel amply rewarded. However, I shall not feel hurt if my thoughts will find no response in the hearts of my listeners.

We all know that the Bible offers two accounts of the creation of man. We are also aware of the theory suggested by Bible critics attributing these two accounts to two different traditions and sources. Of course, since we do not unreservedly accept the unity and integrity of the Scriptures and their divine character, we reject this hypothesis which is based, like much Biblical criticism, on literary categories invented by modern man, ignoring completely the eidetic-noetic content of the Biblical story. It is, of course, true that the two accounts of the creation of man differ considerably. This incongruity was not discovered by the Bible critics. Our sages of old were aware of it.* However, the answer lies not in an alleged dual tradition but in dual man, not in an imaginary contradiction between two versions but in a real contradiction in the nature of man. The two accounts deal with two Adams, two men, two fathers of mankind, two types, two representatives of humanity, and it is no wonder that they are not identical. Let us just read these two accounts.

In Genesis I we read: "So God created man in His own image, in the image of God created He him, male and female created He them. And God blessed them and God said unto them, be fruitful and multiply, and fill the earth and subdue it, and have dominion over the fish of the sea, over the fowl of the heaven, and over the beasts, and all over the earth."

In Genesis 2, the account differs substantially from the one we just read: "And the eternal God formed the man of the dust of the ground and breathed into his nostrils the breath of life and man became a living soul. And the eternal God planted a garden eastward in Eden. . . . And the eternal God took the man and placed him in the Garden of Eden to serve it and to keep it."

I want to point out four major discrepancies between these two accounts:

1. In the story of the creation of Adam the first, it is told that the latter was created in the image of God, *b'tzelem Elokim*, while nothing is said about how his body was formed. In the account of the creation of Adam the second, it is

---

* Vide *Berakhot*, 61a; Nachmanides, Genesis 2:7; *Cuzari*, IV.

stated that he was fashioned from the dust of the ground and God breathed into his nostrils the breath of life.

2. Adam the first received the mandate from the Almighty to fill the earth and subdue it, *u'melu et-ha'aretz v'kivshuhah'* (Gen. 1:28). Adam the second was charged with the duty to cultivate the garden and to keep it, *l'avdah u'lishomrah* (Gen. 2:15).

3. In the story of Adam the first, both male and female were created concurrently, while Adam the second emerged alone, with Eve appearing subsequently as his helpmate and complement.

4. Finally, and this is a discrepancy of which Biblical criticism has made so much, while in the first account only the name of E-lohim appears, in the second, E-lohim is used in conjunction with the Tetragrammaton.

NOTES

1. Shulamith Soloveitchik Meiselman, *The Soloveitchik Heritage: A Daughter's Memoir* (Hoboken, N.J.: Ktav, 1995), 152.

2. Maimonides' twelfth-century law code, *Mishneh Torah*, enjoyed a very high prestige in both the Brisk (*mitnaggdic*) and the Habad (hasidic) traditions.

3. The Yiddish writer Y. L. Peretz caricatured the Brisker Rov in his short story "Between Two Peaks."

4. The vast majority of traditional religious leaders in Eastern Europe opposed Zionism stridently.

5. Apparently, the Rav's many students were bifurcated into those who knew Soloveitchik as a Talmudic giant and those who knew him as a philosopher. His unique integration of the two disciplines has, by and large, proven unrepeatable.

6. It should be noted that Soloveitchik also merited a rabbinic acronym, the GRID (Gaon Rav Yosef Dov).

7. Joseph Soloveitchik, *Halachic Man* (Philadelphia: Jewish Publication Society, 1983), 7.

8. Soloveitchik, *Halachic Man*, 19.

9. Soloveitchik, *The Lonely Man of Faith*, (New York: Doubleday, 1992), 9–10.

10. Here, as elsewhere, the influence of Buber seems pronounced, for this is the very same critique—the confusion of religion with other categories of the human experience—that Buber was so fond of lodging against political Zionists and Nazified Christians.

11. Aharon Lichtenstein, "Joseph Soloveitchik," in *Great Jewish Thinkers*, ed. Simon Noveck (Washington, D.C.: B'nai B'rith, 1963), 282.

Chapter Thirteen

Abraham Joshua Heschel

Universal Hasidism

HESCHEL'S LIFE AND TIMES (1907–1972)

I try not to be stale, I try to remain young. I have one talent and that is the capacity to be tremendously surprised, surprised at life, at ideas. This to me is the supreme hasidic imperative. Don't be old. Don't be stale. See life as all doors. Some are open, some are closed. You have to know how to open them.[1]

The important features of the life of Abraham Joshua Heschel help account for this great thinker's lifelong project and achievement; so we begin our discussion with his biography. Born in 1907 in Warsaw, Heschel was the descendant, maternally and paternally, of a long line of hasidic rabbis. "With ancestry like that, it is not surprising that Heschel grew up in an atmosphere of genuine hasidic piety and learning, nurtured by a great wealth of hasidic traditions and tales."[2] The emphasis here was on spiritual intensity and a conviction that God was everywhere available to the one who sought him. At the same time, the young Heschel received a classical Jewish education, and by the time he was a teenager, he had already mastered the seminal texts of the Jewish tradition—the Bible, the Babylonian and Palestinian Talmuds, the midrash, and the great works of the medieval thinkers. His intellectual brilliance as well as his enormous learning were, by that time, already widely respected. Thus, Heschel had

gained during the formative years of his childhood and youth two things that are manifest on every page of his published work: a knowledge and an understanding. The *knowledge* of the Jewish religious heritage was acquired through an undeviating attention during most of his waking hours to the study of rabbinical

literature. . . . The *understanding* for the realness of the spirit and for the holy
dimension of all existence was not primarily the result of book learning but the
cumulative effect of life lived among people who "were sure that everything
hinted at something transcendent"; that the presence of God was a daily experience and the sanctification of life a daily task.[3]

While still in his teens Heschel began to thirst for another kind of knowledge to complement his erudition in the classic texts of Judaism. The great resources of the Western intellectual tradition, the products of rational method
and empirical research, beckoned. And so Heschel matriculated at the University of Berlin in order to study philosophy, theology, and semitics with
some of the outstanding scholars of the day. At Berlin he mastered the language and methods of modern scientific and humanistic research. But, at the
same time, Heschel found himself puzzled, even irritated, by what seemed to
him a characteristic blindness that afflicted his brilliant professors: "To them,
religion was a feeling. God was an idea, a postulate of reason. They granted
Him the status of being a logical possibility. But to assume that He had existence would have been a crime against epistemology."[4] He chafed as well at
the professorial claim that "everything lay open to rational inquiry,"[5] that sovereign reason could solve all problems and dissolve all mysteries.

At the root of Heschel's concern was his recognition that his professors had
uncritically managed to subordinate religion to assumptions and categories
foreign to it. Real religion cannot be reduced to psychology (religion as feeling) or philosophy (God as an idea). It had to be understood in its own terms
and contemplated by viewing the actual practices and ideas of those who felt
its vibrancy and significance. These reflections led Heschel to write his doctoral dissertation on the biblical prophets, in which he sought to understand
these ancient giants of the spirit, these authentic spokesmen of genuine religion, in their own terms, to draw out the power of their own essentially non-
Western perspective, to comprehend the foundations of a worldview in which
a personal God calls prophets to further his purposes on earth. At the same
time, Heschel sought to convey his subject matter in the expository language
and with the conceptual tools so familiar to the modern European intellectual.

Heschel's complex education and formative experience, a product of Eastern European pietism, rabbinic literary culture, and Western European rationalism, set the framework for his lifelong commitments and intellectual challenges. His central aim was to convey the subtlety and power of traditional
texts and the authenticity of religious practices, phenomena that were either
largely unknown or seriously misunderstood by moderns, academic and
nonacademic alike. But Heschel sought more than description; he also
wanted to awaken his audience, alienated from their own spiritual capacities,
to the joy and meaning that the Jewish tradition can provide.

Yet, Heschel's synthesis of rabbinic phenomenology, Western methodology, and hasidic psychology would remain but a series of abstractions unless he could find a way to show their relevance to the real lives of his readers, to their perplexities and challenges, their fears and hopes. What modern advocates of religion, authors and preachers alike, have failed to show, Heschel maintained, was that living religion is fundamentally a fabric of *responses* to life's persisting questions. What kind of universe do I inhabit? Is it friendly to human striving or is it indifferent, even hostile? What can I understand and what are the limits of understanding? What is the purpose of my life? What can I hope to accomplish and by what activities? Why do I suffer and die? And so Heschel developed, in a way similar to the great Protestant theologian Paul Tillich, a kind of "answering theology" in which religion provides the responses to the questions that come from life. In other words, authentic religion and its contributions to a life purposefully lived is not just for those who are already religious.

Heschel's moral seriousness and intellectual honesty, his unwillingness to blame modernity or secularism for religion's current problems, and his desire to see religion regain its power to speak to life's challenges are clearly in evidence in the opening paragraph of his magnum opus, *God in Search of Man*:

> It is customary to blame secular science and anti-religious philosophy for the eclipse of religion in modern society. It would be more honest to blame religion for its own defeats. Religion declined not because it was refuted, but because it became irrelevant, dull, oppressive, insipid. When faith is completely replaced by creed, worship by discipline, love by habit; when the crisis of today is ignored because of the splendor of the past; when faith becomes an heirloom rather than a living fountain; when religion speaks only in the name of authority rather than with the voice of compassion—its message becomes meaningless. *Religion is an answer to man's ultimate questions.* The moment we become oblivious to ultimate questions, religion becomes irrelevant, and its crisis sets in.[6]

According to Heschel, religion's decisive conviction is that a holy dimension exists within and behind the world of appearances; its chief task is to make that dimension palpable and accessible, and its central challenge is to make plain the various ways to God.

> There are three starting points of contemplation about God: three trails that lead to Him. The first is the way of sensing the presence of God in the world, in things; the second is the way of sensing His presence in the Bible; and the third is the way of sensing His presence in sacred deeds. . . . These three ways correspond in our tradition to the main aspects of religious existence: worship, learning, and action. The three are one, and we must go all three ways to reach the

one destination. For this is what Israel [read: Judaism] discovered: the God of
nature is the God of history, and the way to know Him is to do His will.[7]

Several features of this passage deserve our attention. First is Heschel's
empirical method. He does not begin with dogmas or faith assertions that
would leave the unconvinced behind. He begins by asking us to look and to
listen, to draw inferences from what we experience, to allow ourselves to
sense the holy dimension "all around us." If we observe our world with a willingness to see its depth dimensions, we may be stunned at what we discover.
It all depends upon "how" we look. In this regard we have two choices: we
can observe with the eyes of acceptance or with the eyes of wonder. If we
simply accept what we see, we stop there and take life for granted. Our seeing becomes one-dimensional, limiting, and merely pragmatic. On the other
hand, we can choose to see the world through the eyes of wonder; and in two
quite different ways. There is the way of science and the way of religion. Scientific "wonder," which Heschel defines as curiosity, is fascinated by what it
sees and looks below the data of experience in search of the laws and principles of nature.[8] As science discovers laws and principles, the curiosity that
generated the search diminishes. The legitimate aim of science is total comprehension and therefore the end of curiosity. Religion also looks at the phenomenal world through the eyes of wonder, but of a different kind. Religion
is not animated by intellectual curiosity and it is not interested in scientific
laws or explanations. Religious wonder senses the power and grandeur of all
that exists, and it aims to touch the source behind all things while realizing
that it can never fully understand it. Religion is willing to abide in the mystery, to apprehend more than it comprehends.[9] "What is the structure and origin of this tree?" This is a scientific question. "Why is there a tree at all?"
This is a religious exclamation. Heschel then provides another name for religious wonder: he calls it radical amazement. Radical amazement stands in the
presence of the power and mystery of existence, marvels at it in awe, and
through the experience finds life enlarged and deepened.

The second thing to note in the paragraph above is Heschel's insistence that
the way to the "holy dimension" is found not by avoiding but by embracing
our ordinary world. Judaism has rarely been world-denying or world-avoiding
because it has insisted that the world of things is a window onto the holy dimension, a pointer toward the transcendent. "The world," Heschel says, "is an
allusion to God."[10]

Third, note Heschel's claim that religion provides multiple ways to God, to
the holy. We can find God in nature, through sacred texts, in history, and
through good deeds. Take the Bible, for example. We can read it for the information it provides about ancient history and language, about the methods

and purposes of its authors, and as clues for, and corroboration of, archaeo-
logical investigation. This is the way of curiosity, the way of science, and it
has its legitimate place. But read in another way, as a prism through which to
discover the "answer to the question: how to sanctify life,"[11] the Bible can
"show us the way of God with man and the way of man with God,"[12] and it
can point toward profound responses to the deep questions of life.

> The Bible is primarily not man's vision of God but God's vision of man. The
> Bible is not man's theology but God's anthropology, dealing with man and what
> He asks of him rather than with the nature of God. God did not reveal to the
> prophets eternal mysteries but His knowledge and love of man. It was not the
> aspiration of Israel to know the Absolute but to ascertain what He asks of man;
> to commune with His will rather than with His essence.[13]

In other words, the Bible is not primarily history but norm. It calls out to man
and makes demands on him. And, just as nature opens onto a domain beyond
and deeper than itself while preserving the ultimate mystery, so too does the
Bible both reveal God's will while concealing his essence. These two "path-
ways to God" convey both meaning and mystery; there is something *for us*
and something *beyond us* in the holy dimension. In showing how Judaism
seeks to balance the meaning and the mystery, Heschel once again endeavors
to lay bare the claims of authentic religion in modern terms.

The third way to God is the way of deeds. In exploring the role of actions
in religious life, Heschel means to say something more radical than that belief in God will lead to the performance of the *mitzvot*. While it may be quite
true (Heschel certainly believes that it is) that actions flow *from* a belief in
God, his central claim, a product again of his empirical approach and his personal experience, is that actions may lead *to* God, may themselves clear a
path to a recognition of, and a belief in, the holy dimension. We learn by doing, even in the absence of prior belief. In this way Heschel is suggesting that,
while belief itself may be quite difficult for twentieth-century, university-
educated individuals, an intense spirituality can be awakened by the very act
of keeping kosher or lighting Shabbat candles or dispensing *tzedakah*.

Now, Heschel does not draw forth the meaning of the *mitzvot* in a discur-
sive and systematic, that is to say, philosophical, way; rather, he creates a
composite portrait of the person of piety-in-action. What he describes is none
other than the exemplary figure of his youth, the Hasid. Heschel concludes
his great study of religion, *Man Is Not Alone*, with a chapter entitled simply
"The Pious Man." "Piety," writes Heschel, "is . . . a mode of living. It is the
orientation of human inwardness toward the holy. It is a predominant interest
in the ultimate value of all acts, feeling and thoughts." He continues, echoing

his remarks about the ethical focus of the Bible, by noting that "the pious man's main interest is concern for the concern of God, which thus becomes the driving force controlling the course of his actions and decisions, molding his aspirations and behavior."[14]

In language reminiscent of Hasidism's emphasis on everyday life, on the spiritual possibilities inherent in the ordinary, on the kind of piety available to the learned and unlearned alike, Heschel deepens his consideration of the pious man in action:

> [He] needs no miraculous communication to make him aware of God's presence; nor is a crisis necessary to awaken him to the meaning and appeal of that presence. His awareness may be overlaid momentarily or concealed by some violent shift in consciousness, but it never fades away.[15]

Finally, in an extraordinarily luminous passage that summarizes much of Heschel's approach to religion, especially Judaism, he says that

> the greatest problem is not how to continue but how to exalt our existence. The cry for a life beyond that grave is presumptuous, if there is no cry for eternal life prior to our descending to the grave. Eternity is not perpetual future but perpetual presence. He has planted in us the seed of eternal life. The world to come is not only a hereafter but also a *herenow*.[16]

Up to this point, we have been exploring Heschel's views on the holy dimension and the many paths that illuminate it. God, of course, has figured prominently in our discussion. Now we must pause to examine Heschel's quite distinctive, even revolutionary, understanding of God. It is here that we can see most dramatically his commitment to a biblical worldview and his insistence that we not describe religion in categories foreign to it. Most of us, Heschel points out, have obtained our conception of God (whether or not we believe in this God) through the categories of the Western intellectual tradition, a tradition that goes back to the ancient Greeks. And so we have come to think of God as "the embodiment of ultimate perfection,"[17] as a being so self-sufficient and so austere as to be totally removed from all the changes and imperfections of our earthly existence. How, indeed, could a perfect God be involved in, let alone be subject to, the messiness of the world? This is why Aristotle was led to define God as "the Unmoved Mover"; for, if God could be moved, this would make him dependent on that which moved him. But how could God be dependent on or affected by things (including persons) less perfect than himself? Such a God cannot hear prayer, does not send prophets or deliver people from bondage; such a God, in short, "simply [does] not care about the spiritual and moral state of society."[18]

But if we put aside the categories and logic of Greek philosophy and try to understand biblical religion in its own terms, we will soon discover that the God of the Bible is not Aristotle's impassive, unmoved mover at all; he can only be described as "the Most Moved Mover."[19] Between "unmoved" and "most moved" lies the vast gulf that separates Aristotelian/philosophical and biblical/religious conceptions of God. According to the Bible, the single most important thing about God is not his perfection but his concern for his world. God created the world and from that moment on exhibits concern for his creation.[20] The God of the Bible is not aloof but involved, not distant but near, not immune from, but vulnerable to what happens in his world and what his creatures choose to do. In a word, God seeks intimacy. He is especially "in search of man," desiring relationship and cherishing the hope that, out of this relationship (the biblical term for the fullness of this relationship is *covenant*) will come proper human actions and just societies. God has a stake in our behavior. Thus, he cries when we fail and rejoices when we succeed. He weeps when we ignore widows, exploit orphans, and abuse strangers; and when we violate the norms he has taken pains to communicate to us, he angrily sends prophets to chastise and warn us. What all this means is that God is filled with feeling, with pathos. Strange as this might be to Aristotle, it is the very essence of biblical religion and of the Judaism that arose from it.

It is hardly surprising that Abraham Joshua Heschel, whose scholarship and life converged on the conviction that "the presence of God [is] a daily experience and the sanctification of life a daily task," should himself have expressed his own piety through sustained involvement in the affairs of the world. Spirituality and worldliness are not opposites to Hasidism nor were they to Heschel. "Man is not made," he said, "for neutrality, for being aloof or indifferent, nor can the world remain a vacuum; unless we make it an altar to God, it is invaded by demons."[21] The ways in which Heschel attempted to make the world "an altar to God," the very range of his social and political involvements was legendary and still astonishes us more than twenty-five years after his death. In an essay entitled "Religion and Race," delivered as the opening address at the National Conference on Religion and Race in January 1963, he echoed the passion and the moral outrage of the biblical prophets when he said that "prayer and prejudice cannot dwell in the same heart. Worship without compassion is worse than self-deception; it is an abomination."[22] Two years later he put his convictions into action by participating with Martin Luther King in the decisive protest in Selma, Alabama. Upon returning Heschel proclaimed that, while marching, he felt as if his feet were praying.

Heschel was an early opponent of the war in Vietnam, and in an essay entitled "The Moral Outrage of Vietnam," he asserted memorably that "we must continue to remind ourselves that in a free society, all are involved in what some are doing. *Some are guilty, all are responsible.*"[23] He was also a tireless proponent of Jewish-Christian understanding and, in the early 1960s, served as a trusted advisor to Augustin Cardinal Bea on Christian-Jewish matters during the Second Vatican Council. Moreover, he was the first Jewish theologian to assume a visiting professorship at the (Protestant) Union Theological Seminary in New York City. His inaugural address, "No Religion Is an Island," boldly assessed the differences and conflicts between Judaism and Christianity while also emphasizing the important similarities of purpose that should make them allies in a troubled world. His sensitivity to the common goals as well as the distinctive features of all genuine religions is wonderfully captured in another memorable Heschel sentence: "Different are the languages of prayer, but the tears are the same."[24] Heschel's enormous impact on those who heard him and worked with him was poignantly captured in the words of one of Heschel's eulogists, the Protestant theologian John C. Bennett. Heschel, he said, "belonged to the whole American religious community," and although "he was profoundly Jewish he was yet a religious inspiration to Christians and to many searching people beyond the familiar religious boundaries."[25]

QUESTIONS FOR HESCHEL, "DEPTH THEOLOGY" (FROM *THE INSECURITY OF FREEDOM*)

What is the problem, in Heschel's view, of talking about religion as a discrete subject?

How is Heschel similar to Buber and Rosenzweig on this point?

How has religion been "reduced" by both the "secular" and the "religious"?

If religion is generally misapprehended, what, in Heschel's view, is religion?

Heschel specifies four components of the religious experience. What are they, and where does Heschel place his emphases in the subsequent discussion?

What is depth theology as opposed to theology in general?

Can you explain why Heschel relates his anecdote about the Hasid's rejection of speculative theology?

STUDIES BY AND ABOUT HESCHEL

The two best places to start acquainting yourself with Heschel's thought are Susannah Heschel's *Moral Grandeur and Spiritual Audacity* (Farrar, Straus and Giroux, 1996), which is a collection of (mostly shorter) Heschel essays; and Fritz Rothschild's *Between God and Man* (New York: Harper, 1959), which contains selections drawn from Heschel's larger works. As mentioned in the introduction to this section, I find Heschel's evocation of Eastern European Jewry, *The Earth Is the Lord's* (New York: H. Schuman, 1950), and his book *The Sabbath*, rev. ed. (New York: Farrar, Straus and Giroux, 2005) very moving, though not reflective of what is most original in Heschel's thought.

A huge quantity of secondary literature has been devoted to an analysis of Heschel's theology. Edward Kaplan and Samuel Dresner, *Abraham Joshua Heschel: Prophetic Witness* (New Haven, Conn.: Yale University Press, 1998); John C. Merkle, *The Genesis of Faith: The Depth Theology of Abraham Joshua Heschel* (New York: Macmillan, 1985); Daniel Breslauer, *The Ecumenical Perspective and the Modernization of Jewish Religion* (Missoula, Mont.: Scholars Press, 1978); and Donald Moore, *The Human and the Holy* (New York: Fordham University Press, 1989) are all recommended.

From "Depth Theology"

Abraham Joshua Heschel

Where is religion to be found? What sort of entity is it? What is its mode of being?

He who is in search of art will find it in works of art as preserved, for example, in art collections. He who is in search of literature will find it in books as preserved in libraries. But where is the place of religion? Do visible symbols as preserved in temples, doctrines and dogmas as contained in books, contain the totality of religion?

It seems preposterous to regard religion as an isolated, self-subsisting entity, as a *Ding an sich*. Indeed, there is an inherent weakness of religion not to take offense at the segregation of God, to forget that the true sanctuary has no walls. Religion has often suffered from the tendency to become an end in itself, to seclude the holy, to become parochial, self-indulgent, self-seeking; as if the task were not to ennoble human nature, but to enhance the power and beauty of its institutions or to enlarge the body of doctrines. It has often done more to canonize prejudices than to wrestle for truth; to petrify the sacred than to sanctify the secular. Yet the task of religion is to be a challenge to the stabilization of values.

Religion has been reduced to institution, symbol, theology. It does not affect the pretheological situation, the presymbolic depth of existence. To redirect the trend, we must lay bare what is involved in religious existence; we

must recover the situations which both precede and correspond to the theological formulations; we must recall the questions which religious doctrines
are trying to answer, *the antecedents of religious commitment*, the presuppo-
sitions of faith. A major task of philosophy of religion is, as said above, to rediscover the questions to which religion is an answer. The inquiry must proceed both by delving into the consciousness of man and by delving into the
teachings and attitudes of the religious tradition.

The urgent problem is not only the truth of religion, but man's capacity to
sense the truth of religion, the authenticity of religious concern. Religious
truth does not shine in a vacuum. It is certainly not comprehensible when the
antecedents of religious insight and commitment are wasted away; when the
mind is dazzled by ideologies which either obscure or misrepresent man's ultimate questions; when life is lived in a way which tends to abuse and to
squander the gold mines, the challenging resources of human existence. The
primary issue of theology is *pretheological*; it is the total situation of man and
his attitudes toward life and the world. It is from this point of view that we
must realize that there are four dimensions in religion.

What are the four dimensions of religious existence? To the eye of the
spectator, religion seems to consist exclusively of two components: of ritual
and myth, of sacrament and dogma, of deed and scripture. The importance of
these components is beyond dispute; the emphasis in different systems upon
either of the two only indicates the indispensability of both. To some the truth
of religion is in its ritual, to others the essence of religion is in its dogma.

There is another component, however, which may be regarded as the vital
ingredient, and yet because of its imponderable nature it often escapes the eye
of the observer. It is that which goes on within the person: the innerness of religion. Vague and often indescribable, it is the heart of religious existence.
Ritual and myth, dogma and deed remain externals unless there is a response
from within the person, a moment of identification and penetration to make
them internals. We must distinguish between four dimensions of religious existence, four necessary components of man's relationships to God: a) the
teaching, the essentials of which are summarized in the form of a creed; it is
the creed that contains norms and principles about matters sacred or eternal,
the dimension of the doctrine; b) faith, inwardness, the direction of one's
heart, the intimacy of religion, the dimension of privacy; c) the law, or the sacred act to be carried out in the sanctuary, in society or at home, the dimension of the deed; d) the context in which creed, faith and ritual come to pass,
such as the community or the covenant, history, tradition, the dimension of
transcendence. Are these dimensions always present? There are situations in
which the dimension of depth is missing: the word is proclaimed, the deed is
done, but the soul is silent. There are also situations in which nothing is hap-

pening to the sense, but the whole soul is aflame. Some consider the objective performance to be so sacred and effective that the inner component is of little account. What is the worth of one individual's evanescent response compared with the majesty of a revealed world, the preciousness of a ritual? Others regard the inner moment as the vital principle or the culmination of existence. The study of ritual is like phonetics, the science of sounds; the study of dogma is like grammar, the science of the inflections of language; while the study of inner acts is like semantics, the science of meanings.

We do not have a word for the understanding of these moments, for the events that make up the secret history of religion, or for the records in which these instants are captured. Theology is the doctrine of God, but these moments are neither doctrine nor exclusively divine. They are human as well as divine. The Psalms are not records of theology. The Psalms are the birthpangs of theology; their words plummet-lines reaching into the depth of the divine-human situation out of which genuine theology arises.

Theology has often suffered from a preoccupation with the dogma, the content of believing. The act of believing; the questions, What happens within the person to bring about faith? What does it mean to believe?—all this is the concern of a special type of inquiry which may be called "depth theology."

The theme of theology is the content of believing; the theme of depth theology is the act of believing, its purpose being to explore the depth of faith, the substratum out of which belief arises. It deals with acts which precede articulation and defy definition.

Thus many issues of religious existence may be looked upon in two ways: from the perspective of depth theology and from the perspective of theology.

The principle of the Mosaic authorship of the Pentateuch rests upon two premises: One, that Moses was a prophet, that is, inspired by God, the recipient of divine revelation; two, that Moses wrote the Pentateuch. The first premise refers to a mystery which we can neither imagine nor define; the second premise refers to an act that can be described in categories of time and space. Theology would stress the second premise; depth theology would stress the first premise.

Miracles happen simultaneously in two realms: in the realm of time and space, and in the realm of the soul. Is only an event in the physical world to be considered a marvel, while man's marvel at the miracle, the illumination of the soul, is to be considered inferior in importance?

When the people Israel crossed the Red Sea, two things happened: the waters split, and between man and God all distance was gone. There was no veil, no vagueness. There was only His presence: This is my God, the Israelite exclaimed. Most miracles that happen in space are lost in the heart; the miracle of the Red Sea became a song, "The Song of the Red Sea."

Theology declares: depth theology evokes; theology demands believing and obedience: depth theology hopes for responding and appreciation.

Theology deals with permanent facts; depth theology deals with moments. Dogma and ritual are permanent possessions of religion; moments come and go. Theology abstracts and generalizes. It subsists apart from all that goes on in the world. It preserves the legacy; it perpetuates traditions. Yet without the spontaneity of the person, response and inner identification, without the sympathy of understanding, the body of tradition crumbles between the fingers. What is the ultimate nature of the sacred words which tradition preserves? These words are not made of paper but of life. The task is not to reproduce in sound what is preserved in graphic signs; the task is to resurrect its life, to feel its pulse, so that the life within the words should reproduce its kind within our lives. Indeed, there is a heritage of insight as there is a tradition of words and rituals. It is a heritage easily forfeited, easily forgotten.

We stay away from depth theology because its themes are not easily captured in words, because we are afraid of vagueness. There is no casuistry of the inner life, no codification of innerness. Yet a life made explicit, a soul efficiently organized, would be devoid of its resources.

Theology speaks for the people; depth theology speaks for the individual. Theology strives for communication, for universality; depth theology strives for insight, for uniqueness.

Theology is like sculpture, depth theology like music. Theology is in the books; depth theology is in the hearts. The former is doctrine, the latter an event. Theologies divide us; depth theology unites us.

Depth theology seeks to meet the person in moments in which the whole person is involved, in moments which are affected by all a person thinks, feels, and acts. It draws upon that which happens to man in moments of confrontation with ultimate reality. It is in such moments that decisive insights are born. Some of these insights lend themselves to conceptualization, while others seem to overflow the vessels of our conceptual powers.

To convey these insights, man must use a language which is compatible with his sense of the ineffable, the terms of which do not pretend to describe, but to indicate; to point to, rather than to capture. These terms are not always imaginative; they are often paradoxical, radical, or negative. The chief danger to philosophy of religion lies in the temptation to generalize what is essentially unique, to explicate what is intrinsically inexplicable, to adjust the uncommon to our common sense.

Depth theology warns us against intellectual self-righteousness, against self-certainty and smugness. It insists upon the inadequacy of our faith, upon *the incongruity of dogma and mystery.* The depth of insight is never fathomed, never expressed. Who can be sure of his own faith? Or who can find Him in the mirror of his concepts?

A story is told of a Hasid who was listening to an expert in medieval Jewish scholasticism, holding forth upon the attributes of God, setting forth with logical exactness which statements may be predicted of God. After the discourse came to an end, the Hasid remarked: "If God were the way you described Him, I would not believe in Him. . . ."

Speculative theology, concerned as it is with achieving final formulations of the ideas of faith, is always in danger of taking itself too seriously, of believing to have found adequate expression in an area in which no words are ever adequate.

By the standards of speculative theology, the image and language of Psalm 19 appear to be objectionable. Surely terms such as "King," "Creator," "Master" are more acceptable, since they convey the supremacy and majesty of God as well as man's dependence on Him. In contrast the term "Shepherd" implies not only man's dependence on God but also God's need for man. The sheep look to the shepherd for shelter, food, and protection. At the same time the well-being of the shepherd is bound up with the well-being of the sheep. They are to him milk, meat, clothing, and material wealth.

As said above, the theme of theology is the content of believing; the theme of depth theology is the act of believing. The first we call faith, the second creed or dogma. Creed and faith, theology and depth theology depend upon each other.

NOTES

1. Abraham Joshua Heschel, "In Search of Exaltation," *Jewish Heritage* (Fall 1971): 29.
2. John C. Merkle, *The Genesis of Faith: The Depth Theology of Abraham Joshua Heschel* (London: Macmillan, 1985), 5.
3. Fritz A. Rothschild, *Between God and Man*, introduction (New York: Harper, 1959), 7.
4. Fritz A. Rothschild, "Abraham Joshua Heschel (1907–1972): Theologian and Scholar," *American Jewish Yearbook* 74 (1973): 537.
5. Peter Gay, *Freud, Jews, and Other Germans* (New York: Oxford, 1978), 260.
6. Abraham Joshua Heschel, *God in Search of Man: A Philosophy of Judaism* (Northvale, N.J.: Jason Aronson, 1987), 3.
7. Heschel, *God in Search of Man*, 31.
8. As Plato says, "all knowledge begins in wonder."
9. Heschel, *God in Search of Man*, 58.
10. Rothschild, *Between God and Man*, 53ff.
11. Heschel, *God in Search of Man*, 237.
12. Heschel, *God in Search of Man*, 238.
13. A. J. Heschel, *Man is Not Alone: A Philosophy of Religion* (New York: Farrar, Straus and Young, 1951), 128ff.

14. Heschel, *Man Is Not Alone*, 278.

15. Heschel, *Man Is Not Alone*, 284.

16. Heschel, *Man Is Not Alone*, 295.

17. Neil Gillman, *Sacred Fragments: Recovering Theology For the Modern Jew* (Philadelphia; Jewish Publication Society, 1990), 129. (For much of the present discussion I am indebted to Gillman's lucid presentation.)

18. Gillman, *Sacred Fragments*, 129.

19. Fritz A. Rothschild, "Architect and Herald of a New Theology," *Conservative Judaism* (Fall 1973): 58.

20. Aristotle's God did not create the world. Nor, in fact, could he.

21. Heschel, *Man Is Not Alone*, 185. Note that this passage hints at the important idea of "imitating God"; to wit, God is not aloof but involved; so too must human beings engage in worldly affairs and care about the moral state of society.

22. Abraham Joshua Heschel, "Religion and Race," in *The Insecurity of Freedom: Essays on Human Existence* (New York: Farrar, Straus and Giroux, 1966), 87.

23. Abraham Joshua Heschel, "The Moral Outrage of Vietnam," in *The Insecurity of Freedom*, 50.

24. Heschel, *The Insecurity of Freedom*, 180.

25. Rothschild, "Abraham Joshua Heschel," 533.

Conclusion

Mending the World / Mending Israel

Working on my doctorate at Ohio State University, I made a point of attending any lecture with the word *postmodernism* in the title. I never found two speakers who defined that term the same way, so I am still not entirely sure what postmodernity is. Most scholars agree, however, that the Holocaust and the creation of the state of Israel ushered in a new period of Jewish history. One of the tasks of Jewish thinkers in this postmodern era has been *tikkun*. *Tikkun*, the Hebrew word for "repair, mending, or restoration," became an important part of the mystical vocabulary in the wake of the Spanish Expulsion. It referred, above all, to the human role in healing the pain of exile, pain that the mystics believed God shared in fully. Contemporary Jewish thought applies the term *tikkun* more broadly, referring to the Holocaust, to the sexism long embedded in Jewish tradition, to the gap between believers and nonbelievers, and to the quest for a more spiritual orientation toward the Jewish tradition. My goal in this final chapter, however, is a modest one: to highlight some features distinguishing "modern" from "contemporary," as I tried to distinguish "modern" from "premodern" in chapter 2.

The *Holocaust*, or *Shoah*, is the term used to refer to the six million Jews and five million gentiles criminally murdered by the Nazis. Eastern European Jewish culture, from which many of the figures in this book hailed, was destroyed. The Yiddish language, once the mother tongue of millions, is now used colloquially mainly by ultra-Orthodox Jews who regard Hebrew as appropriate only for the study of sacred texts. The loss of life, of course, was primary, the loss of a distinctive Jewish culture and language secondary. Together, these losses shattered the belief in progress that informed so many modern Jewish philosophies. The conviction that loyalty to their host political nations ensured the safety of diaspora Jews, another modern credo, also fell victim to the Nazis. Before World War II, Jewish and Christian thinkers alike continued to be guided by the Enlightenment legacy. This optimistic outlook seemed discredited by the carnage of two world wars.

Many other changes in contemporary Jewish life resulted from the Shoah and the creation of Israel. Eastern European Jewry, long the reservoir of Jewish migrations, is emptying of Jews. Most Jewish populations of Western European nations have also been in decline since World War II. *Sephardic* Jews, from Persia to North Africa, have been relocated; some to France, more to Israel. *Sephardic*, strictly speaking, applies only to descendants of the 1492 exile. Iraqi, Indian, Persian, and sub-Saharan Jewries are far older. As a result of murder, migration, and assimilation, only two major centers of Jewish life remain vibrant at the beginning of the twenty-first century: Israel and America. While Israel seems likely to be the largest and most creative Jewish community in the near future, security concerns and intra-Jewish conflict loom as serious long-term threats. American Jews, blessed by living in the most Jew-friendly society since the Hellenistic world, if not in our entire history, struggle to maintain numbers, participants, and a meaningful Jewish culture. While some American Jews see a return to traditional religion as the only way to preserve Jewish identity, the majority will not embrace this alternative. The long-term relationship between these two major Jewish centers is also in flux, although there are few Jews today who doubt the necessity of Israel, at the very least, as a refuge from persecution.

In light of these unsettled times, a preoccupation with Jewish survival comes as no surprise. This preoccupation with survival has been a long-standing Jewish tradition. Nevertheless, the Shoah put a new emphasis on addressing this issue head-on. Richard Rubenstein, Eliezer Berkovits, Elie Wiesel, Paul Celan, Primo Levi, and a slew of ultra-Orthodox thinkers have joined in the attempt to formulate some response to this catastrophe. The works of Emil Ludwig Fackenheim (1916–2003) arguably represent the most sustained attempt to formulate a philosophical response to this trauma. In striking phrases such as "the commanding voice of Auschwitz" and "the 614th Commandment," Fackenheim insisted on making traditional philosophy respond to the Shoah. In *Encounters between Judaism and Modern Philosophy*, Fackenheim explained his project:

> I urge the reader not to overlook the systematic impulse which animates [this book]. That impulse, in a word, is to join together two disciplines—philosophy and Jewish thought—which, for a variety of reasons . . . I had found myself forced to hold apart for nearly three decades. Obeying that impulse I consider a demand at this hour in Jewish history.[1]

Fackenheim considered traditional religious genres such as midrash a more fruitful mode of Jewish response than Western philosophy. But Fackenheim injected a distinctly postmodern note into what he called "mad midrash":

> Midrashic existence acts as though all depended on man and prays as though all depended on God. It considers itself worth nothing so that it can only wait for redemption; and worth everything so that a single pure deed or prayer may have redemptive power. It holds all these aspects together because it knows itself to stand in mutual, covenantal relation—mutual even though the partners are radically unequal, for the one is man and the other is God. Climatically, midrashic existence endures the strain between these extremes without palliatives or relief. It cannot seek refuge from the real in the "spiritual" world, for it is the existence, not of souls, monks, sectarian individuals, but rather of a flesh and blood—*a people with children*.[2]

Both of these intellectual postures—confronting philosophy with reality; and fusing modernity with tradition—are telltale signs of postmodernism. If a fusing of traditional and modern characterizes postmodernity, then the American career of Menachem Mendel Schneersohn (1902–1994) offers a striking example. Schneersohn, the beloved Rebbe to thousands of observant and nonobservant Jews alike, headed a movement that wore the traditional garb of Eastern European Orthodoxy but made ingenious and extensive use of faxes, beepers, and the Internet to teach its vision of the Torah and to bring on the messianic era. Who would have predicted in 1950 at the end of World War II that a Russian-born Lubavitch dynast would become one of American Jewry's most recognizable spokespersons? The fusing of traditional and modern, in Schneersohn's case, did not end with appearance. Substantively as well, the Rebbe could talk about man, society, and God in a way that touched many Americans, Jewish and Christian, while his discourses abounded with the particular vocabulary of Hasidism. His patent love of Jews in need, which endeared him to so many, contrasted sharply with his complete rejection of non-Orthodox versions of Judaism. If the pessimist-Liberal Fackenheim articulated the Jewish determination to survive, then the optimist-Hasid Schneersohn convincingly presented traditional Judaism as the repository of a vocation for the present.

The observant reader has no doubt observed that this book has failed to include a single Jewish woman as a principal figure. The explanation is simple. The gender roles assigned men and women until very recently have precluded Jewish women from playing a role in constructive Jewish thought. To be even more blunt, Jewish women in the traditional *and* modern settings have been generally assigned to the private-domestic sphere of life and deprived of the opportunity of attaining the same level of textual mastery as men. While figures such as Sarah Schenirer, Bertha Pappenheim, Henrietta Szold, Etty Hilesum, and Rosa Luxembourg emerged as thinkers and activists of considerable importance, only in the last quarter century have women been allowed access to the full panoply of Jewish sources and to the rigors of the academy. Minus that access and training, no great thinker—male or female—could develop. Even a quick glance at the list of entering rabbinic candidates in liberal seminaries or at the program of the annual Association of Jewish Studies conference, will show that this underrepresentation is on the way to correction. Considering that Enlightenment teachings of human equality powered much of what we consider modern, this may seem paradoxical. But as Riv Ellen Prell in "The Vision of Woman in Classical Reform Judaism" *Journal of the American Academy of Religion* 50, no. 4 (1983): 575–89, and as others have argued, liberal Jewish thinkers in the nineteenth century declared their female equals, "honorary men," and then forgot them. I would venture the following cynical definition: Modernity is that period in which gender equality was widely asserted (versus premodern times) but never realized (versus contemporary times).

Since the 1970s, the women's movement has transformed American society in general, including the lives of Jews and the norms of Judaism. The changes wrought by the greater inclusion of women transcends any single discipline. Gender analysis has provided new vantage points from which to view the Bible, rabbinics, literature, and history. A wholesale reconstruction of the role of women in Jewish history has been largely accomplished within a remarkably short time span. For a volume that does justice to the influence of general feminist theory on Jewish practitioners, I recommend Lynn Davidman and Shelly Tenenbaum, eds., *Feminist Perspectives on Jewish Studies* (New Haven, Conn.: Yale University Press, 1994). Ellen Umansky and Dianne Ashton, eds., *Four Centuries of Jewish Women's Spirituality* (Boston: Beacon, 1992); and Judith L. Baskin, ed., *Jewish Women in Historical Perspective* (Detroit, Mich.: Wayne State University Press, 1991) contain, respectively, wonderful primary material and useful introductions by some of the leading scholars in their areas. And these are but the tip of the iceberg.

In Jewish thought, both the newness of the feminist critique and the ongoing revolution in American feminism continue to generate new works. While a host of Jewish women were involved in the American feminist movement in the 1960s (e.g., Bella Abzug, Betty Friedan, and Gloria Steinem), a specifically Jewish feminism did not emerge until the 1970s. By the end of that decade, however, collections such as Elizabeth Koltun's *The Jewish Women* (New York: Schocken, 1976) and Susannah Heschel's *On Being a Jewish*

Feminist: A Reader (New York: Schocken, 1983) demonstrated that Jewish feminists had found their voice. Although *seminal* is an overused word, it surely applies to Judith Plaskow's *Standing Again at Sinai* (San Francisco: Harper and Row, 1990). With her broad reevaluations of central pillars of Jewish theology such as God, the Torah and Israel, Plaskow has helped inspire a new generation of feminist theologians such as Lori Lefkowitz, Laura Levitt, and Miriam Peskowitz . Many have "worked" the texts of the rabbinic tradition more assiduously than Plaskow. For example, Rachel Adler's *Engendering Judaism: An Inclusive Theology and Ethics* (Philadelphia: Jewish Publication Society, 1998) offers, among many other gems, a sample of a nonsexist marriage contract. It may be excessive to claim that "Jewish feminism is the only new idea to have emerged among American Jews since their arrival in 1654" (Aviva Cantor, *Jewish Women/Jewish Men: The Legacy of Patriarchy in Jewish Life*, 1st ed. [San Francisco: HarperSanFrancisco, 1995], 440). But there is no ideology more creative or inspiring on the American Jewish scene today. (The feminist movement in Israel has proceeded along very different paths.)

The whole phenomenon of Jews working in the ostensibly secular, value-neutral academy represents another dividing line between modern and contemporary Jewish thought. The scope of our knowledge about Judaism has been extended immeasurably, as has our thinking about the ends and means of Jewish learning. For many modern Jews, the study of Judaism (as opposed to traditional Jewish *lernen* of the male-only yeshiva), provides an important vehicle for Jewish identity. To take one example: Gershom Scholem, whose name has appeared several places in this book, was more than an ivory-tower student of mysticism. He offered, through the medium of scholarship, a view of Jewish history and of Judaism that served as a surrogate faith. As Yosef Yerushalmi put it, history can be "the faith of fallen Jews." But can "fallen Jews" transmit that faith? And how do the nonfallen integrate scholarship with traditional beliefs? One potent response to these questions, I submit, may be found in the realm of contemporary Jewish Bible scholarship.

An enormous list of first-rate Bible scholars who are also specifically Jewish thinkers could be generated, even without including Israelis, and even without including scholars such as Robert Alter or Ilana Pardes whose training is primarily literary. The works of Adele Berlin, Michael Fishbane, Edward Greenstein, Jon Levenson, Carol Meyers, and Nahum Sarna, among many others, read the Bible with intellectual integrity (i.e., they are not fundamentalists), with knowledge of rabbinic insights into the text, and with deep appreciation for the role that the Torah played and plays in the Jewish world (unlike, say, either Spinoza or nineteenth-century scholarship).

At the very beginning of the modern era, Baruch Spinoza treated the Bible as a wholly human book that could be analyzed in a purely scientific manner. Critical Bible scholarship of the nineteenth-century academy, especially in German Protestant lands, vivisected the biblical texts, finding a multiplicity of authors reflecting a variety of periods and interests. Fundamentalists of all stripes rejected this approach altogether, reaffirming the perfection of the Bible. But where does that leave the rest of us? Most modern Jews do not accept that the Bible was literally dictated by God to Moses at Mount Sinai, even if they have no problem proclaiming that fact when the Torah scrolls are raised in synagogue.[3] Yet most modern Jews, even without a belief in divine authorship, continue to confide in the Bible's eternal importance as a moral and historical patent of Jewish legitimacy.

The answer to the question "Where does that leave the rest of us?" was partially anticipated in Martin Buber's dialogical approach to Scripture. Buber suggested that the interaction between the reader and the text was the truly important "fact" with respect to the Bible and its readers. More recently, a "rehabilitation" of the Bible has taken place on several fronts: a renewed appreciation for the literary artistry of the Bible; an awareness that the Bible constantly reinterprets itself, thus narrowing the gap between the activities of revelation (divine) and interpretation (human); and an appreciation for the Bible as having started and lived life within a religious community. These developments may have been initiated in the academy, but anyone can see from the recent dramatizations of biblical characters, from Bill Moyers's Genesis project, and from the many biographies of God, that the Bible is "back." The specifically Jewish dimension in this process has been notable. Only in the last twenty to thirty years have a significant number of Jewish scholars entered the academy.

Post-Holocaust theologies, feminist theologies, and recent trends in Bible scholarship share, in my view, a sense of rupture with previous modes of Jewish life and thought and the intense desire to heal wounds left by the cruelty of the nations, the profound underutilization of half the Jewish people, and the arrogance of modernism. These recent developments reflect the same desire to see Jewish life proceed with integrity, meaning, and conviction as did their predecessors. They are sufficiently different, however, to merit the appellation *contemporary* rather than *modern*. Other trends in contemporary Jewish thought, including the mushrooming interest in spirituality, transdenominationalism, and the compatibility of Judaism with Eastern forms of religion are undeniably important. They seem to this author, however, to be topics well handled elsewhere, and also peripheral to the conversation initiated by Spinoza, the famous Amsterdam heretic, some three-and-a-half centuries ago.

NOTES

1. Michael Morgan, *Dilemmas in Modern Jewish Thought* (Bloomington: Indiana University Press, 1992), 112.

2. Michael Morgan, *The Jewish Thought of Emil Fackenheim* (Detroit, Mich.: Wayne State University Press, 1987), 201–34.

3. As Franz Rosenzweig brilliantly quipped, the story of Balaam (Num. 22–24) is the word of God when read in synagogue as the weekly *parsha* (portion), but a fable the rest of the year.

Index

About the Author

Alan T. Levenson teaches Jewish history and thought at Siegal College in Cleveland, Ohio. He received his BA and MA from Brown University and his doctorate from Ohio State University. He has been a visiting professor at the College of William and Mary and at Case Western Reserve University. He is author of *Between Philosemitism and Antisemitism: Defenses of Jews and Judaism in Germany, 1871–1932*, and *The Story of Joseph: A Journey of Jewish Interpretation*. His publications on German Jewry, modern Jewish thought, and Jewish pedagogy have appeared in a variety of academic and nonacademic journals. He has received fellowships from Tel Aviv University, the Lucius Littauer Foundation, the German Academic Exchange Program, the Memorial Foundation for Jewish Culture, and the American Council of Learned Societies. Currently on sabbatical in New York, he resides permanently in Shaker Heights, Ohio, with his wife, Hilary, and their son, Benjamin Ze'ev.